MUTUAL FUNDS
—THE—
MONEY MULTIPLIER

MUTUAL FUNDS
— THE —
MONEY MULTIPLIER

Lalitha Thamaraipandy

Notion Press

Old No. 38, New No. 6
McNichols Road, Chetpet
Chennai - 600 031

First Published by Notion Press 2017
Copyright © Lalitha Thamaraipandy 2017
All Rights Reserved.

ISBN 978-1-946641-19-9

This book has been published with all reasonable efforts taken to make the material error-free after the consent of the author. No part of this book shall be used, reproduced in any manner whatsoever without written permission from the author, except in the case of brief quotations embodied in critical articles and reviews.

The Author of this book is solely responsible and liable for its content including but not limited to the views, representations, descriptions, statements, information, opinions and references ["Content"]. The Content of this book shall not constitute or be construed or deemed to reflect the opinion or expression of the Publisher or Editor. Neither the Publisher nor Editor endorse or approve the Content of this book or guarantee the reliability, accuracy or completeness of the Content published herein and do not make any representations or warranties of any kind, express or implied, including but not limited to the implied warranties of merchantability, fitness for a particular purpose. The Publisher and Editor shall not be liable whatsoever for any errors, omissions, whether such errors or omissions result from negligence, accident, or any other cause or claims for loss or damages of any kind, including without limitation, indirect or consequential loss or damage arising out of use, inability to use, or about the reliability, accuracy or sufficiency of the information contained in this book.

Dedicated to

THE ALMIGHTY

without whose grace this book would not have seen the light of the day

Contents

Preface ... xi

SECTION I: INTRODUCTION

1. What is a Mutual Fund? ... 3
   Back to Basics

SECTION II: FUND ORGANISATION

2. Mutual Fund Constituents ... 9
   Function Follows Form
3. Mutual Fund Structure ... 19
   More Than a Legal Curiosity
4. Legal and Regulatory Framework ... 25
   The Resilient Enabler

SECTION III: FUND CONCEPTS

5. Core Concepts ... 35
   Reinforcing the Roots
6. Myths Exploded! ... 49
   Uprooting NFO and Dividend Weeds
7. Unloaded! ... 55
   Yet Burdened?
8. Expenses Exposed! ... 65
   Outlaw the Outlay

SECTION IV: FUND FLAVOURS

9. Passing Through the Portals of Portfolio Classification ... 79
   Across Asset Classes
10. On to Operational Classification ... 101
    Of Liquidity, Strategies, Selection and Capitalisation

11.	Geographical Classification of Funds *The Logic Behind Logistics*	109
12.	Speciality Funds *Speciality Genres*	115

SECTION V: FUND CHOICE

13.	Comparison With Other Investment Avenues *One up on Counterparts*	167
14.	Raison d'etre *Ingenious Investment*	181

SECTION VI: FUND PERFORMANCE

15.	Becoming an Informed Investor *Right Use of Knowledge*	189
16.	Performance Evaluation *Returns – the First Dimension*	211
17.	Understanding the Risks *Risk – the Second Dimension*	225
18.	Delving Deep for Debt Funds *Returns Revisited – the First Dimension*	235
19.	The Taxing Question – Which Option to Opt For? *Keep All Options Open*	239
20.	Turn to Towering Taxes *The Third Dimension*	243
21.	Systematically Narrow Down Your Choices *Yardsticks to Reach the Final Yard*	257

SECTION VII: FUND PLANS AND SERVICES

22.	Mutual Fund Investment Plans *Compounding – the Eighth Wonder of the World*	265
23.	Mutual Fund Investment Services *At Your Service*	275

24.	Advent of Online Investing *Torrential Technological Triumph*	297

SECTION VIII: FUND FAREWELL

25.	Behold, Hold and Fold *Nothing Lasts a Lifetime*	317

SECTION IX: FUND ADVICE

26.	Do You Need a Financial Adviser? *A Caring Gardener…*	327
27.	How to Choose Your Financial Adviser *…Who Nurtures Plants That Bear Fine Fruits*	331

Epilogue — *335*

Preface

The high decibel advertisements for mutual funds cannot but be drowned in the ensuing din. Such is the voracity with which they are marketed. Books on this much-touted topic by stalwarts in the financial circles are available a dime a dozen. Therefore, the rationale for another book on this topic does not hold water.

What then could be the motivation for yet another book on *Mutual Funds*? There is a dearth of books on this topic by Indian authors. It is my intention to encapsulate all that is there for you to know about Indian mutual funds in a lucid and concise style with a mark of authenticity, of course. In this book, it will be my endeavour to demystify the concept of mutual funds so that even a layman can reap the benefits it offers and build his wealth. This book is not intended for professional investors but for ordinary investors, who need guidance while investing.

The genesis of this book dates back to nearly a decade ago when I started writing a blog on the site www.indianmutualfund.blogspot.com titled "The Money Multiplying Matrix of Mutual Funds". The rousing reception the site had with the investing public, notably the novices in this field, prompted me to go ahead with this book on mutual funds.

The sole source of inspiration for this book was none other than my life partner, P. Palavesa Muthu, whose single-minded devotion and constant encouragement was instrumental in the transformation of my blog into a book. The entire credit for editing and fine tuning this book and giving it the present shape goes to my father, who instilled in me the love for the written word as a child. The willing co-operation of my family members – my mother, brother, sister, son and daughter – deserves special mention.

Last but not least, I am indebted to the entire team of Notion Press for the excellent job done by them.

Lalitha
Kuwait,
February 2017

SECTION I
INTRODUCTION

As Benjamin Franklin succinctly put it, "An investment in knowledge always pays the best interest."

Mutual fund – a globally proven investment vehicle – is slowly but steadily finding a place in the investment itinerary of Indians. There is no magic formula for successful mutual fund investing… all it requires is common sense, emotional discipline and a clear understanding of the concept.

John C. Bogle, in his preface to *Common Sense on Mutual Funds: New Imperatives for the Intelligent Investor* rightly pointed out, "intelligent investing turns out to be little more than common sense and sound reason. The sooner investors realise that elemental principle, the better will be their ability to accumulate the maximum possible amount of capital for their financial security."

"To invest successfully over a lifetime does not require a stratospheric IQ, unusual business insights, or inside information. What's needed is a sound intellectual framework for making decisions and the ability to keep emotions from corroding that framework", so said Warren Buffet in his preface to the fourth edition of Benjamin Graham's *The Intelligent Investor*.

In this book, *Mutual Funds: The Money Multiplier*, the concept of mutual funds has been introduced against the backdrop of investment planning. Such a holistic view will enable readers to place mutual fund investing in a proper perspective. Due care has been taken to ensure that readers understand the concept and enrich their knowledge and wealth. Minute details are dealt with precision and clarity to drive home the concept and prepare the readers to fearlessly enter the world of mutual funds.

Welcome to the world of Mutual Funds…

Chapter 1
What is a Mutual Fund?
Back to Basics

Mutual Funds Defined and Explained

SEBI (Mutual Fund) Regulations, 1993, define a mutual fund as "a fund established in the form of a trust by a sponsor to raise money by the trustees through the sale of units to the public under one or more schemes for investing in securities in accordance with these regulations."

At the outset, it would be best to limit ourselves to explaining mutual funds in layman's terms. A graphic description of the constituents and legal composition of mutual funds in the subsequent section will serve as a self-explanatory follow-up to the formal, legalistic definition above.

In common parlance, a mutual fund is an investment vehicle that enables a number of investors with common financial goals to pool their money and have it jointly managed by a professional investment manager. A mutual fund pools the money of many investors and invests it in shares or debentures, bonds, etc. The fund manager invests the money in a portfolio of marketable securities in accordance with specific investment criteria, which are spelled out in the prospectus, the official booklet that describes the mutual fund. Investors, therefore, know what they are getting into and can match their investment objective to that of a fund.

The pooled money has greater buying power than one investor alone can command. A fund can own hundreds of different securities. Thus, its success is not dependent on how just one or two companies perform, but on the performance of all the stocks or securities which the fund is holding. The ownership remains in the hands of the investors who have pooled in the funds. A mutual fund is, thus, a financial intermediary that is managed by investment professionals and other service providers, who earn a fee from the fund for their services. Mutual fund is the purest form of financial intermediary because there is almost perfect pass through of money between investors and the securities in which the fund invests. Investors are indicated *a priori* in what type of securities their funds will be invested. The investor's share in the fund is denominated by units whose value is updated on a daily basis.

Mutual Funds against the Backdrop of Investment Planning

To properly understand mutual funds, we need to take a step back. If you want to invest, say, in shares or debentures of companies, how do you go about it?

At the outset, you determine the level of risk you are willing to take and the kind of returns you are expecting. Your decision at this stage will determine the amount of investment you will make in shares (equities) and debentures (debt). Shares represent ownership in a public company, say, Reliance Industries, Infosys, Tata Steel, etc. and are traded on the stock exchanges. Bonds/debentures are basically a chance for you to lend your money either to the Government or a company. You can receive interest and your principal back over predetermined periods of time. They are the most common lending instruments traded on the market. There are many types of investments other than shares and debentures (insurance, real estate, precious metals, etc.), but a majority of mutual funds invest in shares and/or debentures. Normally, shares carry a higher risk and also offer higher returns while debentures carry a lower risk and have lower returns. This allocation of your money among various types of investments is known as **asset allocation**.

Having decided on your asset allocation, you have to select the shares and debentures you want to invest in. You can do this by independently researching companies or acting on tips. The latter is not recommended, unless it comes from the horse's mouth – your financial adviser. This process of choosing specific investments is known as **investment selection**.

If you have selected shares quoted in the stock markets, you will have to call up your broker and **place the order**. Alternatively, if you have selected a company whose share is available by way of a public issue, you will have to fill up the necessary application form and pray that you will get allotted some shares, especially if the public issue is considered attractive. Similarly, you can buy debentures, which are listed on the stock markets, or **apply for them in public issues**.

Now that you are invested in the companies of your choice and in the manner you choose, equity and/or debt, you have to continually **monitor your investments**. You have to track the company's performance, collect your dividends and interest payments and take that most crucial decision of selling your shares when you feel you have achieved your target price, or live with your losses if the share prices/investments have tanked.

Seems a lot of work, doesn't it? Wish there was someone who would do it all for you?

Well, that is what a mutual fund does. It collects money from a large number of small investors and invests it on their behalf. The most important characteristic of a mutual fund is that the contributors and the beneficiaries are the investors. **The term "mutual" implies that investors contribute to the pool and also benefit from the pool.** The pool of funds held mutually by investors is the mutual fund. A mutual fund is a trust that is mutually beneficial to all those who have put their money in the trust.

Mutual Fund Mechanics

Figure 1.1 below clearly explains the working of a mutual fund.

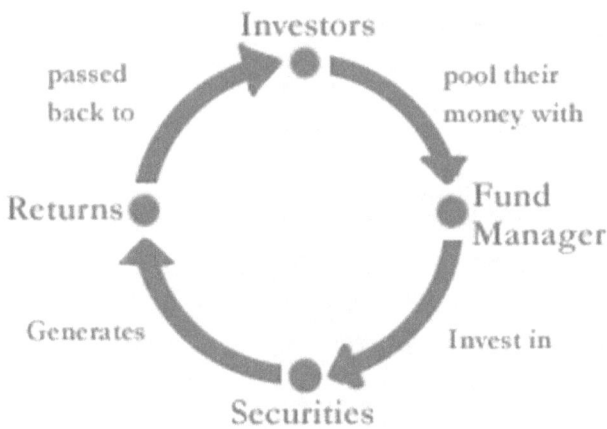

Source: AMFI Website

Figure 1.1 Mutual Fund Mechanics

Thus, **investors** with common financial objectives **pool their money with** the **fund manager**. The mutual fund issues units to investors in exchange for cash. Investors get mutual fund units on a proportionate basis for the sum contributed to the pool. It is interesting to note that funds do not issue a predetermined number of units as most companies do; instead, new units are issued as each new investment is made.

The money collected from investors is **invested in** shares, debentures and other securities by the fund manager. The investment pattern depends on the mutual fund's stated investment objective. The fund manager keeps a constant watch on the financial markets and adjusts the portfolio to achieve the highest returns. The fund manager is responsible for the investment decisions. The fund manager is ably assisted by the research team, dealers/brokers, custodians, etc. The research team provides him information on various investment opportunities. The dealers execute the decisions. The deals are placed through the brokers. Custodians take care of the back-office work. By owning a part of a fund, the hard work of selecting, investing and monitoring stocks and bonds is done for investors by the fund manager.

The primary assets of the fund are the **securities** it invests in. These securities **generate** dividends, interest and sales proceeds. At the close of every trading day, a mutual fund tallies the market value of all the securities in its portfolio and deducts its expenses, i.e. management fees, administrative expenses, advertising costs, etc. The balance is divided by the number of units owned by the unit-holders to arrive at the value of one unit of the mutual fund or the Net Asset Value, or NAV.

The **returns** are **passed on to the investors**. They get a proportional share of the fund's income and losses.

And the Cycle Continues...

When investors purchase a mutual fund, they own a piece of an investment portfolio. Investors, thus, become part-owners of the fund itself and, thereby, the assets of the fund. Thus, buying a mutual fund is like buying a small slice of a big pizza!

SECTION II
FUND ORGANISATION

Majority of mutual fund investors are quite oblivious of the way the mutual fund is organised – they have no inkling of its constituents, structure, or the regulatory framework, least of all pay attention to it. It does not matter as long as they are well protected and reap the requisite returns. Little do they realise that the fund's organisational structure can have a tremendous impact on their protection as well as their returns. To borrow John Bogle's words, "it (structure of a mutual fund organisation) is a fundamental determinant of the relationship between the fund complex and the fund shareholder."

Let us delve at length (or rather depth!) on the bedrock of a mutual fund, namely, fund organisation.

Chapter 2

Mutual Fund Constituents

Function Follows Form

Let us now see the parties involved in the initiation and operation of mutual funds.

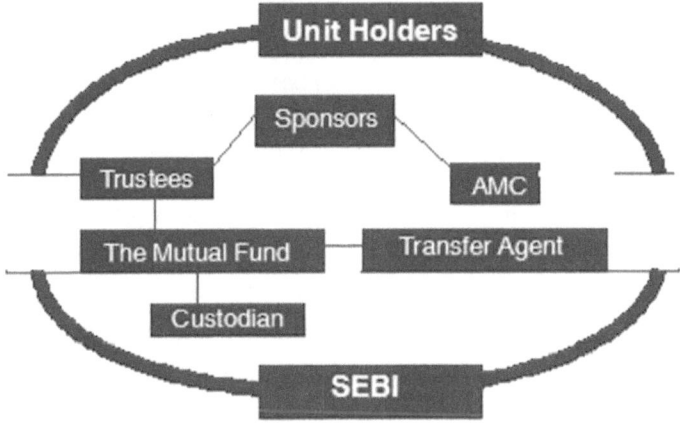

Source: AMFI Website

Figure 2.1   Mutual Fund Constituents in India

The sponsor is the promoter who, acting alone or in combination with another body corporate, creates the mutual fund as a trust under the Indian Trusts Act, 1882 and appoints trustees to manage the trust with the approval of Securities and Exchange Board of India (SEBI), creates an Asset Management Company (AMC or the Investment Manager) under the Companies Act, 2013 and gets the trust registered with SEBI. There can be one or more sponsors. The sponsor initiates the idea to set up a mutual fund and invests in the capital of the AMC. It could be a domestic or foreign registered company, scheduled bank, or financial institution.

Since sponsors are the pivotal persons in the establishment of a mutual fund, they need to abide by stringent standards specified by the prime regulator of mutual funds, SEBI. The sponsor must have at least a five-year track record of business interest in the financial markets and a reputation of fairness and integrity in all its business transactions. The sponsor should have a positive net worth in all the preceding 5 years. The net worth of the sponsors in the immediately preceding year should be more than the capital contribution to the AMC. The sponsor should contribute at least 40% of the net worth of the AMC. The sponsor must have been making profit in at least 3 out of the last 5 years, including the last year.

With prior approval of SEBI and in accordance with SEBI regulations, the sponsor appoints the trustees, custodian and the AMC. Once the AMC is formed, the sponsor is just the stakeholder. The sponsor is not responsible or liable for any loss or shortfall resulting from the operation of the schemes beyond the initial contribution made by it towards setting up of the mutual fund. However, sponsors do play a role in bailing out any AMC during a crisis.

Trustee is usually a company (corporate body) or a Board of Trustees (body of at least 4 individuals). The trustee is appointed by the sponsor by executing and registering a trust deed with prior approval of SEBI. The trustee is authorised to accept funds from various investors for management in accordance with a specified objective. The trustee of the mutual fund holds its property for the benefit of the unit-holders. The trustee safeguards the interest of investors in the mutual fund and also ensures that the operations of the fund comply with the Securities and Exchange Board of India (Mutual Funds) Regulations, 1996, the provisions of the Trust Deed and the Offer Documents of the respective schemes.

The AMC and the other functionaries are functionally accountable to the trustee. The trustee is vested with the general power of superintendence and direction over the AMC. The trustee is responsible for ensuring that the AMC has all its systems in place and all key personnel have been appointed prior to the launch of any scheme. The trustee floats and markets schemes and secures necessary approvals. The trustees, however, do not directly manage the portfolio of securities. The portfolio is managed by the AMC as per the defined objectives, in accordance with Trust Deed and SEBI (Mutual Funds) Regulations. The trustee checks if the AMC's investments are within defined limits, whether the fund's assets are protected and also ensures that the unit-holders get their due returns. The trustee also reviews any due diligence done by the AMC. For major decisions concerning the fund, the trustee has to take the consent of the unit-holders. The trustee is obliged to perform a quarterly review of all transactions carried out amongst the mutual fund schemes, AMC and its associates. The trustee submits reports to SEBI once in every 6 months.

The trustees, being the primary guardians of the unit-holder's funds and assets, have to be persons of high repute and integrity. SEBI Regulations require that at least two-thirds of the directors or board of trustees must be independent, i.e. they should not be associated with the sponsors.

The Asset Management Company is appointed by the sponsor or the trustee, if so authorised by the trust deed, as the investment manager of the trust through an agreement called Investment Management Agreement. The AMC cannot be an AMC or trustee of another mutual fund. AMCs are owned by banks, financial institutions, Indian private sector companies, foreign institutional players, or jointly owned by Indian and foreign sponsors.

Though the trust is the mutual fund, the AMC is the business face of the mutual fund as it manages all the affairs of the fund. The AMC is, thus, the operational arm of the mutual fund. The AMC structures various schemes, launches the schemes and mobilises the initial amount, manages the funds and offers services to the investors. The AMC takes investment decisions, compensates investors through dividends, maintains proper accounting and information for pricing of units, calculates the NAV and provides information on listed schemes and secondary market unit transactions. It also exercises due diligence on investments and submits quarterly reports to the trustee. AMCs are required to do exception reporting on a bi-monthly basis. AMCs are required to report only the exceptions in the Compliance Test Reports or CTR to SEBI and the CTR has to be placed before the trustees. The AMC should submit the Annual Statistical Report (ASR) to SEBI in the prescribed format by the 30th of April each year. AMCs are required to develop a suitable Management Information System for reporting to the trustees. The Half-Yearly Report on the activities of the mutual fund to be submitted by the trustees to the Board under the mutual fund regulations shall cover all issues mentioned in the prescribed format as well as any other issue relevant to the operation of the mutual fund. It is mandatory for all mutual funds to submit a Daily Transaction Report with details of transactions in the secondary market on a daily basis in a prescribed format to the Board.

For effective discharge of their responsibilities under the mutual fund regulations, the AMCs shall provide infrastructure and administrative support. The AMC employs professionals to manage the funds. The AMC is headed by a **Managing Director, Executive Director, or Chief Executive Officer. The Chief Investment Officer** is responsible for the overall investments of the mutual fund. He is ably assisted by the **fund manager**. Every scheme requires a fund manager, according to SEBI regulations, but a fund manager is allowed to manage multiple schemes. The fund manager is supported by **research analysts** and mutual fund scheme's purchase and sale transactions are executed by **securities dealers**. The **Chief Marketing Officer** is responsible for mobilising money for various schemes of the fund. The Chief Marketing Officer is supported by the **Direct Sales Team**, which generally focus on large investors, **Channel Managers**, who manage the distributors and the **Advertising and Sales Promotion Team**. All operational issues are handled by the **Chief Operations Officer**. There is a **Compliance Officer** who ensures all legal compliances. He signs a due diligence certificate to the effect that all regulations have been complied with and all intermediaries mentioned in the offer document have the requisite statutory registrations and approvals. The Compliance Officer reports directly to the head of the AMC so as to safeguard his independence. He also works closely with the trustees on various compliance and regulatory issues.

SEBI regulations stipulate that 50% of the directors of the AMC must be independent. The AMC must have a minimum net worth of at least Rs. 50 crore at all times and should not indulge in any business other than that of asset management nor act for any other fund. SEBI can pull up an AMC if it deviates from its prescribed role.

Portfolio Management – at the Heart of the Mutual Fund Activity-Chain

Portfolio manager, popularly known as fund manager, carries on the portfolio management function. Each scheme of a mutual fund has a designated fund manager who is responsible for constructing, managing and protecting portfolios in order to achieve the predefined investment objectives.

Normally mutual funds have separate departments/cells/wings performing these activities. Investment advisory department/department of securities research provides research support to the department of fund management. Given the types of schemes the mutual fund has, its fund management department specifies a set of securities that have to be regularly tracked. For such securities, various reports may be prepared by the research department.

Research analysts study the financials of the companies in detail and prepare valuation reports. They interact with the managements of the respective companies, understand their strategies and their plans for the future. They create a risk-return profile of the companies and prepare their reports on the basis of these inputs. This department provides research support not only to the fund management team but also to the investment monitoring department.

Each analyst tracks one or more industries on a regular basis. Industry allocation enables the analyst to develop a better understanding of the critical success factors for a company in that industry and to assess the performance of the industry in future. The underlying idea behind securities evaluation is to understand the business strengths of the company and project the company's performance years down the line in terms of the likely returns to its shareholders. The analysts attempt to understand whether the companies can create and sustain shareholder value. The intrinsic worth of the stock is calculated by discounting future cash flows and the current market price is compared with the intrinsic worth to derive the extent of undervaluation/over-valuation. Based on this and other qualitative analysis a risk-return profile of the security is prepared. Quality of management of the company, general industry scenario, competitive position of the company and financial analysis are some of the criteria that are given due consideration while arriving at the intrinsic value of a stock.

With effect from December 1, 2014, every individual or entity desiring to function as a research analyst needs to get registered after meeting the criteria prescribed by SEBI regarding qualifications, capital adequacy, establishment of internal policies and procedures, firewalls against conflict of interest, sufficient and timely disclosures, etc. in SEBI (Research Analysts) Regulations, 2014.

The department of research prepares periodic reports on specific securities in addition to reports based on specific request made by the fund managers. The department of securities research normally issues a recommendation list for companies for a period of say, one or two years in the form of Buy, Market out-performer, Market performer, Market under-performer, or, Sell. The frequency of these recommendation lists could be weekly/fortnightly/monthly depending upon the needs of the fund management department. These recommendations are not binding on the fund managers. Whether the fund manager accepts these recommendations or not is his/her prerogative.

> Department of securities research normally maintains model portfolios. The objective of this portfolio is to be reflective of the research recommendations of the department. These model portfolios are actively managed and are made available to fund managers. This is also used by the fund managers to compare the actual performance of their schemes *vis-à-vis* the model portfolio.
>
> Department of dealing acts as a support function to the fund management activity. It handles activities relating to the secondary market operations and tries to obtain the best possible price for purchase/sale of securities. The department of dealing is responsible for trading in the market. After it receives purchase/sale requisitions from the fund managers for various schemes, it places orders with various brokers. Dealers also interact with the brokers during and after the trading hours. Since it directly deals with the brokers, it provides feedback to the fund managers on market information.

There exists a conflict of interest between the sponsors of mutual funds, the trustees and the AMC. SEBI addressed the issue by ordering that AMCs, trustees and managements should have different sets of individuals. SEBI erected a "Chinese Wall" between the activities of the various constituents of mutual funds. But, many AMCs carry out practically all activities pertaining to the fund on behalf of the trustees. The AMC is virtually the face and mouthpiece of the fund. The reason for concern is because trustees are expected to be the first level of regulators to safeguard the interests of mutual fund investors. The report submitted by the trustees to SEBI on the functioning of the AMC, rely heavily on the data provided by the AMC. Trustee companies, in practice, do not have employees. In fact, only the AMC has employees to manage the interests of the mutual funds. The first school of thought feels AMCs and trustees have similar objectives and so there cannot be a conflict of interest. The second school of thought says that there is a conflict of interest as the trustees are appointed by the AMC, besides being regulated and controlled by it. In a way, the trustees owe their jobs to the AMCs. By the very nature of appointment and compensation, they are controlled by AMCs.

The AMC is the first functionary to be appointed and is involved in the appointment of all other functionaries including the custodian, depository participants, registrar and transfer agent, collection bankers, brokers, selling and distribution agents, legal advisers, auditors and fund accountants. All the functionaries are required to report to the trustees, who lay down the ground rules and monitor their working.

The Custodian, normally a bank or any other financially sound institution, is responsible for the custody of the assets (in material form) of the fund and for safeguarding the interests of the fund arising from the assets. Only institutions with substantial organisational strength, service capability in terms of computerisation and other infrastructure facilities are approved to act as custodians. SEBI mandates that the custody of the portfolio should not be with the AMC but with a custodian, specifically approved by SEBI. The custodian must be totally de-linked from the AMC and must be registered with SEBI. The custodian is appointed by the mutual fund. A custodial agreement is entered into between the trustees and the custodian. Though the securities are bought and held in the name of trustees, they are not kept with them. The responsibility of safe keeping the securities is on the custodian. Securities, which are in material form, are kept in safe custody of a custodian and securities, which are in "dematerialised" form, are kept with a depository participant, who acts on the advice of the custodian.

Custodians can service more than one AMC. Stock Holding Corporation of India is the custodian for most fund houses in India. They discharge the important back-office function by ensuring that securities which are bought are delivered and transferred to the books of the mutual funds and that funds are paid out when a mutual fund sells securities. They keep the investment account of the mutual fund and collect the dividend and interest payments due on the mutual fund's investments. They track corporate actions such as bonus issues, rights issues, offer for sale, buy-back and open offer for acquisition and act on these actions on the advice of the fund managers. The custodian normally charges portfolio fees, transaction fees and out-of-pocket expenses in accordance with the terms of the Custody Agreement. Their charges range between 0.15 and 0.20% of the net value of the holding.

Depository Participants (DPs) hold the securities of mutual funds in dematerialised form. They handle the operational aspects of actually making or receiving the delivery of securities into the accounts of the mutual fund from the company or stock exchange in dematerialised form, on instructions from the custodian. They also communicate the custodian's instructions on corporate actions to the company.

The Registrar and Transfer Agent (RTA) to the mutual fund is appointed by the AMC, if so authorised by the trust deed. It is not compulsory to appoint a registrar and transfer agent. The AMC can choose to handle this activity in-house. All RTAs need to register with SEBI. The registrar and transfer agent, responsible for the investor-servicing functions, maintains and updates the records of the unit-holders and handles communications with them. The registrar processes the application form, redemption requests and dispatches account statements to the unit-holders. Investors can get information about various investments in different schemes of different fund houses at a single place. It would be challenging, impractical and expensive for mutual funds to have workforce all over India for this purpose. The offices of registrar and transfer agents in various centres serve as Investor Service Centres. Registrar and transfer agents ensure quality services at reasonable costs. In addition, they track investor behaviour for selling and distribution agents.

The money invested by the investors in the scheme goes into the bank account of the scheme they have invested in. These bank accounts are maintained with **collection bankers** who are appointed by the AMC. They accept applications of investors in most of their branches. Payment instruments against applications handed over to branches of the AMC or the RTA need to be banked with the collecting bankers, to ensure that money is available for investment by the scheme. Thus, the banks enable collection and payment of funds for the schemes.

Brokers are registered members of the stock exchange whose services are utilised by AMCs to buy and sell securities on the stock exchanges. Many brokers also provide the Investment Manager (AMC) with research reports on the performance of various companies, sector and market outlook, investment recommendations, etc. Regulations have imposed restrictions on the involvement of brokers in the investment process of any mutual fund. If a broker is related to the sponsor or its associate, then the AMC shall not purchase or sell securities through that broker in excess of 5% of the aggregate of purchase and sale of securities made by the mutual fund in all its schemes. For transactions through any other broker, the AMC can exceed the limit of 5%, provided it has recorded justification in writing and report of such excess has been sent to the trustee on a quarterly basis.

Selling and Distribution Agents, by acting as an intermediary between mutual funds and investors, enable the wide reach of mutual fund products throughout the length and breadth of the country. The selling and distribution agents are individual agents, distribution companies, banks, NBFCs, or direct marketing channels. These agents are compensated by way of commission – initial commission paid on mobilisation of funds and trail commission paid depending on the length of the investment holding period of the investor in the mutual fund (discussed in detail in Chapter 7). Mutual funds are advised to ensure that their agents/distributors do not indulge in any kind of malpractice or unethical practice while selling/marketing mutual fund units. SEBI has prescribed a detailed code of conduct for the mutual fund intermediaries, i.e. agents and distributors. With a view to implementing this code of conduct effectively, the AMFI (Association of Mutual Funds in India) certification examination was made mandatory for all distributors and agents of mutual funds. Regulations require that these agents should be AMFI certified and have a valid ARN (AMFI Registration Number) number allotted. The mutual fund agent certification process has come under the purview of the National Institute of Securities Market (NISM) from June 1, 2010.

Legal Advisers advise mutual funds on regulatory and taxation issues. A Compliance Officer works under their advice. The compliance officer ensures the compliance of the mutual fund schemes with SEBI regulations. He receives circulars and notifications from SEBI and forwards the same to the respective departments for necessary action. The officer receives relevant information from various departments/officers of the trust, compiles the same into standard formats and submits to SEBI/AMFI, etc. He vets the offer document to ensure that the offer document discloses all the information as required by SEBI. This helps SEBI to do continuous off-site inspection.

Investors' money is held by the trustees in the trust. The accounts of the scheme are actually the accounts of the pool in which the investors have invested in. The SEBI (Mutual Funds) Regulations, 1996 have ensured proper accounting norms to ensure fair and responsible record keeping of investor's money. Separate books of accounts are maintained for each scheme of the mutual fund and individual annual report is prepared. The books of accounts and the annual reports of the scheme are audited by **auditors**. The AMC is a company under the Companies Act, 2013 and is, therefore, required to get its accounts audited as per the provisions of the Companies Act. In order to maintain high standards of integrity and transparency, regulations stipulate that the auditor of the mutual fund schemes and the auditor of the AMC will have to be different. While the scheme auditor is appointed by the trustees, the AMC auditor is appointed by the AMC. The audit fees that auditors charge is paid by the AMC out of its income. Barring a few top fund houses which do fund accounting in-house, most fund houses have outsourced their back-office activities to custodians, who are outside the ambit of regulations as far as fund accounting and administration are concerned.

The **fund accountant** is responsible for calculating the NAV, by collecting scheme-wise information about the assets and liabilities. The AMC can either handle this activity in-house, or outsource it. A fund accountant need not register with SEBI to undertake this activity.

Chapter 3

Mutual Fund Structure
More Than a Legal Curiosity

Mutual funds can be organised in two ways – **the trust structure and the company structure**. In both these structures, there is an entity which undertakes the designing and marketing of schemes, raises money from the public under the schemes and manages the money on behalf of its owners. This entity is the fund manager or an AMC. To segregate the collected funds from this entity's own funds, the corpus is placed in a legal vehicle. **If this vehicle is a corporate entity, then the fund acquires the name of an investment company as in the United States (US); if the entity is a trust, the fund acquires the name of mutual fund as in India.** A mutual fund in the US is typically externally managed. It is not an operating company with employees in the traditional sense. Instead, a fund assembles services from third parties to carry out its business activities, i.e. investing funds in securities. In the United Kingdom, there are unit trusts and investment trusts. Irrespective of the nature of the structure, what is more fundamental is that in view of the fiduciary role of the AMC or the fund manager towards the public, there is a need for supervision of the activities of the AMC or fund manager by a separate body. A fiduciary manages the assets for the benefit of the other person rather than for his or her own profit. The supervisory role is fulfilled by the Board of Trustees in the case of a trust and in a corporate structure, by the Board of Directors of the investment company. The duties of trustees and directors are essentially identical. The trustees and directors must perform their responsibilities with the care expected of a "prudent person".

Mutual funds or unit trusts are one of the three types of investment companies, the other two being investment trusts or closed-end funds and unit investment trusts.

A **Unit Trust** is a fund which collects money and the pool of money is divided into units. Each unit accurately reflects the underlying investments.

Unit Trusts are open-end funds created by the trust deed. They have trustees who safeguard the unit-holders' interests. Assets of the unit trusts are held by the trustees on behalf of the beneficiaries – the unit-holders. The trustee may be a bank or a large insurance company appointed by the unit trust management group on a fee-paying basis to represent the unit-holders' interests. Trustees are required to make their own report in the annual accounts that, the managers have managed the fund in accordance with the trust deed and, where they have not, in what way they have transgressed.

An **Investment Trust or Closed-end Fund** is an investment company that issues a fixed number of units (new investors can buy only from existing investors) that trade on a stock exchange or in the over-the-counter market. As a result, the price of a closed-end fund's share fluctuates based on supply and demand. If the share price is more than the value of its assets, then the fund is trading at a premium; if the share price is less, then it is trading at a discount. Assets of a closed-end fund are professionally managed in accordance with the fund's investment objectives and policies and may be invested in stocks, bonds, or other securities.

Unit Investment Trusts (UITs) are public limited companies traded on the stock market and incorporated under the company law. Investors in such investment trusts are the shareholders who enjoy the same rights and privileges as shareholders in any other company. They own the company and it is up to them to choose the company's directors. A Unit Investment Trust is an investment company that buys and holds a generally fixed portfolio of stocks, bonds, or other securities and issues a fixed number of units for sale. "Units" in the trust are sold to investors, or "unit-holders," who, during the life of the trust, receive their proportionate share of dividends or interest paid by the trust. Unlike other investment companies, a UIT has a stated date for termination, which varies according to the investments held in its portfolio. At termination, investors receive their proportionate share of the UIT's net assets. UITs often have a fixed number of shares or "units" that are sold to investors in an initial public offering. If some shareholders redeem units, the UIT or its sponsor may purchase them and re-offer them to the public.

Although an **Exchange Traded Fund (ETF)** (dealt with in detail in Chapter 12), is an investment company (either a unit trust, i.e. traditional mutual fund or UIT), its structure and the trading of its shares differ significantly from traditional mutual funds or UITs. Indeed, unlike other mutual funds or UITs, ETF shares are traded intra-day on stock exchanges at market-determined prices. As such, an ETF has the features of an investment company (diversified portfolio and professional management), but its shares trade in the retail market similar to an equity security. Unlike mutual funds, investors must buy or sell ETF shares through a broker as in the case of the shares of any publicly traded company.

At this juncture, it would be useful to understand the legal composition of a mutual fund. A mutual fund is a legal entity. In India, it is organised in the form of a trust. The legal definition of mutual fund introduced in the first chapter imposes three limitations on a mutual fund and determines its basic legal character. First, it requires the mutual fund to be set up in the form of a Trust under the Indian Trusts Act, 1882. Second, it allows the mutual fund to raise resources through sale of units to the public. Third, it permits the mutual fund to invest only in securities prescribed in the SEBI (Mutual Funds) Regulations, 1996. This implies that mutual funds cannot invest in commodities other than gold, as the securities prescribed in the regulations are only shares, debentures, equity linked instruments, gold and now real estate. In India, SEBI (Mutual Funds) Regulations, 1996, regulate the structure of mutual funds. As per these regulations, **mutual funds should have a three-tier structure – Sponsor, Trustee and AMC.**

Organisation Structure of the Unit Trust of India

The first mutual fund of India was the Unit Trust of India (UTI). Unit Trust of India, which had a structure different from the three-tiered structure of other mutual funds in India, was established by the Government of India to encourage private savings and investment. It was formed under a special Act of Parliament, *viz*. The Unit Trust of India Act, 1963, as a corporate body. The promoter-sponsor of UTI was the Government of India through the Reserve Bank and financial institutions. In the true sense, however, they were the only owners of the initial units of the UTI. Different provisions of the UTI Act laid down the structure of management, scope of business, powers and functions of the trust as well as accounting, disclosures and regulatory requirements for the trust.

The management structure of UTI was thus distinct from the remaining mutual funds in more than one way. First, unlike other mutual funds, it was a statutory body corporate and not a trust under the Indian Trusts Act, 1882. Second, there was no separate asset management company with a separate board of directors of AMC to manage the schemes. The functions of the Board of directors of the AMC and the trustees were combined in the Executive Committee and Board of UTI. The sponsors existed in the form of Government and Industrial Development Bank of India (IDBI), though they did not hold any equity in the trustee company or AMC for none existed.

It was a trust, custodian and investment manager all in one. It was capable of buying property and borrowing/lending money for project finance. SEBI regulated UTI through a special regulatory dispensation effective from July 1, 1994, which *inter alia* required UTI to file offer documents in accordance with the SEBI (Mutual Funds) Regulations and allowed SEBI to inspect UTI. In 2003, the UTI Act was repealed.

In February 2003, following the repeal of the Unit Trust of India Act, 1963, UTI was bifurcated into two separate entities. One is the UTI Mutual Fund Ltd., sponsored by State Bank of India (SBI), Punjab National Bank (PNB), Bank of Baroda (BOB) and Life Insurance Corporation (LIC). It is registered with SEBI and functions under the Mutual Fund Regulations. The second is the Specified Undertaking of the Unit Trust of India (SUUTI) with assets under management of Rs. 29,835 crore as at the end of January 2003, representing broadly the assets of Unit 64 Scheme, assured returns and certain other schemes of the beleaguered behemoth. The Specified Undertaking of Unit Trust of India functions under an administrator and under the rules framed by the Government of India. It does not come under the purview of SEBI (Mutual Funds) Regulations, 1996.

Organisation Structure of Mutual Funds of Public Sector Banks

In 1987, the public sector banks were allowed to set up mutual funds. State Bank of India was the first one to set up a mutual fund. It preferred to adopt the trust route and set up the mutual fund as a trust under the Indian Trusts Act, 1882. Later, other mutual funds followed suit and thus trusts set up under the Indian Trusts Act became the adopted legal form of mutual funds in India. These mutual funds combined the roles of trustee, fund manager and custodian in the sponsoring bank. There was little demarcation in the roles and responsibilities and the structure was open to conflict of interests.

With the establishment of SEBI under the SEBI Act, 1992, mutual funds other than the UTI, were brought under the regulatory purview of SEBI. SEBI found that mutual funds had been set up by public sector banks adopting the trust route because using the route of the Companies Act appeared to be more complex as it could have also led to multiple regulatory jurisdictions. The SEBI (Mutual Funds) Regulations provided for setting up of mutual funds as trusts under the Indian Trusts Act of 1882.

In the context of Indian mutual funds, it needs to be mentioned that the Indian Trusts Act was enacted in 1882, essentially to govern private trusts and charitable institutions. Trust form of organisation appears suitable to meet the requirements of the investors who are unable to play the role of principals in their investment management process. The trust structure attempts to bifurcate the role of the principal (that is, the owner) into two parts – the beneficial owner (the investor) and the registered owner (the trustee). The trustee assumes the role of the principal and intercedes between the investor and the asset manager. He exercises the oversight function on the investment manager. **Trustees are the fictitious owners of trust property**. The relationship between the beneficiary and the trustee is one of principal and agent. However, between the trustee and a third person, the trustee assumes the role of fictitious owner of the trust property. This enables the trustee to represent the beneficiary in his dealings with the world at large. The trustee has the right to possess the title deeds of the trust property and to reimburse himself expenses incurred in the execution of the trust. He can also indemnify against breach of trust. As per trust law, a trustee is bound to keep clear and accurate accounts of the trust property. Further, he is bound to furnish the beneficiary full and accurate information as to the state of the trust property at all reasonable times. The effectiveness of the trust structure depends on how trustworthy the trustees are. The SEBI (Mutual Funds) Regulations, 1996 provide stringent qualifications for the appointment of trustees. Persons with ability, integrity and standing can be appointed as trustees. The regulations had spelled out the rights and obligations of the trustees, the disqualifications from being appointed as trustees, etc. to ensure that they carry out their fiduciary responsibilities in the best interest of the unit-holders. The act has delineated a code of conduct to be abided by the trustees. As per SEBI Regulations, the instrument of trust should be in the form of a deed. The trust deed contains clauses for safeguarding the interests of the unit-holders.

Mutual funds are repositories of trust and of investors' hard-earned money. The task of providing protection to them is a difficult one. Considering the inherent fiduciary nature of the functions, arm's length relationships were sought to be built into the various constituents of a mutual fund by the existing SEBI (Mutual Funds) Regulations, through separation of various entities which constitute a mutual fund – sponsor, trustees, asset management companies and custodian. Besides, the SEBI (Mutual Funds) Regulations require that two-thirds of the trustees and half of the board of directors of the AMC must be independent of sponsor or its affiliates. The beneficial owners of the trust, i.e. the unit-holders, have also been given a role, as their approval is required by the fund/AMC to enable it to bring about certain changes in the fund or to wind up a scheme. The SEBI regulations have made it mandatory that the trustees shall obtain the consent of the unit-holders in important matters. The trustees shall ensure that no change in the fundamental attributes of any scheme or the trust or fees and expenses payable or any other change which would modify the scheme and affect the interest of unit-holders, shall be carried out unless it is made known to the unit-holders and the unit-holders are given an option to exit at the prevailing Net Asset Value without any exit load. The unit-holders have a right to terminate the AMC. The appointment of an AMC can be terminated by majority of the trustees or by seventy-five per cent of the unit-holders of the scheme. Any change in the appointment of the AMC shall be subject to prior approval of SEBI and the unit-holders ('Rights of Unit-holders' is dealt with in detail in the next chapter).

Chapter 4

Legal and Regulatory Framework
The Resilient Enabler

Mutual funds have emerged as an important segment of financial markets and have so far delivered value to the investors. But no industry can flourish without a proper regulatory mechanism in place. SEBI has played a vital role in regulating the mutual fund business. From time to time, it has tried to plug the loopholes prevailing in the system and safeguard the interest of investors, who have been the backbone of this unprecedented growth.

SEBI, the apex regulator of the capital markets, is the primary regulator of mutual funds in India. **SEBI has framed the SEBI (Mutual Funds) Regulations, 1996, which provide for the establishment, management and regulation of mutual funds in India**. Registration with SEBI is mandatory for all mutual funds in India. Every mutual fund must be constituted in the form of a trust in accordance with the provisions of the Indian Trusts Act, 1882. The instrument of trust must be in the form of a deed between the sponsor and the trustees of the mutual fund duly registered under the provisions of the Indian Registration Act, 1908. The structure and formation of mutual funds, appointment, rights and obligations and regulation of the principal constituents, operations of the mutual fund, accounting and disclosure norms, investment restrictions, compliance and penalties come under the purview of the SEBI (Mutual Funds) Regulations, 1996. Mutual funds have to provide reports about their operations, including half-yearly compliance reports. SEBI is also entitled to inspect the mutual funds to ensure compliance with the SEBI (Mutual Funds) Regulations, 1996.

An applicant proposing to sponsor a mutual fund in India, must apply in Form A with a fee of Rs. 25,000. The application is examined and once the sponsor satisfies certain conditions (already discussed under 'Sponsors' in Chapter 2), it is required to complete the remaining formalities for setting up a mutual fund. These include, *inter alia*, executing the trust deed and investment management agreement, setting up a trustee company/board of trustees comprising two-thirds independent trustees, incorporating the AMC and appointing a custodian. Upon satisfying these conditions, the registration certificate is issued subject to the payment of registration fee of Rs. 25 lakh.

Each mutual fund scheme floated by the mutual fund has to be approved by the trustees and the offer document is required to be filed with SEBI. The offer document should contain disclosures that are adequate enough to enable the investors to make an informed investment decision. There are obligations on the AMC and the trustee to ensure that the statements made in the offer documents are true and correct. SEBI has prescribed an advertising code that has to be observed while launching a new scheme. SEBI has restricted mutual funds from giving guaranteed returns in a scheme unless such returns are fully guaranteed by the sponsor or the AMC, or a statement indicating the name of the person who will guarantee the returns is made in the offer document. Besides, there are some investment criteria that need to be adhered to by the mutual funds.

Investors would find the name of the contact person whom they may approach in case of any query, complaints or grievances, in the offer document of the mutual fund scheme. The names of the directors of the AMC and trustees are also given in the offer document. Investors can also approach SEBI to redress their complaints. On receipt of complaints, SEBI takes up the matter with the concerned mutual fund and follows up with them till the matter is resolved. *(Kindly refer to the official website of SEBI, www.sebi.gov.in, for the comprehensive and updated regulations on mutual funds.)*

Rights of Unit-holders Specified by SEBI

SEBI has clearly stated your rights and limitations as a unit-holder. The salient rights are elaborated below. It is imperative that you understand them and use them as and when the need arises.

- NFOs (New Fund Offers) can remain open for a maximum of 15 days (30 days in the case of ELSS [Equity Linked Savings Scheme]). Units have to be allotted/refunded within 5 days of the NFO (15 days in the case of ELSS). In the case of open-end funds, the scheme has to reopen for continuous sale and redemption within 5 business days of allotment. In the event of delays in refunds, unit-holders are to be paid interest at the rate of 15% p.a. for the period of the delay. This interest cannot be charged to the scheme.

- Units of all mutual fund schemes held in demat form are freely transferable. Unit-holders have the option to receive allotment of mutual fund units of open-end and closed-end schemes in their demat account. Only in the case of ELSS schemes, free transferability of units (whether demat or physical) is curtailed for the statutory minimum holding period of 3 years.
- Statement of Accounts is to be sent to unit-holders as follows:
  - Within 5 business days of closure of the NFO in the case of NFOs
  - Within 10 business days of the investment in the case of post-NFO investment
  - Within 10 business days of initial transaction and once every calendar quarter (March, June, September, December) within 10 business days of the end of the quarter in the case of SIP/ STP/ SWP
  - On specific request by the unit-holder, it will be dispatched to him within 5 business days free of cost. If mandated by the unit-holder, soft-copy shall be e-mailed to him every month.
  - Dormant investors, i.e. investors who have not transacted during the previous 6 months shall be sent Statement of Accounts along with the Portfolio Statement/Annual Return, with the latest position on the number and value of units held.
  - Unit-holders can ask for a Unit Certificate for their Unit Holding. This is different from a Statement of Accounts. A Statement of Accounts shows the opening balance, transactions during the period and closing balance. A Unit Certificate only mentions the number of units held by the investor. In a way, the Statement of Accounts is similar to a bank pass book, while the Unit Certificate is comparable to a Balance Confirmation Certificate issued by the bank. Since Unit Certificates are non-transferable, they do not offer any real transactional convenience for the unit-holder. However, if a unit-holder asks for it, the AMC is bound to issue the Unit Certificate within 5 business days of receipt of request.
- Half-yearly results and the entire portfolio have to be published in at least one national daily, at least once in 6 months. Such disclosure has to be done within 30 days of the six-monthly account closing date of the fund.
- Unit-holders have the right to ask the trustees about any information that may have an adverse bearing on their investments and trustees are bound to disclose such information to the unit-holders.

- Unit-holders have the right to inspect copies of the Trust Deed, investment management agreement, agreements with fund constituents, memorandum and articles of association of the AMC and unabridged balance sheets of the mutual fund schemes, sponsor and the AMC.
- Unit-holders are entitled to receive dividend warrants within 30 days of the date of declaration of dividend and interest @15% has to be paid by the AMC or sponsor in case of delay in payment.
- Unit-holders are entitled to receive redemption proceeds within 10 business days and interest @15% has to be paid by the AMC or sponsor in case of delay in payment.
- Unit-holders can recover unclaimed dividend and redemption amounts. If they claim the money within 3 years, then payment is based on the prevailing NAV after adding the income earned on the unclaimed money. If they claim after 3 years, then payment is based on the NAV at the end of 3 years.
- Unit-holders can appoint a maximum of 3 nominees. They will be entitled to the units in the event of the unit-holder's death. The unit-holder can specify the proportion in which the units can be distributed among the nominees. If no distribution is indicated, an equal distribution among the nominees will be presumed.
- Unit-holders can also pledge the units. This is most commonly done to offer security to a financier.
- Unit-holders can opt for a change in their distributor or go direct. On a written request by the unit-holder, AMCs will need to comply without insisting on any kind of No Objection Certificate from the existing distributor.
- If 75% of the unit-holders so decide, a scheme can be wound up or a meeting of the unit-holders can be called, or the appointment of the AMC of the mutual fund can be terminated.
- If there is change in any of the fundamental attributes of the scheme, the unit-holders have to be informed in writing and they have to be given an option to redeem their holdings at NAV without any load.
- In the event of any issue with the AMC or the scheme, the unit-holder can initially approach the Investor Service Centre. If the issue is not sorted out, in spite of taking it up with the senior echelons of the AMC, the unit-holder can seek redressal from SEBI. Offer Documents have details of the number of complaints received and their disposal. Pending investor complaints can be a ground for SEBI to refuse permission to the AMC to launch new schemes.

- The trustees are bound to obtain consent of 75% of the unit-holders whenever required to do so by SEBI, in the interest of the unit-holders, when the trustees decide to wind up or prematurely redeem the scheme.
- If a unit-holder feels that the trustees have not fulfilled their obligations, he can file a suit against the trustees for breach of trust.

Limitation of Rights of Unit-holders

- Under the law, a trust is a notional entity. Therefore, unit-holders cannot sue the trust (but they can file suits against trustees).
- The principle of *caveat emptor* (let the buyer beware) applies to mutual fund investments. So, the unit-holder cannot seek legal protection on the grounds of not being aware, especially when it comes to the provisions of law and matters fairly and transparently stated in the Offer Document.
- Unit-holders have a right to proceed against the AMC or trustees in certain cases. However, a proposed investor, i.e. someone who has not invested in the scheme does not have the same rights.
- The Companies Act, 2013 offers some protection to shareholders and people who invest in fixed deposits in companies. A unit-holder in a scheme is, however, neither a shareholder, nor a fixed deposit-holder – and the scheme is in any case not a company. Therefore, these protections under the Companies Act, 2013 are not available to unit-holders in a scheme.

Reserve Bank of India (RBI), the regulator of the banking system and the monetary authority of India, is involved with the mutual fund industry only to the limited extent of being the regulator of the sponsors of bank-sponsored mutual funds. RBI regulates the Government securities market and money markets in India. Earlier, bank-sponsored mutual funds, gilt mutual funds and money market mutual funds were under the dual control of RBI and SEBI. At present, gilt mutual funds and money market mutual funds are regulated by SEBI. Mutual funds are affected by the RBI stipulations on the structure, issuance, pricing and trading of Government securities.

The Ministry of Finance (MoF), the supervisor for both SEBI and RBI, is the appellate authority under SEBI Regulations. Aggrieved parties can make appeals to the MoF on the SEBI rulings relating to mutual funds.

Mutual funds come under the purview of **the Office of the Public Trustee** since they are structured and registered as trusts under the

Indian Trusts Act, 1882. The public trustee, in turn, reports to the Charity Commissioner.

Since the AMCs are structured as limited companies, the provisions of the Companies Act, 2013 are applicable and they come under the purview of the **Company Law Board (CLB)**. CLB has to be approached for filing complaints against directors of the AMC and trustee company. Periodic reports and annual accounts have to be filed with the **Registrar of Companies (ROC)**. The formulation and modification of laws relating to companies and the prosecution of directors for non-compliance with the provisions of the Act rests with the **Department of Company Affairs (DCA)**.

Mutual funds (closed-end funds) that list their units in **Stock Exchanges** are governed by **the listing agreement,** which necessitates periodic notifications and disclosure of information that may impact the trading of listed units.

Association of Mutual Funds in India (AMFI) is the apex body of mutual funds in India incorporated on August 22, 1995 with a view to promoting the interests of mutual funds and unit-holders, to set ethical, commercial and professional standards and to increase public awareness of the mutual fund industry. True to its objectives, it has been providing yeoman service to the mutual fund industry as well as to the investor. Till date, all Indian AMCs registered with SEBI are its members. It functions under the supervision and guidance of the Board of Directors and is headed by a full-time chairman. AMFI functions through a number of committees, some of them standing committees, in order to address areas requiring constant vigil and improvements. *Ad hoc* committees are also constituted to address specific issues. These committees consist of industry professionals from member mutual funds. It has functioned as a formidable forum, where mutual funds have been able to present their views, debate and participate in creating their own regulatory framework. AMFI was originally created as a body that would lobby with the regulator to ensure that the viewpoint of the funds was heard. Today, it is usually consulted on matters long before regulations are framed and it often initiates regulatory changes that prevent malpractices that crop up from time to time. At present, AMFI can only issue guidelines to its members and it cannot enforce regulations.

Self-Regulatory Organisations (SROs) regulate their own members. Statutory regulatory bodies confine themselves to laying down the broad policy framework and leave the micro regulation to SROs, wherever SROs exist. Mutual funds in India are directly regulated by SEBI since they have not constituted an SRO for themselves.

Mergers and Takeovers in the Mutual Fund Industry

Mergers of mutual fund schemes are quite common. The main reason for this is that there are often too many funds within the AMC with a similar objective. This automatically leads to higher costs for the AMC as it has to maintain records under different fund names, print different forms and so on. However, when this happens, there is a tax implication for individual investors.

When two schemes merge, investors of the scheme, which is being merged, would get units of the scheme into which their scheme has been absorbed. The NAVs of the two schemes determine the exchange ratio of units at that point of time. Scheme mergers are treated as sale of funds or redemption and long-term investors are deemed fresh investors the moment a scheme is merged with another one and taxed accordingly. From April 1, 2017 scheme mergers will no longer be considered as fresh investments. There will be no tax impact at the time of merger. Only the holding period and the cost of acquisition of the units in erstwhile schemes will be taken into consideration for taxation purposes.

SEBI regulations require that SEBI and trustees of both funds must approve of the merger. The mutual funds have to demonstrate that the circumstances merit the merger of the scheme and the interests of the unit-holders are not adversely affected. After approval by the boards of AMCs and trustees, mutual funds will have to file such a proposal with SEBI. The regulator would then communicate its observations on the proposal. The letter to unit-holders would be issued only after the final observations communicated by SEBI have been incorporated and final copies of the same have been filed with SEBI. Unit-holders must be notified of the merger and be provided the option to exit at NAV without load. An exit option is an opportunity for existing investors of acquired schemes to withdraw their investments without paying an exit load. For instance, a fund house is merging scheme 'B' with scheme 'A', then as per the existing norms, mutual funds have to give exit option to the unit-holders of both the schemes at the current NAV.

Common forms of Mergers and Acquisitions in the mutual fund industry in India are illustrated below, in brief, with examples:

Merger of AMCs: The AMC merges with another AMC and a new merged AMC takes care of the schemes of both the AMCs. Example: Merger of the AMCs of HB Mutual Fund and Taurus Mutual Fund.

AMC Takeover: The AMC is taken over by another sponsor. Example: Takeover of Pioneer ITI AMC by Franklin Templeton Mutual Fund.

Scheme Takeover: The scheme is taken over by another AMC. Example: Takeover of Apple Mutual Fund's schemes by Birla Mutual Fund, where the management of the fund was transferred from Apple AMC to Birla AMC.

Winding Up of Schemes

In the case of winding up of a scheme, the mutual funds pay a sum based on the prevailing NAV after adjustment of expenses. Unit-holders are entitled to receive a report on winding up from the mutual funds giving all necessary details.

There have been wide ranging regulations, covering aspects from the way mutual funds invest to the way mutual funds are sold. The Indian mutual fund industry has changed over the past few years, possibly beyond recognition. The new regulations have broken the shackles of traditional practices and have made mutual funds one of the most affordable and accessible financial instruments for the Indian investor.

SECTION III
FUND CONCEPTS

> "Thoughts without content are empty, intuition without concepts are blind."
>
> – Immanuel Kant

Blind man's buff is a traditional children's game in which a blindfolded player tries to catch and identify the other players. This is a game of chance, wherein you do not have control over the odds. You need to just beat the other players to win the game. Thankfully, successful mutual fund investment is akin to a game of chance in which you have control over the odds. You cannot control whether the funds you buy will outperform the market. But you can control your return expectations, your risk, your costs and above all, your own behaviour.

> "The fault, dear investor, is not in our stars – and not in our stocks – but in ourselves…"
>
> – Benjamin Graham

Be patient, disciplined and eager to learn. Harness your emotions and think for yourself. As you begin to master concepts in mutual fund investment, you are increasing your odds of achieving investment success.

We start this section by elucidating the core concepts of mutual funds, followed by demystifying certain myths prevalent in the fund industry. To conclude, we dedicate two chapters to the concepts related to costs, an important dimension of mutual fund returns and analyse them threadbare. That cost matters cannot but be overemphasised.

Chapter 5

Core Concepts
Reinforcing the Roots

There are certain concepts to be clarified before we deal with mutual fund investing.

The mutual fund is a trust registered under the Indian Trusts Act. It is initiated by a sponsor. A **sponsor** is a person, who acts alone or with a corporate, to establish a mutual fund. The sponsor then appoints a **trustee** to safeguard your interests and an **AMC** to manage the investment, marketing, accounting and other functions pertaining to the fund. For instance, HDFC Trustee Company Limited is appointed as the trustee to the mutual fund trust, HDFC Mutual Fund by the sponsors, Housing Development Finance Corporation Limited and Standard Life Investments Limited. HDFC Asset Management Company Limited is appointed as its investment manager (AMC).

An AMC is the fund house or the company that manages the investor's money. A **fund house** has a group of **funds/schemes** with diverse objectives managed under one umbrella. The terms **funds** and **schemes** are used interchangeably. The most basic fund family would include equity, debt and money market portfolio, although many fund houses have variants including sector funds, balanced funds, etc. For instance, HDFC Mutual Fund is a fund house with several funds under it. HDFC Equity Fund, HDFC Prudence Fund, etc. are all independent schemes managed by HDFC Mutual Fund. Mutual fund schemes, with a range of investment objectives offer varying degree of return and corresponding risk. You are essentially buying into the scheme's investment philosophy when you invest in a scheme. Scheme is the notional entity for which books of accounts are maintained.

It is easier to **switch** between the various funds in the same fund house. Funds will also usually give you a choice either to receive a cheque for distribution of dividend or to reinvest the earnings or dividends (myth associated with dividends by mutual funds will be dealt with in the subsequent chapter) and get more units. For instance, HDFC Equity Fund – Growth, HDFC Equity Fund – Dividend Reinvestment and HDFC Equity Fund – Dividend are all the various **options** (to be dealt with in detail later) offered by the fund house under the scheme. The books of accounts and investment portfolio are kept at the scheme level and *pro rata* adjustments/transaction differences are made to reflect the differences between options/plans. For instance, there would be a single revenue account, based on which, the amount to be distributed as dividend under the scheme would be decided. This dividend amount would be apportioned between the various options based on the value of assets under each option. The dividend amount that is apportioned to 'dividend option' would be distributed among those investors, who have chosen that option. The dividend amount that is apportioned to 'reinvestment option' and 'growth option' would be added to the assets of those investors who have chosen those options. Thus, the retained earnings for the different options would be different.

New Fund Offering (NFO) is the term given to a new mutual fund scheme. Every scheme has an investment portfolio. **Portfolio** is the term, which refers to all the investments made by the fund as well as the amount held in cash. Let us assume that a very small mutual fund has an initial investment of 1,000 units and each unit is worth Rs. 10, also known as the face value. Face value assumes importance from the accounting perspective. Now, the total amount with the fund, i.e. the number of units multiplied by the face value of each unit is Rs. 10,000. This is referred to as the **corpus or the unit capital**. Later, some other investors invest Rs. 2,000. Now, the corpus will be Rs. 12,000 (Rs. 10,000 + Rs. 2,000). The total amount of money invested (Rs. 12,000) in the fund is called the corpus. **Asset under Management (AUM)** is the total value of all the investments currently being managed by the fund. Let us say the corpus is Rs. 12,000 but due to a rise in the market price of the shares it has invested in, the value of the units has increased. So, Rs. 12,000 invested is now worth Rs. 15,000. This figure is referred to as the AUM. The fund's AUM is declared once every quarter. It is the total value of the portfolio that the fund is invested in on that particular day. In simple terms, it is the total of the NAV multiplied by the total number of units. Hence, the AUM fluctuates with the changing NAV, redemptions and even additional purchases done.

Fund Pricing: NAV and the Pricing Process

By law, you are able to redeem mutual fund units each business day. As a result, fund units are very liquid investments. Most mutual funds also continually offer new units to you. Many fund companies also allow you to transfer money or make "exchanges" (switches) from one fund to another within the same fund family. Mutual funds process your request for redemptions and exchanges as a normal part of daily business activity and must ensure that all transactions receive the appropriate price.

Your contribution to the pool of funds is converted into standard units so as to inform you regarding the value of your investment on any given day and to keep track of your investments while entering and exiting on different dates, including partial exiting. The pool of funds earns **interest income or dividend income** on the investments it holds. Further, when it purchases and sells investments, it earns capital gains or incurs capital losses. These are called **realised capital gains or realised capital losses** as the case may be. Investments owned by the pool of funds may be quoted in the market at higher than the cost paid. Such gains in values on securities held are called **valuation gains**. Similarly, there can be **valuation losses** when securities are quoted in the market at a price below the cost at which the scheme acquired them. Running the scheme leads to its share of **operating expenses**.

Investments can be said to have been handled profitably, if the following **profitability measure** is positive:

(A) + Interest income

(B) + Dividend income

(C) + Realised capital gains

(D) + Valuation gains

(E) − Realised capital losses

(F) − Valuation losses

(G) − Scheme expenses

When the investment activity is profitable, the true worth of a unit goes up; when there are losses, the true worth of a unit goes down. **The true worth of a unit of the scheme is otherwise called Net Asset Value (NAV) of the scheme.**

NAV is a term that you will often hear in the context of mutual fund investment (the myth associated with NAV is discussed in the subsequent chapter). The price per unit at which units are redeemed is known as the NAV. NAV is the current market value of all the assets of the fund minus its liabilities (e.g. fund expenses), divided by the total number of outstanding units. NAV is the net asset of the scheme divided by the number of units outstanding on the valuation date. So, Net Asset Value is the market value of a unit of a scheme after accounting for all expenses on any given business day. The market value of the investments is determined on the basis of their closing prices at the principal stock exchange. The process of valuing assets by using market prices is known as **marking to market**. The NAV should reflect the true worth of each unit of the scheme, because you buy or sell units on the basis of the information contained in the NAV. If investments are not marked to market, then the investment portfolio will end up being valued at the cost at which each security was bought. Valuing shares of a company at their acquisition cost, say Rs. 20, is meaningless, if those shares have appreciated to, say Rs. 70. If the scheme were to sell the shares at that time, it would recover Rs. 70 – not Rs. 20. When the NAV captures the movement of the share from Rs. 20 to Rs. 70, then it is meaningful for you. Thus, marking to market helps you buy and sell units of a scheme at fair prices, which are determined based on transparently calculated and freely shared information on NAV.

Net Assets = Market value of investments + current assets and other assets + accrued income – current liabilities and other liabilities – accrued expenses.

This calculation ensures that the value of each unit in the fund is identical. You may determine the value of your *pro rata* share of the mutual fund by multiplying the number of units held by the fund's NAV.

Some mutual funds own securities, which are not regularly traded on any formal exchange. These may be shares in very small or bankrupt companies, or derivatives, or private investments in unregistered financial instruments (such as stock in a non-public company). In the absence of a public market for these securities, it is the responsibility of the fund manager to form an estimate of their value when computing the NAV. As to how much of a fund's assets may be invested in such securities is stated in the fund's prospectus.

> **Fund Pricing in the United States**
>
> **Determining Share Price**
>
> Fund x owns a portfolio of stocks worth $6 million; its liabilities are $60,000; its shareholders own 500,000 shares.
>
> Share Price
> or
> Net Asset Value (NAV) = $11.88
>
> Market Value in Dollars of Securities Minus Liabilities ($6,000,000 - $60,000) / Number of Investor Shares Outstanding (500,000)
>
> Share prices appear in the financial pages of most major newspapers. A share price can also be found in semiannual and annual reports.

Source: ICI Website

Figure 5.1 Determination of NAV in the USA

The price at which a fund's shares (units are called shares in the USA) may be purchased is its NAV per share plus any applicable front end sales charge (the offering price of a fund without a sales charge would be the same as its NAV per share). The NAV must reflect the current value of the fund's securities. The value of these securities is determined either by a market quotation for those securities in which a market quotation is readily available, or if a market quotation is not readily available, at fair value as determined in good faith by the fund.

The Investment Company Act of 1940 requires "forward pricing," meaning that shareholders who purchase or redeem shares must receive the next computed share price (NAV) following the fund's receipt of the transaction order. Under forward pricing, orders received prior to 4 p.m. receive the price determined on the same day at 4 p.m.; orders received after 4 p.m. receive the price determined at 4 p.m. on the next business day. Most funds price their securities at 4 p.m. Eastern time, when the New York Stock Exchange closes. A mutual fund typically obtains the prices for securities it holds from a market data vendor, which is a company that collects prices on a wide variety of securities. Fund accounting agents internally validate the prices received from a vendor by subjecting them to various control procedures. In many instances, funds may use more than one pricing service either to ensure accuracy or to receive prices for a wide variety of securities held in its portfolio (e.g. stocks or bonds).

The vast majority of mutual funds submit their daily NAVs to NASDAQ by 6 p.m. Eastern time so that they may be published in the next day's morning newspapers. As NASDAQ receives prices, they are instantaneously transmitted to news-wire services and other subscribers. Daily fund prices are available in newspapers and other sources such as through a fund's toll-free telephone service or website.

Federal law (in the USA) as well as SEBI guidelines (in India) require that a fund's NAV be calculated each trading day. NAV based on market prices and valuation in the past is known as **historical pricing.** The **prospective NAV** is that which is based on that day's NAV or the next business day's prices and valuation. Earlier, mutual funds used to prescribe their own cut-off times. Now, SEBI has issued guidelines in this regard, which is mandatory.

All funds other than liquid funds have a different cut-off. For valid purchase and redemption applications for amounts less than Rs. 2 lakh received up to 3 p.m., the closing NAV of the day on which the application is received is applicable. In case valid applications are received after 3 p.m., the closing NAV of the next business day is applicable. In respect of valid applications for an amount of Rs. 2 lakh or more received at the official points of acceptance up to 3 p.m. by the mutual fund and the funds are available for utilisation on the same day before the cut-off time (3 p.m.) – the closing NAV of the day on which the funds are available for utilisation shall be applicable. In respect of valid applications received at the official points of acceptance after 3 p.m. by the mutual fund and the funds are available for utilisation on the same day – the closing NAV of the business day following the day on which the funds are available for utilisation shall be applicable. However, irrespective of the time of receipt of application, where the funds are not available for utilisation on the day of the application, the closing NAV of the business day on which the funds are available for utilisation before the cut-off time (3 p.m.) shall be applicable provided the application is received at the official points of acceptance prior to availability of the funds. For determining the availability of funds for utilisation, the funds for the entire amount of subscription/purchase (including switch-in) as per the application should be credited to the bank account of the scheme before the cut-off time and the funds are available for utilisation before the cut-off time without availing any credit facility whether intra-day or otherwise, by the respective scheme.

In the case of liquid funds, for valid purchase applications received up to 2 p.m., the closing NAV of the day immediately before the day on which funds are available for utilisation is applicable. In case the purchase application is received after 2 p.m. and the funds are available for utilisation on the same day, closing NAV of the same day is applied. Irrespective of the time of receipt of application, where funds are not available for utilisation on the day of the application, the closing NAV of the day immediately preceding the day on which the funds are available for utilisation is applicable. The entire amount of the application must also be credited to the bank account of the respective scheme before the cut-off time. In respect of valid redemption applications received up to 3 p.m., the closing NAV of day immediately preceding the next business day is applicable. If valid redemption applications are received after 3 p.m. by the mutual fund, the closing NAV of the next business day is applicable.

Mutual funds post the NAV on the website of AMFI (www.amfiindia.com) by 9 p.m. every day. Thus, you can access NAVs of all mutual funds at one place. The NAVs are also available on the websites of mutual funds. Mutual funds also make the NAV of their schemes available over phone, using the 24-hour voice mail facility. While open-end funds compute and disclose NAVs every day, closed-end funds compute NAVs every week (updated every Thursday) while disclosures have to be made every day. Closed-end schemes, not listed by mandate on stock exchanges, can publish NAV periodically (each month or quarter) as permitted by SEBI.

Fund Expenses (to be dealt with in detail later)

NAV is the most important measure of performance of a mutual fund. Let us say you have invested Rs. 10,000 in a scheme at Rs. 13 a unit and now its NAV is Rs. 15. Quite simply, that means your investment has appreciated by more than 15%. But, wait before you jump in joy – you may not actually get that much when you redeem your units. That is because of the load charged by mutual funds. The expense ratio is calculated on an ongoing basis and already factored in the NAV declared.

Let me introduce you to some concepts associated with mutual fund expenses before we proceed with the example. **A mutual fund's costs are categorised as sales charges (Loads) and operating expenses (Expense Ratio).**

Loads include distributors' commission and marketing and selling expenses that are charged directly to you. **Front End Load or Entry Load** (abolished w.e.f. August 1, 2009) was a fee that was charged upfront, when you purchased the mutual fund units. It was charged on a percentage basis on the face value, based on the amount of purchase. **Point of Purchase Price (POP), or Resale Price, or Sales Price** was the price you paid to purchase a unit of the fund. **Back End or Rear End Load or Exit**

Load is a fee that is charged at redemption. **Redemption Price** is the price received by the investor on selling units of an open-end scheme to the fund. The difference between the Sales Price and the NAV is called the entry load and the difference between the Redemption Price and the NAV is called the exit load. The loads that are charged depending upon your period of holding your scheme investment are called **Contingent Deferred Sales Charge (CDSC).** CDSC is a fee imposed by certain funds on units redeemed within a specific period following their purchase. These charges are usually assessed on a sliding scale, such as 4% to 1% of the amounts redeemed, with the fee reduced each year the units are held. Imposition of CDSC serves as an incentive to invest for the long term.

Expense Ratio is an annual operating expense expressed as a percentage of the fund's average daily net assets. It refers to costs incurred in operating a mutual fund and is paid out of the fund's earnings. It includes advisory fees paid to investment managers, audit fees, custodial fees, transfer agent fees, trustee fees, legal expenses, etc. Operating expenses are calculated on an annualised basis and are normally accrued on a daily basis. Therefore, you pay expenses prorated for the time you remain invested in the fund.

Let us return to our example. Since entry load has been abolished, the price at which you invest is Rs. 13 and you receive 769.231 units (10,000/13) as against 761.615 (10,000/13.13) units earlier, when entry load was levied since sales price and the NAV are the same (assuming an entry load of 1%, sales price per unit worked out to 13.13 =13+13*1/100).

Let us now assume that you decide to redeem your 769.231 units and the exit load is 0.50%. The Redemption Price per unit works out to Rs. 14.925 (15–15*0.5/100). Earlier, when the entry load was charged, you would have received Rs. 11,367.10 (761.615 × 14.925). The returns would have reduced to 13.6% of the investment as a result of entry and exit loads. Now, with entry loads no longer levied, you would receive Rs. 11,480.77 (769.231 × 14.925) and the returns would reduce to 14.8% only.

Repurchase Price is different from **Redemption Price** and refers to the price at which a closed-end scheme repurchases its units. Repurchase can either be at NAV or can have an exit load. (Open-end and Closed-end Funds will be discussed in the section on Fund Flavour).

Now, you can appreciate the extent to which mutual fund loads and expenses eat into your real returns. The associated cost for mutual funds is still very low when compared to making investments directly in equities. This notwithstanding, a proper understanding of mutual fund expenses will stand you in good stead when you have to choose from among equally well-performing funds.

Fund Account Statement

In today's ever-growing mutual fund market, mutual funds have become a part of every investor's portfolio. Despite this fact, how many of you can confidently state the exact number of mutual fund units in your portfolio or at what NAV your money has been invested? Does your fund levy a load? What was the rate at which you got your monthly dividend? All this is possible if you have a regular look at the mutual fund account statement that the fund houses mail to you periodically. Here is a small guide to understand your **Fund Account Statement**.

Mutual funds issue account statements with the facility to hold units in fractions up to 3 decimal units. A mutual fund statement is just like your bank account statement. It is a complete summary of your investments. It is generated within 4 to 5 days of your investment in a particular scheme and received by you within 7 to 10 business days. So, for any delay more than the stated period, you have to contact your broker or the fund house. The frequency of the account statement is stated in the offer document. In most cases, you receive an annual statement if there are no transactions in a year. You can use the latest phone service or internet service, to check the balances in your accounts and effect transactions through the phone or the internet.

The statement date is the date on which the fund house issues the statement as requested by you. "For the period" states the period for which the statement is issued. Say from January 1, 2015 to December 31, 2015.

To understand the statement, we need to break it into parts starting with:

- **Customer folio/account number:** This is mentioned on the top of the statement. Just like your bank account number, this is the fund account number, which is also your reference number. For any correspondence, the folio/account number is a prerequisite. Therefore, besides maintaining a record of the statements, it is also important to make a note of the folio/account number. While funds, including Franklin Templeton Mutual Fund, allot account numbers for each scheme, it clubs all your investments with the fund house under one single umbrella, called a folio and allots you a unique number, called a folio number.

* **Personal details:** The name, address and phone numbers of the first holder, the names of the second and third holders and Permanent Account Number (PAN) of all unit-holders are stated.
* **Other details:** Tax status, mode of holding and bank account details are stated.

Make sure that the personal details, as mentioned in the statement, are as per the data furnished by you. If there are any discrepancies, inform the fund house immediately and get it rectified.

In the main body of the statement, you will get all the information relating to your transaction(s). The transaction details in the fund account statement are produced below:

Table 5.1   Transaction Details in the Fund Account Statement

Fund Account Statement for the period January 1, 2015 to December 31, 2015

Account/Folio Number

ABC Fund – Dividend Reinvestment						
Date	Transaction Type	Amount (Rs.)	NAV (Rs.)	Price (Rs.)	Units	Unit Balance
28/01/15	Dividend Payout @ Rs.0.14032016 per unit	140.32	0	0	0	1,000
20/02/15	Systematic Purchase (SIP) Instalment 1/12	5,000	10	10	500	1,500
28/03/15	Switch out to XYZ Fund	5,000	10	10	500	1,000
28/04/15	Switch in from XYZ Fund	5,000	10	10	500	1,500

ABC Fund – Dividend Reinvestment						
Date	Transaction Type	Amount (Rs.)	NAV (Rs.)	Price (Rs.)	Units	Unit Balance
25/06/15	Purchase	10,000	10	10	1,000	2,500
07/08/15	Dividend Reinvest. @ Rs.0.14032016 per unit	140.32	10	10	14.032	2,514.032
10/10/15	Redemption	20,000	10	10	2,000	514.032

These are some of the mutual fund transactions that you may generally see in your statement. Interpretation of this part is where most of you get stuck. Let us have a look at it in more detail.

* **Fund name** is mentioned along with the option you have selected, for example: growth, dividend payout, or dividend reinvestment.

* **Date** on which the transaction takes place.

* **Transaction type** states the type of transaction you have opted for – purchase, systematic investment plan (SIP), along with the number of the instalment or transfer (STP) or withdrawal (SWP) or switch in or switch out or redemption. Transactions such as "switch out" and "redemption" involve incidence of Securities Transaction Tax (STT) and exit load, which have not been reflected in Table 5.1.

Transactions involving dividend payout or reinvestment options are mentioned along with percentage or rupees per unit at which the dividend will be reinvested or paid out. Say, dividend payout @ Rs. 0.14032016 means dividend will be paid at Rs. 0.14032016 per unit. Similarly, dividend reinvestment @ Rs. 0.14032016 means dividend admissible at Rs. 0.14032016 per unit was reinvested at the prevailing NAV. Where STP is concerned, the fund name to which you are transferring your investments will be mentioned. If your account is an old one and you have asked for a statement only for a particular period, it will give the opening balance, which states your balance of units as on the starting date of the relevant period.

* **Amount** refers to the amount, which you have invested, transferred or withdrawn, or the dividend amount being paid or reinvested.

* **NAV** means the Net Asset Value or the per unit price.

- **Price** is the actual price at which your amount gets invested or redeemed.

The sum of entry load and the NAV was the price at which your money was invested. If you are redeeming your funds before a period of 12 months, or more in some cases, exit load will be deducted from the NAV, which is the price at which your units will be redeemed. At the time of redemption, Securities Transaction Tax (STT) will be deducted from the NAV. ***(With effect from August 1, 2009, entry load has been abolished. The NAV will be the price and your amount will get invested at NAV.)***

- **Units** refer to the number of units allotted or redeemed.
- **Unit balance** shows the number of units accumulated as on a particular date.

Say, in the above example, in dividend reinvestment option, 14.032 units are allotted. They are added to your outstanding units and the unit balance as on August 7, 2015 would be 2,514.032. As for dividend payout, your unit balance will remain the same as the initial purchase or the unit balance on the date of declaration of dividend as the case may be. If you had opted for an STP from one fund, then units are deducted from that particular fund based on the price resulting in an ongoing reduction in the unit balance. As for the fund to which you are transferring, unit balance will keep on increasing. After the above particulars, the **summary of the account** is given, where, at a glance, you can have all the details of the account:

- **NAV** as on a particular date.
- **Current cost (inclusive of dividend reinvestment)** means total investment plus any dividend reinvested by the fund house based on your option.
- **Current value** shows the current value of investment on that particular date, which is equal to unit balance multiplied by NAV on that particular day.
- **Dividend earned (inclusive of dividend reinvestment)** shows the total dividend earned by way of payout or reinvestment.
- **Load structure** gives the entry load (now abolished) and exit load of the fund.

- **Agent/Broker code and name** gives the details of the agent or broker. If there is more than one broker, then it will just show 'Multiple brokers'.

- **Bank details** as submitted by you.

- **Mode of payment** as opted for dividend payout or redemption.

At the bottom of the statement is the transaction slip for additional purchase or other requests such as redemption or switch or change of address or change of bank details.

This guide can be understood best if read along with an account statement by the side.

SEBI has mandated all fund houses to send monthly Consolidated Account Statement (CAS) to their unit-holders with effect from October 2011. Consolidated Account Statement is a single account statement that consolidates financial transactions in all folios of an investor across all schemes of all mutual funds (More on CAS in Chapter 23).

Chapter 6

Myths Exploded!
Uprooting NFO and Dividend Weeds

NAVia Mania

The NAV (Net Asset Value) is what one share or unit is worth presently. You do not invest in a mutual fund by buying a fixed number of units but rather by a lump sum investment amount such as Rs. 1,000. Since it would be a fluke for the unit price to be an exact even multiple of your investment, you will be issued some partial units to make up enough to cover your investment to the paise. Say, the NAV of the fund is Rs. 52 and you have invested Rs. 1000 in it. There being no entry load, the number of units allotted will be 19.231 (1000/52).

People carry the perception that a fund with a lower NAV is cheaper than that with a higher NAV since they are under the notion that the NAV of a mutual fund is similar to the market price of an equity share. This, however, is not true. There is no concept as market value for the mutual fund unit. Therefore, when you buy mutual fund units at NAV, you are buying at book value. You are paying the right price of the assets whether it is Rs. 10 or Rs. 100. There is no such thing as a higher or lower price. But the market price of a stock is generally different from its book value depending on its fundamentals, the perception of the company's future performance and the demand-supply scenario.

NFO NAV at Rs. 10 is cheap – this myth surrounding the NAV is the underlying reason why mutual fund NFOs, have been selling like hot cakes. Mutual fund NAV merely represents the market value or the book value of the portfolio minus its liabilities backed by each unit. In the case of a stock, the book value (its intrinsic worth) and market value (determined by market factors) are divorced from one another. The appreciation of an existing fund due to appreciation in its portfolio over a given period of time results in a higher NAV. The NAV of an NFO (with an identical portfolio) is Rs. 10. The higher NAV of the existing fund does not make it expensive *vis-à-vis* an NFO, since the returns over a given period of time will be the same from an existing portfolio (with a higher NAV) and an identical new portfolio (with Rs. 10 NAV).

Now, let me make this concept clear by using an analogy. Consider this: If you are investing Rs. 1,00,000 in a Fixed Deposit (FD), there would be 4 Fixed Deposit Receipts (FDRs) if the denomination is Rs. 25,000 and two FDRs, if the denomination is Rs. 50,000. If you have Rs. 1,00,000 to invest, you will get either 2 or 4 fixed deposit receipts on which your income (interest earning) will remain the same. If you choose to invest in 4 FDs of denomination Rs. 25,000, it does not mean you have got those cheaper and, therefore, you will earn more interest.

Please appreciate that the level of NAV is as irrelevant in your mutual fund investment decision as the number of FDRs while investing in FD. It is just an equation; as long as the numerator (investment amount) does not change, the denominator (NAV/ number of FDRs) does not have ANY material impact on the return potential of your investment.

The following illustration will clarify that returns from mutual fund schemes are independent of the NAV:

Table 6.1 Illustration of Independence of Mutual Fund Returns from NAV

Description	New Scheme with NAV at par (X)	Existing Scheme with NAV at Rs. 50 (Y)
NAV	Rs. 10	Rs. 50
Your investment	Rs. 10,00,000	Rs. 10,00,000
No. of units allotted to you	1,00,000	20,000
Market value of assets after one year	Rs. 12,00,000	Rs. 12,00,000
Corresponding NAV after one year	Rs. 12	Rs. 60
Current value of your investment	Rs. 12,00,000	Rs. 12,00,000
Return on investment (%)	20%	20%

Say, you have Rs. 10,00,000 to invest. You have two investment options – Fund X and Fund Y. Both the funds have the same portfolio. But say, Fund X has an NAV of Rs. 10 and Fund Y has an NAV of Rs. 50. You will get 1,00,000 units of Fund X or 20,000 units of Fund Y. After one year, both funds would have grown equally as their portfolio is the same, say by 20%. Then the NAV after one year would be Rs. 12 for Fund X and Rs. 60 for Fund Y. The value of your investment would be 1,00,000*12 = Rs. 12,00,000 for Fund X and 20,000*60 = Rs. 12,00,000 for Fund Y. Thus, your returns would be the same irrespective of the NAV.

A few **valuable lessons that need to be learnt – An NFO NAV at par has absolutely no role to play in your future returns. The quality of the portfolio, rapid and prudent deployment of resources and in-built flexibility are the key to fund performance.** It is the quality of the fund, which would make the difference to your returns. In fact, broadly, this logic would apply for equity shares also. An IT company's share at say Rs. 1,000 may give a better return than say a jute company's share at Rs. 50, since the IT sector would show a much higher growth rate than the jute industry (Of course, the IT company's share at Rs. 1,000 may fundamentally be over-priced or under-priced, which will not be the case with a mutual fund NAV).

Uniqueness of NFO Makes Eminent Sense

Ideally a new fund should have something unique to offer. Derivative Funds, Fund of Funds, Gold Funds, etc. are some of the examples of new concepts. But no sooner one theme hits the market than scores of similar funds follow. HDFC Core and Satellite Fund, Magnum Comma Fund and Benchmark Split Capital Fund (redeemed in August 2008) are among the more unique funds that have not been replicated so far. In a move to snap NFO clones, **SEBI has now restricted AMCs from coming out with NFOs unless they can justify the uniqueness of the investment strategy and risks.**

Business (non) Sense

Fund management is a business. Fund management companies (AMCs) make money on the money they are able to collect from the public through schemes.

AMCs prefer to launch new funds in different flavours whether you need them or not. But AMCs are better off focusing on their existing offerings rather than adding NFOs that have little value and make a guinea pig of you.

From Guinea Pig to King

There is a case for evaluating an NFO as a probable investment if the NFO is from a well-managed and process-driven fund house, has a unique theme to offer, matches your investment objectives, adds diversity, is open for a limited time period and you are comfortable with its risk profile.

Otherwise, avoid using the NFO route to increase your exposure to mutual funds. Investing in a series of NFOs could saddle you with an unwieldy portfolio.

If you have invested in an NFO, give the fund a chance to perform. A good fund or theme may under-perform for a brief period due to difficult market conditions. Evaluate its performance for a year and hold on if the performance has been impressive or switch to a well-established fund if it dramatically trails the benchmark index for several months. A benchmark index gives you a point of reference for evaluating a fund's performance.

An NFO must establish a track record over the long term (at least three years for an equity-oriented fund) before meriting inclusion in your portfolio. Established funds with inherent strength and consistent performance should rightly enjoy a royal treatment in your portfolio as opposed to run-of-the-mill funds or NFOs, which are, in reality, a gigantic gamble. This will go a long way in establishing a regime where you, the investor, are the king!

Tightening the (NFO) Noose

The SEBI regulations to fast-track NFOs to reduce their NFO subscription period from 30 days to fifteen and posting of unit allotment, refunds and statement of accounts to investors within 5 business days from the closure of the NFO and to approve NFOs only if a certain amount of minimum corpus is invested in it by the public – Rs. 10 crore for equity funds and Rs. 20 crore for debt funds – had dealt a severe blow to the sagging NFO market. If the new fund is not able to attract enough funds (Rs. 10 or 20 crore as the case may be), then the fund has to be closed and the money invested by the investors has to be returned in the next 15–20 days. If the refund fails to happen within the next 6 weeks (from date of closure), the fund house is required to pay an interest of 15% to the investors. SEBI is planning to deny approval to new offerings from fund houses whose schemes have been consistently underperforming over the last few years. SEBI hopes that this will put pressure on such mutual funds to deliver returns closer to or better than the benchmark indices. But, with Indian stock indices scaling new highs, new equity launches by the country's mutual fund industry is gaining traction.

Ideally, the investment cycle should start by an investor wanting to buy a fund because it fits his needs and not by hearing of a hot new NFO. This shift will require a long time, but the changed rules of the game had ensured that this shift had begun. The hand of God had arrested the lay investor's leanings towards NFOs during the lean period... But, now that the cycle has turned, will the investor view NFOs against the backdrop of the myth just busted?

Capital Returned

The concept of **dividend** in the context of mutual funds is fundamentally different from that used in the context of equity shares. Let's say, I borrow Rs. 5,000 from you today and return Rs. 2,000 back to you in a few days; so, now I owe you Rs. 3,000. Will you consider your return on investment to be 40%? No, certainly not! I pay you Rs. 2,000 and yet continue to owe Rs. 5,000 – it is only under such circumstances that you can say the return is 40%. But since I paid back Rs. 2,000 and still owed you Rs. 3,000, the Rs. 2,000 is return OF capital and not return ON capital. **Any dividend received from a mutual fund is essentially return of capital and not return on capital.** The problem is on account of usage of the term 'dividend' in relation to mutual funds. Investors mistake it to have a similar significance as the term has with respect to stocks. Now, when Reliance gives you a dividend, it transfers money from its hand to your hand. To that extent, Reliance becomes poorer and you become richer. However, when a mutual fund gives you dividend, it is transferring money from your left hand to your right hand. After the dividend, neither is the mutual fund poorer nor are you any richer. **It is only your money coming back to you. In other words, the value of your investment (NAV) falls to the extent of the dividend.** Let me explain this with an example. As on October 4, 2016, the NAV of the growth option of HDFC Equity Fund was Rs. 511.946, whereas that of the dividend option was Rs. 52.844. The difference of Rs. 459.102 per unit (Rs. 511.946 minus Rs. 52.844) is largely nothing but your own money paid back to you (in the name of dividend). An investor choosing the growth option will get Rs. 511.946 (Rs. 459.102.102 + Rs. 52.844) per unit from the scheme, whereas an investor choosing the dividend option will get only Rs. 52.844. At this juncture, I would like you to draw parallels between the example that we started out with and this one.

The scenario becomes more baffling when it comes to ELSS funds. Say, for instance, the NAV of an ELSS fund is Rs. 100. It declares a dividend of say 20% or Rs. 20 per unit. Looks enticing…doesn't it? A 20% return from dividend in addition to 30% return due to the tax saving resulting in a total of 50% return on the initial investment! This 50% is only the frill added to the returns generated from the exhilarating performance of the fund (if it manages to do so!). The flaw in this calculation stems from the improper understanding of the concept of dividend in the context of mutual funds. In the first place, as lucidly explained, the 20% return is not *on* capital but *of* capital. As soon as you receive Rs. 20 as dividend, the NAV falls to Rs. 80. The 30% tax deduction spread over the three-year lock-in period boils down to a 10% return on an annual basis. Lock-in period is the period during which an investment cannot be redeemed without incurring penalties.

A mutual fund dividend is nothing but redemption in disguise. For the dividend-paying plan, funds simply sell off part of the assets and pay out of the sale proceeds. Getting mutual fund dividend is a zero-sum game. Dividends have no impact on the return you are getting from your investment.

Mutual fund NFOs were initially called initial public offerings (IPOs). To enable you to differentiate between a mutual fund IPO as against a company IPO and prevent any misunderstanding on your part or mis-selling on the distributors' part, the term NFO for new offers from mutual funds was introduced. The time is now ripe for a similar change in the nomenclature for 'dividend' from mutual funds.

Chapter 7

Unloaded!
Yet Burdened?

The normal expenses of running a mutual fund scheme are adjusted while calculating the NAV, implying that it is recovered from all its investors on a proportionate basis. There might be certain specific expenses which an AMC would prefer to adjust from some of its investors only and not charge them on the entire scheme. For instance, costs incurred by the mutual fund in paying commissions to agents to bring in new investments and the cost incurred by the fund in liquidating the portfolio and paying off the investors are specific expenses recovered in the form of loads.

Loads are expenses recovered by mutual funds against compensation paid to sales intermediaries such as brokers, distributors, etc. These expenses are generally called **sales loads.**

These expenses were recovered from the scheme's investors in two ways:

Entry Load: At the time of your entry into the fund, by deducting a specific amount from your initial contribution and investing the remaining;

Exit Load/CDSC: At the time of your exit from the fund, by deducting a specific amount from the amount payable to you on redemption/switch (exit load); or, by amortising and charging the scheme with a fixed amount each year until the maturity of the scheme or for a stated number of years (CDSC).

Exit load is a load charged when you exit before a stipulated period, as defined in the offer document, regardless of the amount you have invested and your period of holding. CDSC is a load charged depending on two factors – your investment amount and tenure of your investment. In other words, CDSC is a charge imposed when the units of a fund are redeemed during the first few years of ownership.

But now, with the abolition of entry load from August 1, 2009 and the SEBI stipulation on August 16, 2012, that the entire amount of exit load will be put back into the fund, i.e. it will enhance the NAV of the fund and contribute to your returns instead of going to the AMC, both the methods of recovering expenses from you are no longer applicable. (Earlier, of the exit load or CDSC charged to you, a maximum of 1% of the redemption proceeds had to be maintained in a separate account, which could be used by the AMC to pay commissions to the distributors and to take care of the marketing and selling expenses and any balance had to be credited to the scheme immediately).

Loads – the Law Point

The SEBI (Mutual Funds) Regulations Act, 1996, has not clearly defined 'load'. However, the Regulations stipulate that the redemption price cannot be lower than 93% of the NAV, while resale price cannot be higher than 107% of the NAV in the case of open-end schemes. So, **the entry load (no longer applicable) and exit load cannot be more than 7% of the NAV.** The difference between sale price and redemption price cannot be more than 7%, calculated with respect to the sale price. Thus, for a scheme the NAV of which is Rs. 15, if the AMC would prefer to sell new units at Rs. 16.05, the redemption price cannot be lower than Rs. 14.927 (Rs. 16.05 multiplied by 93%); and for the same scheme, if the AMC would rather redeem existing units at Rs. 13.95, it would need to bring the sale price for new units to a maximum of Rs. 15 (Rs. 13.95 divided by 93%). **In the case of closed-end schemes, the repurchase price of units shall not be lower than 95% of the NAV.**

Entry loads generally varied between 1.00% and 2.25%. Exit loads vary between 0.25% and 3.00%. Most Indian equity funds used to charge an entry load of 2.25% till July 31, 2009. SEBI removed entry load on direct mutual fund investment, i.e. when you did not invest through a distributor and instead invested directly with the mutual fund either through the office or website of the AMC, Collection Centres, or Investor Service Centres w.e.f. January 4, 2008. SEBI guidelines further entailed that entry and exit loads should not be charged for units given as bonus or against reinvested dividends.

The entry load charged by the fund houses has been abolished by SEBI with effect from August 1, 2009, for all mutual fund schemes. The restriction of entry load on existing and new mutual funds in 2009 marked a turning point in the functioning of the mutual fund industry. This, in effect, has had a huge impact on the commission structure of distributors, leading fund houses and distributors to restructure their business and operating models in order to arrive at a profitable solution.

Exit load has been made uniform across-the-board w.e.f August 24, 2009 and can be imposed for exit by the investor within one year of investment. Institutional investors, who invest in big chunks, have always got a better deal. Funds have always had lower or zero entry and exit loads for investors who invest large amounts usually ranging from Rs. 1 to 5 crore. After entry loads were abolished on August 1 2009, all AMCs revised (enhanced) their exit loads. However, they generally stuck with zero loads for large investors. This differential treatment meted out to large investors has been banned by SEBI. Generally, exit load is higher when the money is pulled out soon after investment and drops or comes to zero for longer term investments. There are two sets of justifications for exit loads. One, the fund company has spent a certain amount of money in making you invest in their scheme and if you redeem too soon, the fund must get some recompense. And two, when some investors pull out their investments, it does some harm to other investors. Therefore, they must be recompensed by taking some of the redeemers' money and distributing it among the remaining investors. Under this rule, both concerns are addressed.

With effect from October 2012, the exit load charged under the schemes of the mutual fund shall be credited to the respective schemes. Service tax on exit load shall be paid out of the exit load proceeds and exit load net of service tax shall be credited to the schemes.

Initial Issue Expenses

Initial issue expenses are expenses that are incurred in the launch of the fund. It includes costs of registration and fund formation, legal and advisory expenses, costs of launching the scheme, advertisement and promotion expenses, distribution costs and commission to selling agents. For open-end funds, the initial issue expenses were earlier carried in the balance sheet as deferred revenue expenses and were written off over a period not exceeding 5 years. For closed-end funds, they were charged over the life of the scheme on a weekly basis.

In April 2006, SEBI prohibited mutual fund houses from charging and amortising issue expenses on open-end schemes. This move was particularly beneficial to the long-term investors in an open-end fund. It refrained from penalizing the long-term investors, who would have to bear the cost of earlier redemptions by other unit-holders. But the regulation was not of much help as fund houses rushed to launch closed-end schemes. That is because the same ruling stated that fund houses could continue to charge and amortise the initial issue expenses of the closed-end schemes (6% of the corpus) for the entire period they remained close ended – up to 3 years. Amortisation allowed AMCs to show a higher NAV in closed-end schemes. For example, if you buy 100 units of Rs. 10 each in a new closed-end fund, the fund house charges 6% as initial issue expenses, which means that the NAV is Rs. 9.40, but it is shown as Rs. 10 initially. The Rs. 6 charged to the scheme is amortised over a period. But they could not charge an entry load just as the open-end funds did. By the end of January 2008, market regulator SEBI decided to scrap the initial issue expenses for closed-end funds. This resulted in closed-end mutual fund schemes becoming less expensive for investors. Fund houses still launch closed-end schemes if the nature of the scheme warrants such a structure. But it is no longer a monetary move. As they are no longer in a position to pass on the initial issue expenses to you, there remains very little incentive for them to launch such schemes.

Transaction Charges

In 2011, Securities and Exchange Board of India issued guidelines to mutual funds for deducting transaction charge for a subscription of Rs. 10,000 or above. This charge goes to the distributors of the fund products. Transaction charge is meant to enable people with small saving potential to invest and to increase the reach of mutual funds in urban areas and smaller towns. The applicability of this charge is explained below.

For investors in a mutual fund, a distributor is paid Rs. 100 as transaction charge for a subscription of Rs. 10,000 or above. As an incentive to attract new investors, a distributor is paid Rs. 150 as transaction charge for a first-time investor. The terms and conditions relating to transaction charges are mentioned in the scheme information document/key information memorandum. This charge is deducted by the AMC from the subscription amount and paid to the distributor; the balance is invested. This charge depends on the distributor registering for an 'opt-in' or 'opt out' to deduct and receive the transaction charges. If a distributor has registered with the AMFI to opt out, that is, not to receive such a charge, then no charges are applicable even if you apply through such a distributor. Such charges are applicable only if an investor has applied for fund units through a distributor who has opted in to receive such charges. This implied that distributors were either allowed to charge all their clients or not charge at all. This was creating a lot of accounting problems. Since September 2012, SEBI has allowed distributors to opt out of transaction charges on the basis of schemes. Of course, if you invest directly no charge is deducted. If you invest under an existing folio number (mutual fund customer number) which you had created earlier through an agent, then even if you invest now under the same folio number through Computer Age Management Services (CAMS) or directly through websites, commission may still be paid and you may be charged Rs.100. So if you are not currently taking any help from the agent make sure that you remove the agent's name from your folio number and save on this cost.

If you have invested in any mutual fund earlier, you may indicate that you are an existing investor. Application forms contain a section for declaring that. Only if you are a first-time investor in mutual funds, you may indicate the same appropriately on the form and deduction of applicable transaction charges is effected after necessary verification. If you are an existing investor, after deducting Rs. 100, the balance amount is invested and units are allotted for Rs. 9,900. If you are a first-time investor, after deducting Rs. 150, the balance amount is invested and units are allotted for Rs. 9,850. If you invest less than Rs. 10,000, no charge is applicable.

For SIPs, the transaction charge is applicable only if the total commitment through SIPs amounts to Rs. 10,000 or above. For example, if you commit in the application form to invest in an SIP of Rs. 1,000 for 12 months – making that Rs. 12,000 in total – the transaction charge is levied and recovered in 4 instalments. This means that the total amount you have committed to the SIP should be Rs. 10,000 or more. If you start an SIP for Rs. 1,000 for 6 months, making that a commitment of Rs. 6,000, transaction charge is not deducted.

Transaction Charges will not be deducted under the following circumstances:-

- Purchase/Subscription submitted by the investor at the designated collection centres or through AMC's website and which is not routed through any distributor.

- Purchase/Subscription through a distributor for an amount less than Rs. 10,000.

* Switch and STP transactions wherein there is no additional cash flow at a mutual fund level similar to Purchase/Subscription.
* Purchase/Subscriptions through any stock exchange.

Understanding Different Commissions of Mutual Fund Distributors

The investor has the independence to decide on the commission payable to the distributor based on his/her assessment of various factors including the service rendered by the distributor. As the distributor's commission varied depending upon the different schemes and the fund houses, the investor was often kept in the dark about this payment. Now, distributors have to disclose the commission for the schemes.

A proper understanding of the different commissions distributors earn on selling mutual funds is imperative so as to enable you to compensate your distributors. It is important to understand what kind of advice you should demand from your agents (the terms 'distributors' and 'agents' have been used interchangeably) because they earn money out of your investments. You can decide if the advice given by your mutual fund agent is worth the money you are paying or not. There are three components of commissions earned by mutual funds distributors:

Commission from Clients

This is the commission which you pay the distributors for their service. It generally ranges from 0.5% to 2%. It should depend on the quality of advice your agent provides. This is the commission you pay your agent every time you invest. After the abolition of entry loads, you have to compensate the agents directly. So if you invest Rs. 10,000 per month and your agent charges commission @1%, he gets 1% of 10,000, i.e. Rs. 100 every month. This is the amount you have to pay your agent apart from the investment of Rs. 10,000.

Upfront Commission from the AMC

Upfront commission is the amount received for the purpose of getting the initial investment into the fund, i.e. the commission paid by the AMC to the agent in the first year. This is the figure that the distributor will earn immediately and is usually a percentage figure based on the amount that is brought in. Sometimes there is also a flat payment for a large number of applications, especially in the case of a new fund offer. The commission varies from one distributor to another, one product to another and also across different categories of mutual funds.

A fund house pays different commissions to different distributors. An AMC classifies its distributors as **retail** (at the base level), **preferred, premium** and finally **key relationships** that typically have the largest national distributors and bank distributors. Your fund house then prepares various commission structures for each of these categories; higher a distributor's category and higher the business a distributor gets, higher are his or her rewards. Typically, banks and national distributors get paid the most because of the sheer volume of investments that they get, but many independent financial advisers (IFAs), who have grown their businesses, have also seen a rise in their fees and commissions. Fees paid to distributors from beyond the top 15 cities are higher than what distributors get in the top 15 cities.

Pricing also varies from product to product. Products that have the potential to generate higher returns also pay higher commissions. In addition, higher the volatility, higher will be the commissions because such products are difficult to explain to the investor. More effort has to be taken by the distributor to explain its nuances. Sometimes, fund houses focus on garnering inflows in few and select existing schemes. Such schemes could be small-sized and the fund house may want to grow them in size. The fund house then makes such schemes as its focus schemes. For focus schemes, the fund, typically, pays something extra, say, 25 bps extra upfront, in addition to the usual upfront fees it pays.

Equity mutual funds generally give higher upfront commissions, whereas debt funds give lower commissions. Typically, equity funds pay 75–100 bps (.75% – 1%) as upfront commission and about 0.50% as trail fees. Debt funds pay 50–75 bps as upfront charges and about 40–50 bps as trail fees. The Direct Plan has a lower expense ratio as compared to existing plans in the same schemes, as there is no commission to be paid to the distributor under this plan.

An example of commission by investing a lump sum amount in a mutual fund:
Assume your equity fund's expense ratio is 2%. Of this, further assume the fund puts aside twenty-five basis points (bps), i.e. 0.25% for custody charges, registrar and transfer charges and audit fees. A basis point is one-hundredth of a percentage point. This leaves 1.75%, of which, your fund gives some portion to agents as commission and keeps the rest as its own income, also known as management fees. Assume your fund decides to give about 0.75% as upfront fees and 0.50% as trail fees. What remains, 50 bps or 0.50%, is your AMC's own income.

An example of commission earned in SIP:

Assume you enrol for a three-year (36 months) SIP and commit to invest Rs. 2,000 every month. Further, assume your fund pays the distributor an upfront commission of 1% every month (after the instalment comes in on a monthly basis), i.e. 1% of Rs. 2,000 which is Rs. 20 per month. Add another 0.25% special upfront commission. This means, that your agent will earn a total of Rs. 720 (Rs. 20 per month × 36 months) as upfront commission and Rs. 180 as a special commission throughout the SIP tenor. This Rs. 180 gets paid upfront to the distributor when the SIP starts. If the investor leaves prematurely, the advance special commission is recovered back from the distributor.

It takes more effort on the distributor's part to convince investors to invest in an SIP. Moreover, the investment amounts are typically small, in the range of Rs. 1,500 to Rs. 3,000. So, in addition to the usual upfront charges, some fund houses pay a flat charge per application. Some fund houses pay Rs. 50 per application if it is a one year SIP, Rs. 100 for a three-year SIP, Rs. 150 for a five-year SIP and Rs. 200 for a 10-year SIP. These are merely approximate amounts; your fund house may or may not pay such flat charges.

Therefore, even if you do not pay your agent any commission, he will earn an upfront commission from the AMC.

Trail Commission from the AMC

Trail commission is the commission paid on an annual basis to the distributors by the AMC in subsequent years when the investor remains with the fund for a specified period of time on a continuous basis. This commission is mostly hidden from the general public. This is the most important part of distributor commissions and the main earning of mutual fund agents in the long run. Since these are calculated on net assets, distributors benefit from a rise in their assets in the form of higher NAV of funds or sale of more units. The most important point you should be aware of is that trail commission is a percentage of the total AUM (total worth of your investment). So, if the total worth of your investments in a particular year is Rs. 10 lakh and trail commission is 0.5%, the AMC will pay 0.5% of Rs. 10 lakh, i.e. Rs. 5,000 to your agent. This is the commission paid to your agent out of your money and it is adjusted from the NAV. This means that if an agent has 100 clients, who have Rs. 10 lakh of investments (current worth or market value and not initial investment) with an AMC, then total AUM of that agent is the total worth of all the clients, which is Rs. 10 lakh × 100 = Rs. 10,00,00,000 (Rs. 10 crore). So, he will get 0.5% of Rs. 10 crore, i.e. Rs. 5 lakh. Many banks and very big agents, who have AUMs of around Rs. 1,000 crore invested through them, will earn Rs. 5 crore of income per year (0.5% trail commissions). This is one of the biggest reasons why many agents entice clients to shift their current investments to them. This is not to pass judgement on distributor commissions. Commissions are everywhere and you have to pay the price of transactions. This is just to make you aware of how the commission on mutual fund sales is structured. The trail commission is deducted out of NAV anyway, whether you invest directly or through some agent. If you invest directly, the trail commission is pocketed by the AMC itself.

Some fund houses such as Franklin Templeton Investments Ltd. and Canara Robeco AMC have started to offer the option to its distributors to opt for a full-trail model. This means only trail fees and not upfront fees at all. Currently, there is a proposal to ban upfront commission. In addition to the upfront and trail fees, some fund houses pay an additional bonus incentive to distributors. For instance, if 1% is the upfront fee, the mutual fund may choose to pay an additional incentive of 25 bps on all monthly incentives.

Why is it important to understand the commission structure?

For a client, it is important to know about commissions, so that he is not a victim of mis-selling. It might happen that your agent is pushing you to buy a mutual fund which pays higher trail commission. For example, Birla Sun Life pays a trail commission of up to 0.75%, whereas SBI pays a maximum of 0.4%. That means the agent will get much more trail commissions in later years if you buy Birla Sun Life Mutual funds from him, in which case he will try to encourage you to buy higher paying trail commission products, irrespective of the mutual funds which are suitable for you. As a client, understanding the mutual fund commission structure will make sure that you understand the whole situation and figure out if you are being mis-sold a mutual fund or not!

The dynamics have changed. The 2.25% load is no longer there. So, earnings for the distributor and AMCs are definitely coming down. For the distributor, it is a mix of commission and trail fee. Every fund house has a different commission structure.

Mutual funds cannot increase the load beyond the level mentioned in the offer document. Any change in the load will be applicable only to prospective investments and not to the existing investments. In the case of imposition of fresh loads or increase in existing loads, the mutual funds are required to amend their offer documents so that the new investors are aware of loads at the time of investment.

If Exit load/CDSC is within proper limits, do not look at these as a burden. Just think of them as tolls you pay on the highway to big money!

Chapter 8

Expenses Exposed!
Outlaw the Outlay

"Dazzled by performance, indifferent to cost," is a common accusation hurled at mutual fund investors. I would have succeeded in my endeavour if I elevate you, dear reader, to well above the average in the next few pages.

Total Expense Ratio

The Total Expense Ratio (TER) is the total expense of operating a mutual fund expressed as a percentage of the fund's weekly average net assets. The base for calculation of fund expenses is net assets – not unit capital. Net assets could be more than, or less than, unit capital, depending on investment performance and expenses charged to the scheme. Open-end schemes calculate their net assets every day. So fund expenses too are provided for on a daily basis. While fund expenses would be accrued every day, the actual payment by the fund to the AMC and other service providers would be at such frequency as is agreed between them – say, quarterly. Until then, the amount would be shown in the balance sheet as a liability item – "Expenses payable". The expense ratio is disclosed every March and September.

The Major Components of Expense Ratio

The investment advisory fee or the management fee is the money that goes to pay the salaries of the fund managers and other employees of mutual funds. The management fees (which could range from 0.5% to 1.25% of the fund's corpus) are one of the highest expenses incurred by a mutual fund. While it sounds small, this fee ensures that mutual fund managers remain in the country's top echelon of earners. Think about it for a moment. 1% of Rs. 25 crore (a small mutual fund) is Rs. 25 lakh – fund managers are definitely not going hungry!

The investment advisory fees that the AMC proposes to charge the mutual fund used to be disclosed in the offer document.

The regulations prescribed the following limits on the management fee that could be charged by the AMC each year:

* 1.25% of weekly average net assets of the scheme on the first Rs. 100 crore;
* 1% of weekly average net assets in excess of Rs. 100 crore.

The regulations prescribed that the following items would be kept out of net assets for the purposes of calculating management fees:

* Investment by the AMC in the scheme;
* Investment by the scheme in other mutual fund schemes; and
* Issue expenses not written off (now irrelevant).

Earlier, the expense ratio had an internal division of actual expenses and the management fee and distribution expenses. Suppose a fund charged 2.5% as the expense ratio, then it compulsorily had to allocate 1.25% as fund management fees and 0.5% as distribution charges. After accounting for the other actual expenses, the remaining amount was taken as the fund's profits. With effect from October 2012, the expenses charged by the mutual fund from investors are fungible, i.e. they are treated as a single pool, which gives greater flexibility to the fund company to tailor revenue usage to its business needs.

Recurring Expenses

In addition to the management fees, the following recurring expenses can be charged to the fund:

* Marketing and selling expenses, including agents' commission;
* Brokerage and transaction cost;
* Trustees' fees;
* Registrar's charges;
* Audit fees;

* Custodian fees;
* Administrative expenses on investor communication, account statements, dividend/redemption cheques and warrants;
* Expenses on fund transfers;
* Insurance premium paid by the fund;
* Winding up costs for terminating a fund or a scheme;
* Costs of statutory advertisements;
* Cost towards investor education and awareness (at least 2 basis points on an annual basis); and
* Service tax.

One ongoing expense that was not included in the expense ratio prior to October 2012 was **brokerage costs** incurred by a fund as it bought and sold securities. With effect from October 2012, brokerage and transaction costs incurred for the purpose of execution of trade may be capitalised to the extent of 0.12% for cash market transactions and 0.05% for derivatives transactions respectively. Any payment towards brokerage and transaction costs, over and above the said percentage may be charged to the scheme within the maximum limit of total expense ratio. Expenditure in excess of the said prescribed total expense ratio limit (including brokerage and transaction costs, if any) shall be borne by the AMC or by the trustee or sponsors.

Administrative expenses are the costs associated with the daily activities of the fund. These include the costs of record keeping, mailing, maintaining a customer service line, etc. These are all necessary costs, though they vary in size from fund to fund. The thriftiest of funds can keep these costs below 0.20% of the fund assets, while the funds which use engraved paper, colourful graphics, etc. might fail to keep administrative costs below 0.40% of fund assets.

In October 2012, SEBI allowed additional expenses for gross new inflows from specified cities. It laid down the following, with respect to calculation and charging of total expense ratio:

If the new inflows from beyond top 15 cities are at least (a) 30% of gross new inflows in the scheme or (b) 15% of the average assets under management (year to date) of the scheme, whichever is higher, funds can charge additional expense of up to thirty basis points on daily net assets of the scheme.

In case inflows from beyond top 15 cities is less than the higher of (a) or (b) above, additional total expense on daily net assets of the scheme shall be charged as follows:

Daily net assets × 30 basis points × New inflows from beyond top 15 cities/ 365 × Higher of (a) or (b) above

The additional TER on account of inflows from beyond top 15 cities so charged shall be clawed back in case the same is redeemed within a period of one year from the date of investment. The additional TER charged must be utilised for distribution expenses incurred for bringing inflows from such cities.

Earlier the **service tax** was borne by mutual funds themselves. But from October 2012, service tax can be passed on to investors and charged from the AUM of the fund. Provisions with respect to service tax are as follows:

* Mutual funds/AMCs may charge service tax on investment and advisory fees to the scheme in addition to the maximum limit of total expenses allowed for the scheme.
* Service tax on expenses other than investment and advisory fees, if any, is to be borne by the scheme within the maximum limit of total expenses allowed for the scheme.
* Service tax on brokerage and transaction cost paid for execution of trade, if any, must be within the prescribed total expenses limit for the scheme.

Expenses other than the above, which are directly attributable to the scheme, may be charged to the scheme with the approval of the trustees and within the overall limits. However, **the following cannot be charged to the scheme** but are borne either by the sponsor or the AMC:

* Penalties and fines for infraction of laws;
* Interest on delayed payment to the unit-holders;
* Legal, marketing, publication and other general expenses not attributable to any scheme(s);

- Expenses on investment management/general management;
- Expenses on general administration, corporate advertising and infrastructure costs; and
- Depreciation on fixed assets and software development expenses.

The regulations prescribe the following limit on expense ratio (recurring expenses excluding the initial issue expenses and redemption expenses, but including management fees):

Table 8.1   Limit on Expense Ratio

Weekly Average Net Assets	Equity Schemes	Debt Schemes
First Rs. 100 crore	2.5%	2.25%
Next Rs. 300 crore	2.25%	2.00%
Next Rs. 300 crore	2.00%	1.75%
Excess over Rs. 700 crore	1.75%	1.50%

Additional expenses allowed over and above these limits are

- *Expenses for gross new inflows from specified cities of up to 0.3%*
- *Service tax on investment and advisory fees of up to 0.2%*

As the asset size of the fund increases, the cap on expenses as a percentage of assets declines. This is one of the reasons why you find that funds with a larger asset base such as Franklin India Bluechip, HDFC Equity, or Fidelity Equity have lower expense ratios. On equity funds, the limits on expenses are higher by 0.25%. These regulatory ceilings are applied on the weekly average net assets of the mutual fund scheme. Any excess over the specified limits has to be borne by the AMC, the trustees, or the sponsor.

For balanced schemes, the limit would depend on whether the scheme is predominantly invested in equity or debt. Accordingly, either the equity scheme limit or the debt scheme limit would apply. Total expenses of index funds and ETFs shall not exceed 1.5% of the weekly average net assets out of which investment advisory fees shall not exceed 0.75% of the weekly average net assets. In the case of a fund of funds scheme, the total expenses of the scheme, including weighted average of charges levied by the underlying schemes, shall not exceed 2.50% of the daily net assets of the scheme. Expenses above these limits cannot be charged to you. You will generally pay more for specialty or international funds, which require more expertise from managers.

From October 2012, mutual funds launched new schemes under a single plan and ensured that all new investors are subject to single expense structure. Investors, who have already invested according to earlier expense structures based on amount of investment, i.e. retail, institutional, super-institutional, etc. will be subject to single expense structure for all fresh subscription. Other plans shall continue till existing investors remain invested in the plans.

On the whole, expense ratios range from as low as 0.2% (usually for index funds) to as high as 3%. The average equity mutual fund charges around 2.42%, an increase of 17.5% from last year's 2.06%. The reason for the increase in expenses can be attributed to the change in SEBI rules allowing cross-subsidy in order to get funds to expand to smaller cities. So, for getting 30% of assets outside the fifteen largest cities, AMCs can charge an extra percentage of up to 0.3%. Lower percentages will mean a correspondingly smaller extra expense chargeable. In addition, an extra percentage of 0.2% can be charged as service tax on investment and advisory fees. Moreover, service tax used to be paid by the mutual funds but now it is paid by you.

You now have the option of investing through direct plans. Since the direct plans do not entail distributor commissions, they have a lower expense ratio. Direct plans are available for all funds, both existing and new and they have a separate NAV. Typically, direct plans — in which you can circumvent the distributor — are 40–70 basis points cheaper than regular plans. Fund houses pay a commission of 1.5%, nearly half the schemes' expense structure, to distributors. There is definitely a case to invest in direct plans to reduce the impact of expenses.

For actively managed funds, the average expense ratio is on the rise as funds shift fees away from the upfront loads that have now been abolished, into the annual expense ratios where they are more easily hidden. This fee is charged and deducted from the fund regardless of its performance as long as you hold the mutual fund. All these expenses that we have mentioned so far can be thought of as coming out of the portfolio's raw return, skimmed off the top, so to speak.

Comparing Expenses

Mutual fund expense ratios vary greatly from one investment category to another. Understanding why mutual fund expense ratios vary can confuse you. A general rule, often quoted by advisers and fund literature, is that you should try not to pay anything more than 1.5% for an equity fund. As you might expect, funds with higher internal costs (trading costs, administrative costs, etc.) typically also have higher expense ratios.

International funds can be very expensive to operate and tend to have some of the highest expense ratios. International funds invest in many countries and, as a result, often require staff all over the world. Accordingly, international funds tend to have substantially higher payroll and research expenses compared with single country funds that invest in only one country. In addition, international funds often hedge investment exposure by purchasing foreign currency. This strategy is normally employed to offset adverse changes in currency and involves additional cost. According to Morningstar, a well-regarded mutual fund research and ratings organisation, the average international equity fund with assets greater than US$ 5 million (Rs. 25 crore) has a 1.68% gross expense ratio.

Small cap funds tend to have expense ratios higher than the sought-after 1.5% upper limit. Based on Morningstar research, the average expense ratio for a small cap fund with assets greater than Rs. 25 crore is 1.61%. Funds investing in smaller companies typically incur higher costs for research and trading, compared with the costs associated with funds investing in larger companies. Depending upon the method of conducting equity research, we have primary and secondary research. Primary research is first hand collection of information to analyse equities while secondary research is based on already established data such as written reports and books. Small cap stock research can be expensive, partly because it is not nearly as abundant as large cap stock research. As a result, it is very difficult for a small cap fund manager to rely on secondary research as a basis for investment decisions. Accordingly, funds investing in smaller companies very often conduct primary research, which typically requires having several investment analysts contributing to the process. At the same time, small cap funds usually have higher trading costs than large cap funds. Small cap stocks are not as widely traded as large cap stocks and, as a result, normally have higher trading spreads. Normally, the smaller the company, the higher the price you will have to pay to place a trade. In addition, small cap funds tend to have higher turnover ratios than large cap funds, which also affect trading costs. If a small cap fund manager does not sell its winners, it can very easily become a mid-cap fund. Again, according to Morningstar, the average small cap fund has a turnover ratio of 93%, while the average large cap fund has a turnover ratio of 76%.

Large cap funds normally have lower expense ratios than both international funds and small cap funds because the large cap strategy does not necessarily require extensive teams of in-house analysts to support the investment process. Fund managers in this area can easily rely on outside research and there is plenty of high quality research to choose from. In addition, large cap funds also tend to have lower trading costs compared with small cap funds. Large cap stocks are widely traded and normally have much smaller trading spreads. According to Morningstar, the average large cap fund, with assets greater than Rs. 25 crore, has an expense ratio of 1.45%.

Quantitative Funds (or "quant funds") normally have much smaller investment teams than fundamentally managed funds. Funds using a quantitative strategy often rely on models to construct portfolios. Here, models are doing most of the work and not the analysts. On the other hand, quantitative funds tend to have higher turnover than fundamentally managed funds and often have higher trading costs. Trading costs, however, are not nearly as significant as the cost of human capital. In general, funds employing a quantitative strategy should charge less than funds using a fundamental approach.

Index funds: For those of you who believe that fundamental analysis adds little value and that managers cannot outperform benchmarks, there are plenty of index funds available. Index funds normally charge far less than actively managed funds. In addition, index funds are highly tax-efficient, which reduces your overall costs. Index funds can save you money in fees, but this strategy sometimes comes with other costs. For example, index funds do not have the ability to raise cash or alter allocations to address changing market conditions. If securities markets experience a downturn, your portfolio will decline by a similar amount.

Fixed-income funds: Expense ratios also vary significantly across investment categories. Overall, fixed-income fund expenses are lower than those of equity funds, but the amount depends partly on the specific investment category. Similar to equity strategies, bond strategies can vary significantly in terms of personnel, research, trading costs and foreign exchange necessary to effectively implement an investment process.

High-yield funds have some of the highest expense ratios among bond groups. The average high-yield fund normally has a team of highly trained and reputed managers and analysts whose main responsibilities are to conduct fundamental research on corporate securities. Furthermore, fixed-income analysts and managers, who conduct fundamental research, are normally compensated at a level almost comparable to those engaged in equity research. In addition, since high-yield securities have fairly low volume and larger trading spreads, individual trades are more expensive. According to Morningstar, the average high-yield fund with assets greater than Rs. 25 crore sports a gross expense ratio of 1.35%.

International bond funds also have high expense ratios, especially when compared with the more interest rate-sensitive domestic bond funds. Funds investing primarily in foreign bonds also have additional research costs. Investing globally requires knowledge about the many economies, geopolitical structures and markets around the world. At the same time, foreign bond funds often hedge currency exposure. According to Morningstar, funds focusing on foreign bonds have an average gross expense ratio of 1.35%.

Domestic bond funds investing primarily in high quality Government and corporate securities usually have the lowest expense ratios among fixed-income categories. Funds investing mostly in high quality issues have lower trading costs and generally do not require a staff of analysts or a hedging strategy. High quality bonds tend to rise and fall mostly with changes in interest rates. According to Morningstar, the average intermediate bond fund has a gross expense ratio of 1.07%. Fees are a very important factor for anyone deciding whether to purchase a particular fixed-income fund, as there is a high correlation between expenses and fixed-income fund performance.

While comparing the expense ratios of two or more funds, you must make sure that comparison is done between comparable funds, i.e. a diversified equity fund must only be compared with a diversified equity fund. Comparing different types of funds would fail to show the true picture. Hence, index funds, which traditionally tend to have lower expense ratios, should not be compared with diversified equity funds.

Finally, as mentioned earlier, the expense ratio is one amongst the various factors, which needs to be considered while evaluating a mutual fund scheme.

However, it should not be considered in isolation. Higher return is normally associated with high risk. But higher return can be earned hand in hand with lower risk merely by taking the expense ratio into account. You would do well to give this factor its due weight in the evaluation process.

Do Expenses Really Matter?

Now that you know everything about expense ratios, let us see if it really matters. The answer is yes, it does, especially in the case of debt funds. Debt funds generate about 7–9% returns and the expense ratio, whatever the percentage, becomes a substantial amount in the case of such low yields. In a debt fund, a 2.25% expense ratio would shave 25–30% off your returns! Expenses are, thus, crucial in determining the performance of debt funds and should be a factor to consider when buying a fund. Typically, institutional options within debt funds deliver better returns because of the lower expenses required to service bigger customers.

On the other hand, in the case of actively managed equity funds, the issue of expenses is more complicated. The wide divergence of returns between 'good' and 'bad' funds makes the expense ratio secondary. However, if you are stuck between two funds with a similar portfolio, the expense ratio can be a good differentiator. But keep in mind, expense is charged even when the fund's returns are negative. Overall, before you invest in a mutual fund, it is imperative that you check out the fund's expense ratio. But remember that a low expense ratio does not necessarily mean that the fund is good. **A good fund is one that delivers good returns with minimal expenses.**

Let us take an example to understand the effect of expenses on a fund's performance. Consider two similar funds, A and B. The expense ratio of Fund A is 2.25% and that of Fund B is 1.75%. Suppose you invest Rs. 2,00,000 each in both the funds and both the funds charge 2.25% as entry load (abolished w.e.f. August 1, 2009). Assume that the funds register a growth of 15% p.a. and that you stay invested for a 10-year period.

Table 8.2 Lower Fund Expenses…Higher Returns

Fund A vs Fund B

Details	Fund A	Fund B
Initial Investment (Rs.)	2,00,000	2,00,000
Entry Load (%)*	2.25	2.25
Expense Ratio (%)	2.25	1.75
Annual Return (%)	15.00	15.00
Maturity Value in 10 years (Rs.)	6,29,931	6,62,904
Maturity Value in 25 years (Rs.)	36,43,443	41,39,108

*Entry load has been abolished w.e.f. August 1, 2009

The investment of Rs. 2,00,000 in Fund A (which has a relatively higher expense ratio), will appreciate to Rs. 6,29,931 at the end of 10 years. The same amount invested in Fund B (with a lower expense ratio), will grow to Rs. 6,62,904. Effectively, the lower expenses charged by Fund B will fetch you an additional sum of Rs. 32,973 over the ten-year tenure.

Now, assume that the same investments are made over a longer time frame, say 25 years. In that case, the disparity in returns from both the funds widens to approximately Rs. 4,95,665.

The following assumptions have been made in the above calculations:

1. Expense ratios of both the funds have been assumed to be constant throughout the investment tenure. Under normal circumstances, expense ratios could vary over a period of time, especially with a growth in the fund's assets under management.

2. The rate of return has been assumed to stay constant throughout the investment tenure. In reality, the returns may vary across time horizons depending on factors such as the market conditions, among others.

It is evident that as the investment tenure grows, the benefits on account of "conservative" expenses grow exponentially. When you add mutual funds to your investment portfolio as a part of a financial planning exercise, you typically tend to have longer investment horizons. Funds charging lower expenses can play a significant role in aiding you achieve your investment objectives.

While it pays to monitor a fund's expenses, recent performance by equity funds reveals sharply divergent returns. This means that fund manager skills still play a big role in determining equity fund returns in the Indian context. Track record and investment strategy should, therefore, take precedence over expenses. You should check if expenses justify performance. A fund with a low expense ratio may not necessarily be the best performer and *vice versa*. Strangely, index funds reveal differences in returns not only due to expenses but also because of tracking errors. Tracking error is a measurement of how much the return on a portfolio deviates from the return on its benchmark index. Hence, focusing on expense ratios as the sole factor in choosing between equity funds is certainly not advisable. **Expense ratios can be useful in choosing between funds of comparable track record, size and investment strategy. The savings in expenses could compound into a sizeable difference in returns over a long holding period of 5 to 10 years.** Choosing debt funds is a more difficult proposition, given the number of options available in the debt space, from deposits to small savings to mutual funds. Here, expense ratios may help you narrow down your choices. With heavier competition in this segment, funds do keep a tighter leash on expenses. Among debt funds, passive funds such as fixed maturity plans might be more attractive because of the lower expenses involved.

Expenses are a very important consideration when selecting any type of mutual fund, especially fixed-income funds. It is very important to understand why expenses are high or low relative to other funds. Sometimes higher expenses are justified and at other times they are not. Portfolio managers and analysts should be compensated for their work. Compensation, however, should be commensurate with the effort required to manage the product and it is up to you to get involved to decide which expenses – and funds – are suitable for you.

For a full understanding of fund expenses, a careful perusal of the Offer Document and the Annual Report is absolutely essential. An informed investor knows where his money is going. He keeps tab on the toll he doles out on the highway to big money.

Are high fees worth it? You get what you pay for, right? Wrong.

Just about every study ever done has shown no correlation between high expense ratios and high returns. This is a fact. If you want more evidence, consider this quote from the Securities and Exchange Commission's website:

"Higher expense funds do not, on average, perform better than lower expense funds."

SECTION IV
FUND FLAVOURS

If the concept of mutual fund is so simple, why does mutual fund investing seem so complex? A common man is usually so confused about the various kinds of mutual funds that he is afraid of investing in these funds; he cannot differentiate between the various types of mutual funds with fancy names. There are 43 AMCs offering more than 2,300 schemes in India today. A systematic categorisation will put things in the proper perspective and guide you while investing in mutual funds. In this section, we go over the different flavours of funds.

Mutual funds can be classified into the following **four broad categories**:

1. Portfolio
2. Functional
3. Geographical
4. Specialised

Portfolio Classification is on the following basis:

* Equity Funds – Diversified, Sector, Dividend Yield Funds and Index Funds
* Debt/Income Funds – Diversified, Focused, High yield, Assured Return, Floating rate, Bond Funds and Gilt Funds
* Marginal Equity Funds – Capital Protection Funds, Fixed Maturity Plans (FMPs) and Monthly Income Plans (MIPs)
* Balanced Funds
* Asset Allocation Funds
* Hedge Funds
* Leveraged Funds
* Option Income Funds

Functional or Operational Classification is done on the following basis:

- Liquidity – Open-end Funds, Closed-end Funds and Interval Funds
- Investment Strategy – Growth and Value Funds
- Trading Strategy – Active and Passive Funds
- Security Selection – Top-down, Bottom-up and Technical Funds
- Market Capitalisation – Small Cap, Mid Cap and Large Cap Funds

Geographical Classification is done on the following basis:

- Domestic Mutual Funds
- Offshore Mutual Funds
- Regional Funds
- Global Funds
- International Funds

Specialised Funds such as ETFs, Fund of Funds (FoFs), Arbitrage/Derivative Funds, Quant Funds, Commodity Funds, Real Estate Mutual Funds and Real Estate Investment Trusts (REITs), Entertainment Funds, Equity Linked Savings Schemes (ELSS), Contra Funds and Socially Responsible or Ethical Funds, are attempting to take the mutual fund concept to the next level.

"Daring ideas are like chess-men moved forward; they may be beaten, but they may start a winning game." – Goethe

Innovation is the vital spark of all change, improvement and progress. It is a delicate balance of investing in the future and protecting the past and the present. Dream of things that are not and ask, "Why not?" The answers unfold in the concluding part of this section, "The Value of Innovation."

Chapter 9

Passing Through the Portals of Portfolio Classification
Across Asset Classes

Equity Funds

Funds that invest in stocks represent the largest category of mutual funds. Equity funds normally invest most of their corpus in equities. They provide capital appreciation over the medium to long term. They have comparatively high risks. Generally, the investment objective of this class of funds is long-term capital growth with some income. Equity funds invest in stocks but usually follow different investment strategies. Equity funds may look for growth in earnings (**growth stocks**), current market valuations that do not reflect intrinsic value in stocks (**value stocks**), or the most actively traded stocks that go up and down in tune with the market (**momentum stocks**). If you buy an equity fund or a mutual fund that invests in stocks, you must clearly understand that the price of its units will fluctuate with the price of the stocks it owns.

Equity funds from the same mutual fund family could be different depending upon where and in what proportion they invest their money. Since most financial newspapers and magazines do not classify equity funds under separate subcategories, it is important for you to look at the fund's top twenty holdings to see if the investments fit with your financial goals. **Do not take the fund's name at its face value.** A fund could be called a blue-chip fund, but you need to see its holdings to determine if the holdings are truly blue-chip. **Blue-chip funds** invest in stocks of very well-respected companies. The purpose is to build a stock portfolio of conservative stocks so that it does not do worse than the stock market indices. Such funds return less than funds that invest in growth-oriented companies.

Equity funds can be classified as follows:

1. **Diversified Equity Funds** invest mainly (at least 75%) in equities without any concentration on a particular sector or sectors. Being a diversified fund it cannot have more than 5% of the investment in one security and not more than 10% of the outstanding share in one security. Equity is their second name and that is where the bulk of their money goes. But, they also have the mandate to invest a small portion of their corpus in debt and cash (including money market instruments). Within the equity asset class, there are a lot of differentiating factors too. The fund manager enjoys the flexibility to research the market and based on the research which takes into account market inputs, economic conditions and political environment, he can modify his portfolio and vary the proportion. While we talk about diversified equity funds as a category, it will be inaccurate to assume that they all have the same focus. In fact, nothing could be further from the truth. Take a sample of what is on offer. Some funds such as Magnum Midcap, Franklin India Prima, Sundaram Select Midcap and Birla Mid Cap are focused on mid-caps. DSP Top 100 Equity invests in the 100 largest corporates. Funds including DBS Chola Contra, Kotak Contra, Magnum Contra, Tata Contra and UTI Contra employ contrarian investing. They buy into fundamentally sound scrips, which have underperformed in the recent past or have not been discovered. Birla Sun Life Frontline Equity targets the same sectoral weights as the BSE 200 but retains the flexibility of selecting stocks within those sectors. Franklin India Equity Fund invests in stocks (India and overseas) that have an attractive (current or potential) dividend yield. These funds are well-diversified and reduce sector-specific or company-specific risk. However, similar to all other funds, diversified equity funds too are exposed to equity market risk. Diversified equity funds are a varied assortment with diverse investment focus – asset allocation, market cap allocation, sectoral weightages. Since diversified is their first name, that is what you can expect from the dexterous and dynamic diversified equity funds.

2. **Sector Mutual Funds** are those mutual funds that restrict their investments to a particular segment or sector of the economy. At least

65% of the corpus is invested in a particular sector. There are a host of sector-specific funds such as FMCG, MNC, IT, New Technologies, Services, PSUs, Infrastructure, Pharma, Energy, etc. These funds concentrate on only one industry or sector. (There are **theme funds** that focus on a particular theme, a few allied industries together.) The idea is to allow you to place bets on specific industries or sectors, which have strong growth potential. These funds tend to be more volatile than funds holding a diversified portfolio of securities in many industries. Such concentrated portfolios can produce tremendous gains or losses, depending on whether the chosen sector is in or out of favour. If the sector performs well, sector funds yield higher returns when compared to other funds. Sector funds might profit much from windfall gains in one sector. The basic disadvantage of sector funds is that the portfolio manager has to confine his investment to one area. Even if the manager knows that the performance of the sector may not be good, he is forced to do so and is limited because of the scope of the fund.

3. **Equity Income or Dividend Yield Funds** have the objective of earning high recurring income and steady capital appreciation for you by investing in those companies which pay high dividends (such as Power or Utility companies whose share prices fluctuate comparatively lesser than the share prices of other companies). Equity income or dividend yield equity funds are generally exposed to the lowest risk level as compared to other equity funds.

4. **Index Funds** are equity funds that invest in exactly the same stocks (and in the same proportion) that make up the market indices such as the BSE Sensex or the NSE Nifty Index. So, what is the advantage of an index fund? The fund manager can programme a computer to just follow the index and pick stocks without putting in hours of his time in research and stock picking. So, the cost to the mutual fund for managing an index fund is low. It benefits investors in the form of low fees. The maximum expense ratio of index funds is 1.5% as against 2.5% in the case of active funds. Index funds are all-encompassing unlike diversified funds that exhibit a tilt towards certain sectors or stocks. The choice is easy since there are fewer index funds as opposed to hundreds of diversified equity funds. Moreover, it is not fund manager dependent. The other advantage is that you cannot do

worse than the BSE Sensex or the NSE Nifty. Simply because the index fund is replicating the movements of the index, NAVs of such schemes would rise or fall in accordance with the rise or fall in the index, though not exactly by the same percentage due to a factor known as "tracking error" in technical terms. Necessary disclosures in this regard are made in the offer document of the mutual fund scheme. These funds tend to replicate the index as it is, in order to match the returns on the market. This is also known as passive management. It is not possible to beat the market over a sustained period of time through active management and hence it is better to replicate the index. Funds that are not passive are called managed funds. Index schemes are also referred to as **Unmanaged Schemes** (since they are passive) or **Tracker Scheme** (since they track the index). Examples in India are UTI Nifty Index Fund and Franklin India Index Funds. Equity index funds that follow broad indices (S&P CNX Nifty, Sensex) are less risky than equity index funds that follow narrow sectoral indices (BSE BANKEX or CNX Bank Index, etc.). Narrow indices are less diversified and are, therefore, riskier. Alternatively, a mutual fund, through its research, can identify a basket of securities and/or derivatives whose movement is similar to that of the index. Schemes that invest in such baskets can be viewed as '**Active Index Funds'.** Internationally, mutual funds have proprietary models that help create baskets that seek to outperform the market during a boom, while falling lesser in a bearish market.

Enhanced Index Fund is a managed index fund that seeks to beat the performance of its benchmark index by at least 0.1% but no more than 2% (beyond the 2% cap, it becomes an equity mutual fund).

Why are Index Funds not Popular in India?

Index funds are a relatively small part of the overall mutual fund industry in India and this is markedly different from the West, where index funds do quite well and in fact the biggest fund in the US is an index fund (SPY) that tracks the popular S&P 500 index.

There are three aspects to this – the first is that, in India, actively managed funds have performed better than index funds in the past and people expect that to continue in the future as well. Secondly, index funds are not really low cost in India. Finally, there is greater scope for mis-selling funds in India.

In the Indian context, investing in actively managed mutual funds is more popular compared to investing in index funds. The reasons are not hard to find – the track record of index funds proves that they have outperformed actively managed funds only across shorter time frames of 12 months or thereabouts. Over the long term (3–5 year time frame) diversified mutual funds rule the show or so they seem to. In most years, only about a third of actively managed funds beat their benchmark indexes, such as the S & P CNX Nifty or the S & P BSE 200. And managers who succeed in one year often fail in the next, suggesting that many winning results are no more than luck. Numerous studies report that these (actively managed) funds have provided investors with returns significantly below those on the passive benchmarks, on an average. It may seem strange, that all those highly paid portfolio managers as a group, do not seem to be able to display any consistent ability to perform better than a diversified portfolio of stocks chosen on the basis of nothing more than their size, but all of this is exactly as it ought to be. First, let me state something that may appear obvious, but it lies at the heart of a very successful investment strategy: it is mathematically impossible for everyone to be above average. No matter what the average is, there must always be a distribution such that half of all people (or in the case of investing, the managers of half of all invested money) would be below average. If an index is the average, then like it or not half of all the investors are going to do worse than the index, before costs and there is nothing that can be done about it. Of course, half will do better, but no amount of trading or research will stop half of all the investors failing to beat the index. To use an analogy, no matter how hard the athletes train and how good they are, even at the Olympics somebody has to lose. Half the athletes will come in the second half of the field. It makes no difference at all if the athletes as a group are superb, terrible or somewhere in between, the actual ratio of winners to losers was fixed all along. Investment is the same.

In developed economies, such as the United States, stock markets are more efficient and research on companies is widely disseminated. This makes it all the more difficult for actively managed funds to unravel investment opportunities. So, most investors find it worth their while to go with an index fund since a majority of actively managed funds struggle to outperform the index in any case. In addition, no loads and lower recurring fees endear index funds to investors.

This brings us to the second aspect of index fund popularity – cost and tracking error of the index funds themselves. The whole point of an index fund is that it should be extremely low cost since there is no active management needed but that low cost has not really materialised in the Indian market. A majority of index funds charge in excess of 1% recurring expenses and that is simply too high for an index fund. But there have been funds that charge much lower expenses, most notably the IIFL Nifty ETF that has an expense ratio of 0.25% which is the lowest of any index ETF till date. The biggest Nifty ETF – Goldman Sachs Nifty BeES ETF – is also a low-cost ETF which has expenses of about 0.50% and has been around for a decade now. But as a category – the low cost has still not become a norm and that makes a difference to the returns.

The final reason why index funds are so popular in the US is because investors know exactly what they are getting into and investment advisers have little scope to mis-sell an index fund. The mis-selling usually happens when the investment adviser is out to pocket his commission at the cost of the investor's interest. In India, mutual fund agents are not just out to pocket the commissions, they are keen to bag all the prizes doled out in mutual fund contests. So, the risk of the mutual fund investor being saddled with the wrong investment could be pretty high, depending of course, on the number of active mutual fund contests and the level of financial literacy of the investor. Investors are duped by slick managed fund marketing. They do not know the facts or they believe "you get what you pay for" — that paying higher active management fees should buy better results. Maybe they are deferential to "professionals," or believe they are smart enough to pick the active managers who are better than average. All those explanations have one thing in common: They assume investors are not very bright. But investors who embrace active management may, in fact, be behaving perfectly rationally. Investors use active management in a kind of arms race to unearth a limited number of bargain-priced investments.

So, the three main reasons for the popularity of index funds – doing better than active funds, low costs and little scope for mis-selling – have been more or less absent in India so far. When the Indian markets turn around on these parameters, we could see a change of mindset on that front. Till such time, people who want the benefit of passive investing feel that by creating an SIP in an active mutual fund – you enjoy the same kind of benefit and the past returns show that it has been beneficial as well!

Debt/Income Funds

Debt/Income Funds invest in medium to long-term fixed income assets such as corporate debentures, Government securities, bonds and other debt-related instruments issued by private companies, banks, financial institutions, Governments and other entities belonging to various sectors (infrastructure companies, etc.). They also invest in short-term instruments such as call money, certificate of deposit, treasury bills, commercial papers, etc. From October 2012, the total exposure of debt schemes of a mutual fund in a particular sector (excluding investments in bank certificates of deposit, Collateralised Borrowing and Lending Obligations (CBLO), Government securities, Treasury Bills and AAA-rated securities issued by public financial institutions and public sector banks) shall not exceed 30% of the net assets of the respective scheme. CBLO is a money market instrument operated by the Clearing Corporation of India Ltd. for the benefit of the entities which have either no access to the interbank call money market or have restricted access in terms of ceiling on call borrowing and lending transactions.

Debt funds provide capital stability and regular income to you. In order to ensure regular income, debt (or income) funds distribute a large fraction of their surplus to you. However, opportunities of capital appreciation are limited. Such funds are less risky compared to equity funds. In spite of their lower risk, debt funds are subject to interest rate risk (risk of change in NAV due to change in interest rate) as well as credit risk (risk of default) by the issuer at the time of interest or principal payment. To minimise the risk of change in NAV due to change in interest rate, debt funds invest in securities of short-term maturities. The NAV of debt funds that invest in securities of long-term maturities fluctuate widely and are hence riskier. To minimise the risk of default, debt funds usually invest in securities from issuers, who are rated by credit rating agencies and are considered to be of "Investment Grade". Debt funds that target high returns are riskier. Based on different investment objectives, there can be different types of debt funds as follows:

1. **Diversified Debt Funds:** Debt funds that invest in securities issued by entities belonging to all sectors of the market are known as diversified debt funds. The best feature of diversified debt funds is that investments are properly diversified into all sectors which results in risk reduction. Any loss incurred, on account of default by a debt issuer, is shared by all investors, which further reduces risk for an individual investor.

2. **Focused Debt Funds:** Unlike diversified debt funds, focused debt funds are narrow focus funds that are confined to investments in selective debt securities, issued by companies of a specific sector or industry or origin. Some examples of focused debt funds are sector, specialised and offshore debt funds and funds that invest only in tax-free infrastructure or municipal bonds. Because of their narrow orientation, focused debt funds are riskier as compared to diversified debt funds. Although not yet available in India, these funds are conceivable and may be offered to Indian investors also.

3. **High-Yield Debt Funds:** Risk of default is present in all debt funds and, therefore, debt funds generally try to minimise the risk of default by investing in securities issued by only those borrowers, who are considered to be of "investment grade". But, high-yield debt funds adopt a different strategy and prefer securities issued by those issuers, who are considered to be of "below investment grade". The motive behind adopting this sort of risky strategy is to earn higher interest returns from these issuers. These funds are more volatile and bear higher default risk, although they may earn higher returns at times for you.

4. **Assured Return Funds:** Although it is not necessary that a fund will meet its objectives or provide assured returns to you, there can be funds that come with a lock-in period and offer assurance of annual returns to you during the lock-in period. Any shortfall in returns is suffered by the sponsors or the AMCs. These funds are generally debt funds and provide you with a low-risk investment opportunity. However, the security of investments depends upon the net worth of the guarantor (whose name is specified in advance in the offer document). To safeguard the investors' interests, SEBI permits only those funds whose sponsors have adequate net worth to guarantee returns in the future on such schemes. In the past, UTI had offered assured return schemes (i.e. Monthly Income Plans of UTI) that assured specified returns to investors in the future. UTI was not able to fulfil its promises and faced large shortfalls in returns. Eventually, the Government had to intervene and take over UTI's payment obligations on itself. Currently, though possible, no AMC in India offers assured return schemes.

5. **Floating Rate Debt Funds:** Floating rate funds are debt mutual funds which invest about 75% to 100% in instruments which pay a floating rate interest while the rest is invested in fixed income instruments. Floating rate instruments are debt instruments whose interest rate (coupon) is not fixed and is linked to a benchmark rate such as the Mumbai Interbank Offered Rate (MIBOR). For example, a debt security where interest payable is described as 'MIBOR plus 1%', will pay interest rate of 7%, when the MIBOR is 6%; if MIBOR goes down to 3%, then only 4% interest will be payable on that debt security. Each time the benchmark rate fluctuates, the coupon rate is adjusted accordingly. MIBOR is the interest rate at which banks can borrow funds, in marketable size, from other banks in the Indian interbank market. It is calculated everyday by the National Stock Exchange of India as a weighted average of lending rates of a group of banks, on funds lent to first-class borrowers. Since its launch in 1998, MIBOR rates have been used as benchmark rates for the majority of money market deals made in India.

There are two types of floating rate funds — short-term and long-term. The portfolio of the short-term plan is normally skewed towards short-term maturities with higher liquidity and the portfolio of the long-term plan is skewed towards long-term maturities. However, even the long-term funds are positioned more on the lines of short-term funds and are not very aggressive. Moreover, the volatility arising due to investment into long-dated fixed coupon bearing instruments is offset by the presence of floating rate instruments.

The primary advantage of these funds is that they are less volatile than other types of debt funds. This advantage arises due to the inherent structure of the floating rate instruments. In the case of fixed rate instruments, when interest rates in the economy change, the price of the instrument adjusts to make up for the fixed coupon of the instrument. While this happens even in the case of floating rate instrument, the change in the price of the instrument is less drastic due to the periodic change in the coupon of the instrument. The fall in the price of the floating rate instrument will depend upon the reset period. The reset period determines how often the interest rate will be adjusted. The reset could be daily, monthly, quarterly, half-yearly, annually or any other periodicity specified by the issuer. The lesser the gap between the resets, the lower will be the fall in price. These funds, in turn, ensure that the portfolio has a limited interest rate risk. Unlike ordinary debt funds, the yield of a floating rate debt fund remains at par with the market yield. The NAV is, therefore, relatively very stable.

6. **Bond Funds**: Bond funds invest in all kinds of bonds – Government, PSU, or private sector bonds. Some bond funds invest in only certain kinds of bonds. For example, gilt funds invest only in Government of India securities and are the safest type of mutual funds available in India. Certain mutual funds invest only in bonds that have the highest safety rating from credit rating agencies.

A bond fund allows you to invest in a basket of thirty to fifty bonds, which a fund manager can trade in reaction to changing market conditions such as interest rates and the bond issuer's credit ratings. The biggest advantage that bond funds offer is the ability to get in and get out at any time. But unlike a bond, you do not have a fixed interest payment or a time period in which the bond issuer will pay back the loan since the fund is buying and selling bonds constantly.

When you buy a bond fund, be very careful about the average maturity of the fund's bond holdings. Average maturity is the average age of debt securities in a fund portfolio. Bond funds invest in a number of bonds, with each instrument having a different maturity. Since the maturity of the bond does not give a clear picture of the fund's maturity profile, funds usually disclose weighted average maturity. For example, if a bond fund owns three bonds of 3 years (Rs. 1,00,000), 5 years (Rs. 7,00,000) and 10 years (Rs. 2,00,000), the weighted average maturity would be 5.8 years. Average maturity tells you how sensitive a bond fund is to change in interest rates. The longer the bond fund's average maturity period, the greater will be the risk of volatility or fluctuations in the fund's net asset value. When interest rates move down, bond prices move up, thus boosting debt fund's returns and *vice versa*, when rates move up. In addition, find out the credit risk or the possibility that a bond issuer will default, by failing to pay principal and interest in a timely manner. Bond funds from different mutual fund families, or for that matter, different bond funds from the same mutual fund could vary in terms of where and in what proportion they invest their money. Since most financial newspapers and magazines do not classify debt or bond funds under separate subcategories, it is important for you to look at the fund's holdings (regulations require mutual funds to disclose their top twenty holdings) to see if the mutual fund's investments fit your financial goals.

Bond funds make sense for investors who prefer a steady flow of income and do not want their original investment to fluctuate, or those who may need their funds for some other purpose in the short-term.

Broadly, Bond Funds are of the following types:

a) **Money Market Funds:** A Money Market Fund is a mutual fund that invests solely in money market instruments. Money market instruments are forms of debt that mature in less than one year and are very liquid. **Money market fund is also known as Liquid Fund.** It invests only in safe short-term debt instruments such as T-Bills, Certificate of Deposits (CDs), Commercial Papers (CPs) and interbank call money market (a technical term for borrowings between banks for a day). Returns on these schemes fluctuate much lesser compared to other funds. These funds are appropriate for corporate and individual investors as a means to park their surplus funds for short periods. Though a money market mutual fund invests in safe instruments and has rarely defaulted, it gives you no guarantee that you will not lose all or part of your original investment. Money market funds first try to keep your principal intact and then try to get you interest. You do not have to worry about your original investment. It will remain intact because this is the overriding concern the fund has and it sacrifices greater returns by picking absolutely safe short-term investments. Money market funds are as safe as your savings bank account and produce a much better return. They should be used as an alternative to savings bank accounts. You can withdraw your money within 24 hours from these funds and they allow you to write cheques on your balance. What that means is that you get a cheque book and you can write a cheque against your investment.

> ### Liquid Funds vs. Liquid Plus Funds
>
> A minor variant of liquid funds is liquid plus funds. While both are short-term debt funds, these funds can be differentiated on the basis of instruments invested, investment tenure, exit load and risk and returns.
>
> Liquid plus funds have investments almost similar to liquid funds. They invest in money market instruments of residual maturity of up to 91 days. But, nearly 30% of the corpus of liquid plus funds is invested in instruments with longer maturity periods. Liquid funds enjoy lowest volatility in returns as there is no mark-to-market of the portfolio on a daily basis unless there is a trade in the secondary market in the underlying securities. Practically, there is no trade in money market instruments and valuation of the daily NAV happens on an accrual basis, i.e. by adding the coupon accrued for the day without any mark-to-market impact. Valuation of daily NAV of liquid plus funds is done according to the valuation matrix published by the rating agencies. The volatility of returns in liquid plus funds is marginally higher than liquid funds due to the small mark-to-market (MTM) component.
>
> The key differentiating factor between liquid and liquid plus funds is the duration of investment. The debt instruments held by liquid plus funds have a longer tenure than liquid funds, i.e. the portfolios of liquid plus funds have a higher average maturity than those of liquid funds. In effect, while you can invest in liquid funds for as briefly as one day, the holding period for liquid plus funds should be higher than that.
>
> Liquid and liquid plus funds can be redeemed within a day. However, if liquid plus funds are redeemed within a specified period, there can be an exit load (the minimum investment tenure and the exit load vary across fund houses). On the other hand, there is no exit load on liquid funds.
>
> Liquid plus funds are riskier than liquid funds. This is mainly due to two reasons: (a) liquid plus funds hold investments that have a higher maturity and (b) there is no limit on the MTM component of liquid plus funds as opposed to the 10% MTM limit on liquid funds. MTM refers to recording the value of investments to reflect the current market value rather than the book value. They also have different cut-off timings for the present day's NAV (Refer 'Fund Pricing in India' in Chapter 6).

You would do well to take into account the above-mentioned differences while investing in liquid or liquid plus schemes. Those of you, who have a relatively longer investment horizon, can consider investing in liquid plus schemes, provided you are ready to stay invested for the specified duration in order to avoid paying the exit load. Those of you, for whom liquidity is the top priority, can opt for liquid funds.

In order to match the tenure of debt securities in the portfolio with the maturity of the schemes, SEBI has cut the maximum maturity of the papers in which liquid funds could invest. From February 1, 2009, mutual funds were made to invest funds in liquid and liquid plus schemes into debt securities having the tenure of up to 182 days. From May 1, 2009, they were made to invest in securities maturing within 91 days only. SEBI tightened the valuation norms of liquid and liquid plus funds in 2012 by imposing MTM requirements for instruments with a residual maturity period of 60 days and more. SEBI, eventually, wants all instruments irrespective of their tenure and type to be quoted at market rates and the net asset value calculated accordingly. Further, SEBI asked mutual funds to discontinue the nomenclature of "Liquid Plus" schemes since it gave a wrong impression of added liquidity.

SEBI's discomfort with the valuation of debt instruments has been there since 2008. After the Lehman Brothers collapse, a number of fund houses faced severe redemption pressure from companies. For instance, Lotus Mutual Fund sold its business to Religare in November 2008 after it lost almost Rs. 2,500 crore in its liquid and liquid plus schemes in a single month. Fund houses have lost significant money in liquid funds since RBI capped banks' investments in liquid funds at 10% of their net worth in May 2011. At the end of April 2011, liquid funds managed Rs. 2.2 lakh crore, accounting for 28% of the industry. According to AMFI, assets under management of liquid and money market schemes, fell to Rs. 1.83 lakh crore in May 2012 but has risen to Rs. 3.09 lakh crore in September 2016.

(b) **High-yield Bond Funds:** Technically, high-yield bond funds are referred to as "**junk bond funds**". These funds pay higher returns than other bond funds, but invest all or part of their funds in riskier 'below investment grade' bonds such as those that may not have the highest safety rating from credit rating agencies. The risk that a bond or bonds in the fund's portfolio could default is greater. SEBI guidelines limit investment in unrated securities and securities that are below investment grade to 25% of the net assets of any scheme. Hence, it is not possible to have a junk bond scheme in India.

   (c) **High Safety Bond Funds:** High safety bond funds invest their funds in the highest rated corporate bonds or risk-free Government securities only.

7. **Gilt Funds:** Gilt funds invest in Government of India and State Government securities and bonds, with medium to long-term maturity, typically more than a year. These bonds are guaranteed by the Central or State Governments. These mutual funds are the safest type of debt funds available since they invest in bonds backed by the full faith of the Government. Your original investment is as safe as it can be though your returns may be lower than what you can get in a debt mutual fund that invests in corporate debt. Government securities do not carry any credit risk, but they are subject to interest rate risk. For all practical purposes, most of us cannot participate in the bond market. With the massive size of each trade and with most brokers catering only to very large investors, the gilt fund route is the best way to participate in the Government securities market.

Caveat Emptor!

A note of caution before we proceed further...

Be careful of mutual funds that have a lot of money in unlisted securities. A number of mutual funds invest funds in stocks and bonds that are not quoted or for which there is no secondary market. This is dicey, because it gives the fund manager the ability to cover up any losses or drop in value of quoted stocks and bonds by increasing the value of unquoted investments subjectively. Such moves could go unnoticed and explode when the mutual fund is under unusual redemption pressure. Moreover, mutual funds that have money in unlisted investments may not be very liquid or may be unable to pay you if the redemption pressure on the bond fund increases.

Marginal Equity Funds

Marginal Equity Funds are funds which have an investment of at least 75% in debt instruments and the balance in equities. These funds offer the security of debt with the flavour of equities. Capital Protection-oriented Funds, Fixed Maturity Plans (FMPs) and Monthly Income Plans (MIPs) are good examples of marginal equity funds.

Capital Protection Funds

Capital protection funds are structured products that ensure that you get your principal back irrespective of what happens to the market. They are designed to attract risk-averse investors to the stock market. In developed countries, such funds offer capital guarantee. Capital protection funds provide investors with an opportunity to profit from a rise in the equity markets. By allocating a portion to equities, the fund participates in the upside during the bull run and offers downside protection in a bearish market. In India, these are closed-end funds that offer capital protection, without a guarantee.

Capital protection funds are essentially a simplified version of structured products with investments made in high quality debt, which typically commands lower yields, while simultaneously taking a small exposure (up to 20%) to a riskier asset – equity. Structured products are already highly popular in Europe. They are beginning to make their mark in India with a deluge of funds from nearly a dozen reputed fund houses including Franklin Templeton, UTI, Deutsche, DBS Cholamandalam (now L&T), ICICI Prudential, Birla Sun Life, SBI, Sundaram and IDFC taking the AUM of such funds to Rs. 6,577 crore in June 2016. In August 2006, SEBI issued guidelines permitting fund houses to launch "capital protection oriented" schemes. SEBI said capital protection should arise from the way in which the portfolio was constructed and not from any guarantee by the AMC or sponsor. It also required that the scheme be rated by a credit rating agency on the ability of the fund to protect the initial investment. The rating had to be reviewed on a quarterly basis and AMCs had to ensure that the debt component of the portfolio had the highest investment grade rating (AAA or P1+). In addition, these schemes should be closed-end so that you could invest only at the time of the new fund offer and could redeem only on the completion of its term or if it gets listed.

The Modus Operandi

To ensure that you are able to reap maximum benefits by participating in an asset class that gives better returns without compromising on the safety of the capital invested, a portion of the fund is invested in debt instruments that would mature at the value of the initial investment at the time of redemption and the remaining in equity. For example, out of Rs. 100, Rs. 80 may be invested in an interest-paying debt instrument or zero-coupon bonds, whose maturity value is Rs. 100. The remaining Rs. 20 is invested in equity. Over a three to five-year period (which is the tenure of such funds), however, it is reasonable to expect a modest return from equity. Even if equity returns nothing, you still have your capital intact.

This is something that you can easily replicate by parking the funds in a Post Office Monthly Income Scheme (POMIS) and investing the monthly interest in the equity market. However, the advantage that fund houses would bring is the use of sophisticated tools to manage funds between less risky assets and risky assets. The protection is at risk only if the value of the portfolio falls below the floor, Rs. 80 and this is monitored on a continuous basis with built-in triggers.

A Double-Edged Sword...

Capital protection funds aim to protect your rupee investment and inflation is ignored. This means that even if you get the amount that you had invested, effectively you have lost money because of the value erosion in the original investment over the period. Does this mean that you will lose money? Not likely. Capital protection funds are closed-end funds with duration of say, 3 years or 5 years. Since you cannot redeem the fund before its maturity, the fund managers can invest in securities of corresponding maturity and ensure adequate returns and hence, capital protection. But, there is no liquidity, since you cannot get back the money before the maturity of the fund.

You can invest only that portion of your money that can be set aside for 3 to 5 years. The credit rating that SEBI insists on will also provide an added level of security for you. In real life, these funds will rise gently when the market shoots up and will go down less than they went up earlier when the markets reach their nadir.

...The Cutting Edge?

Capital protection oriented funds can make an apt fit if you are a low to moderate risk-taking investor since it offers an opportunity to invest in a market-linked investment avenue without compromising on your risk profile. This fund would be all the more appealing if you are in the highest tax bracket or close to retirement.

Fixed Maturity Plans

FMPs are closed-end products, not listed on stock exchanges, investing predominantly in debt and money market instruments, whose maturity coincides with the maturity of the product – ranging from a fortnight to five years. FMP NFOs are marketed to corporates and high networth individuals before the scheme opens. Since minimum investment is Rs. 5000, retail investors can also invest in FMPs. FMPs usually invest in CDs, CPs, money market instruments, corporate bonds, etc. The fund manager invests in a combination of the instruments mentioned above, of similar maturity that matches with the tenure of the FMP. For instance, if the FMP is for a year, the fund manager invests in instruments maturing in one year. Since the tenure of FMPs is short, the yield can be determined fairly accurately. The yield minus the expense ratio (mentioned in the offer document), which varies from 0.25% to 1%, gives the return which can be expected from the FMP. That way it knows the interest rate that it will earn on its investments, providing the 'indicative return' to investors (SEBI has prohibited FMPs from offering indicative returns). The objective is to lock-in the investment at a specified rate of return (in tune with the ruling interest rate scenario), thereby, immunising the fund against market fluctuations. In effect, FMPs are structured to offer you capital protection (although implicitly). FMPs with a dash of equity (up to 20%) offer the twin advantage of capital protection (taken care of by the debt portfolio) and capital appreciation (provided by the equity portfolio). FMPs are akin to FDs issued by mutual funds instead of banks. When a series of FMPs are issued for different maturities, they are called Serial Funds.

You get the expected yield from a debt instrument if it is held till maturity. If the instrument is sold earlier, the amount recovered will depend on the market situation at that point in time, resulting in a capital gain or loss. FMPs seek to eliminate the risk of capital loss by investing exclusively in a pre-specified debt security. If you stay invested in the scheme for the period envisaged, fixed return is assured. An early exit option is available if the FMP is structured as an open-end scheme. Normally, an assured return is offered if there is a named guarantor, who offers the guarantee. An FMP is an 'assured returns scheme', informally (not on paper) since you are reasonably assured of the expected return (subject to credit risk and reinvestment risk) if the units are held for the originally envisaged period but the return is assured without the named guarantor.

FMPs score high on the following aspects:

* FMPs have less risk of capital loss than equity funds because they invest a lion's share in debt and money market instruments.

* FMPs involve minimum expenditure on fund management as there is no requirement for a periodic review by fund managers to buy/sell the instruments constituting the fund since these instruments are held till maturity.

* Fluctuations in the interest rate and hence market value do not affect your returns from FMPs as securities in the portfolio are not traded but held till maturity.

* FMPs are tax efficient both in the short-term as well as in the long-term.

For the financial year 2016–17, the dividend from FMPs is tax-free in your hands. If you invest in the growth option of the FMP for less than 3 years, the capital gains are added to your income and taxed at your slab rate. If you invest in the growth option of the FMP for over 3 years, you pay 20% with indexation plus surcharge and cess. Indexation is the process by which the inflation is taken into account when computing the tax liability. In indexation, the returns generated on FMPs are adjusted to inflation during the holding period. Assuming that the annual inflation index is 6% and the returns generated on the portfolio of the FMP at the end of the term is 9%, the investor has to pay tax only on the 3% gain that he has additionally made.

Though returns from FMPs are only indicative (hence predictable) as opposed to guaranteed returns offered by FDs, **FMPs end up yielding better post-tax returns than FDs** with the added attractiveness of **'double indexation'** benefit, which is not available in the case of fixed deposits. You can invest in an FMP on March 30, 2015 and withdraw it on April 2, 2016 and enjoy double indexation benefit. This ensures the applicability of indexation benefits for inflationary changes in two financial years since the amount remains invested for a period slightly greater than a year. Double indexation, in some cases, can even lead to a net loss figure, even though there is a profit and thus expunges your tax obligation (if you had invested before, or just before, the previous financial year (2015–16) in the hope of getting double indexation benefits, you would be taxed at the higher rate of 20%, if your funds come up for redemption before they complete three years). Moreover, interest from deposits of more than Rs. 1 lakh is taxed at the marginal rate making FMPs a better option for deposits of higher amounts. Dividends declared by all mutual funds are tax-free in the hands of the investors. Equity funds (funds that invest over 65% of their corpus in Indian equity) are exempt from dividend distribution tax. However, non-equity funds pay a dividend distribution tax before paying out dividend. According to tax rates for the financial year 2016–17, for short-term FMPs, dividend distribution tax (DDT) of 28.84% makes the choice of dividend option unattractive whereas for long-term FMPs, growth option would be ideal since only 20% capital gains tax (including surcharge and cess) with indexation is applicable. Indexation benefits lure retail investors to FMPs. However, indexation benefits may be scrapped if the Government implements the Direct Taxes Code or DTC.

Monthly Income Plans

Monthly Income Plans, or MIPs, as they are more popularly known, are a category of mutual funds that invest predominantly in debt instruments (up to 95%). Only about 5–15% of the assets are allocated to equity stocks to ensure higher returns. This can go up to 30%, thereby, boosting the risk component. But the very name – Monthly Income Plan – is a misnomer, as these funds do not guarantee a monthly income. Similar to any other fund, the returns are market driven. Though many fund houses strive to declare a monthly dividend, they have no such obligation. MIPs are launched with the objective of giving a monthly income to you, but the periodicity depends upon the option chosen by you. These are generally monthly, quarterly, half-yearly and annual options. A growth option is also available, where you do not receive regular dividends, but gain in the form of capital appreciation.

The concept of MIP evolves from the requirement to provide enhanced returns to risk-averse investors. MIPs give a conservative investor the double advantage of stability of debt and the growth potential of equities. Thus, it gives you an opportunity to upgrade from low return investments in fixed deposits and bonds to the higher return MIP schemes, without taking excessive risks. MIPs are typically suitable for investors, who want to largely play it safe, but do not mind taking a little risk in order to increase the potential returns that pure income/debt funds would provide. Unlike a bank deposit, you can redeem your funds any time. In addition to the liquidity advantage, the dividends received from an MIP are tax-free. The capital gain at the time of redemption though, would be subject to tax similar to any other debt fund – at the regular income tax slab of the individual if it is short-term in nature (less than three years) and at 20% with indexation plus surcharge and cess, in case it is long-term. These tax rates are applicable for the financial year 2016–17.

Those who are looking for a market-linked solution that provides a monthly income, or those who intend to invest into schemes with moderate to medium risk, can look at MIP.

Balanced Funds

If you depend upon the marketing efforts of the AMCs or distributors to get to know about mutual funds, chances are that you do not have any money invested in balanced mutual funds. A peek into the track record of NFOs makes things more clear. Since the stock market started rising in 2003, 12 equity-oriented balanced funds were launched as against 160 equity funds during the same time period. That boils down to thirteen equity funds for every balanced fund. The same ratio was 2.4:1 in 2002 – 48 equity funds to twenty balanced funds. The objective of these funds is to provide a balanced mixture of safety, income and capital appreciation. The strategy of balanced funds is to invest in a combination of fixed-income securities and equities. The fixed-income part is generally Government or corporate debt of various types. They stick to a fairly well-defined ratio between these two types of assets. Also known as **Hybrid Funds, Balanced Funds** invest in a mix of equity and debt in almost equal proportions. A minimum of 65% in equity is mandatory to get the tax benefits of equity investments. In view of their conservative approach, they are less risky than equity funds while providing commensurately lower returns.

Balanced funds are ideal for diversifying investments without spending time on the process. NAVs of such funds are likely to be less volatile compared to pure equity funds. Balanced funds do better than equity funds in times of economic downturns since shares are usually poor performers during such times. They do better than bond funds in times of economic upturns since the stock investments in these funds help them to post better returns. To maintain the ratio, the fund manager has to periodically sell whichever investment has done better. With the proceeds of the sale, he has to buy the other type of investment to regain the balance. While this sounds counter intuitive to the average investor, it ensures that the profits from equity are being regularly realised and protected by investing them in safe debt investments. It ensures that you are buying equities when the markets are falling and the equities are cheap. Invariably, this is the best strategy that can be adopted in order to combine profits and safety in the long-term. However, individual investors seldom have the discipline to strictly adhere to this game plan since it is counter intuitive to sell whatever is rising and buy whatever is falling. Over a complete market cycle, with its ups and downs, this invariably produces reasonable returns with far less volatility and heartburn. Every time you sell, you have to pay capital gains tax. Every time a fund sells, you are not taxed. When you hold any type of fixed-income instrument, it is liable for long-term capital gains tax unlike equity income (which is exempt from long-term capital gains tax). However, if a balanced fund retains the equity allocation at 65%, then the entire investment is treated as equity for tax purposes and is thus free from long-term capital gains tax.

Asset Allocation Funds

A similar type of fund is known as an Asset Allocation Fund. The objectives are similar to those of a balanced fund, but these kinds of funds typically do not have to hold a specified percentage of any asset class. The portfolio manager is given freedom to switch the ratio of asset classes as the economy moves through the business cycles. Mutual funds may invest in financial assets such as equity, debt, money market, or non-financial (physical) assets including real estate, commodities, etc. Asset allocation funds adopt a variable asset allocation strategy that allows fund managers to switch over from one asset class to another at any time depending upon their outlook for specific markets. In other words, fund managers may switch over to equity if they expect the equity market to provide good returns and switch over to debt if they expect the debt market to provide better returns. It should be noted that switching over from one asset class to another is a decision taken by the fund manager based on his own judgement and understanding of specific markets and, therefore, the success of these funds depends upon the skill of a fund manager in anticipating market trends.

Hedge Funds

Hedge Funds employ speculative trading principles – buy rising shares and sell shares whose prices are likely to fall. Hedge funds are extremely risky leveraged funds where the fund manager invests a mix of funds belonging to the investors and funds borrowed from lenders. Leveraging the two funds would mean that for every Re. 1 of unit capital, an additional Rs. 2 is borrowed, thus investing Rs. 3 in the market. Borrowed funds have interest and repayment obligations, which are independent of how the market performs. Thus, in bad market conditions, while a non-leveraged fund only needs to bear the loss, a leveraged fund would also need to generate additional resources to meet the interest and repayment obligations on borrowed funds. However, when the returns on the borrowed funds are higher than the cost of borrowed capital, the investor earns super normal profit. Hedge funds are popular in the United States. Hedge funds have been one of the worst casualties of the global financial crisis. So far, by limiting the scope for borrowing by the Indian mutual funds, the regulatory framework has kept hedge funds at arm's length in India.

Leveraged Funds

Leveraged Funds make speculative and risky investments, similar to short-sales to take advantage of a declining market. The main objective of the fund is to increase the value of the portfolio by attempting to make gains that exceed the cost of borrowed funds. They are not common in India.

Option Income Funds

While not yet available in India (though permitted, none has been launched so far), Option Income Funds write options on a large fraction of their portfolio. Otherwise considered as a risky instrument, proper use of options can help to reduce volatility. These funds invest in big, high dividend-yielding companies and then sell options against their stock positions, which generate stable income for you.

Chapter 10

On to Operational Classification
Of Liquidity, Strategies, Selection and Capitalisation

A. By Liquidity

Open-end Funds

Open-end funds are similar to bank accounts. Such funds enable you to invest and redeem your money any time! They are always open to accept money from you and return the money to you. During the initial offer period, they are offered for sale at a pre-specified price, say Rs. 10. After a pre-specified period say, 15 days (reduced from the earlier 30 days according to the March 2010 SEBI circular), the fund reopens for further sales and repurchases after the NFO is closed. There is no fixed tenure of the scheme. Units are continuously offered for sale (new units are sold to investors desirous of participating in the fund) and continuously bought back (repurchased) from investors who wish to exit/redeem their units. The units of the fund can be bought from and sold back only to the mutual fund. There is no secondary market trading for units of an open-end fund. They do not have a fixed number of units nor do they have a fixed maturity period. Units are bought and sold at their current net asset value calculated and disclosed on a daily basis. They offer better liquidity due to continuous repurchase. The corpus of an open-end fund is variable because of continuous selling (to investors) and repurchases (from the investors) by the fund. In the short-term, the fund manager has to face liquidity pressure as well as pressure of good returns. Since redemptions can occur any time, the fund manager has constraints in taking a long-term view on his investment. Occasionally, open-end funds can and do close the scheme to new investors because of high cash inflows that cannot be invested profitably in a timely manner. They do not become closed-end funds, however, because current unit-holders can continue to buy or redeem units from the fund or reinvest profits. An open-end fund is not required to keep selling new units to investors at all times but is required to always repurchase from its existing investors. Irrespective of what they invest in, most mutual funds hold 5–15% of their funds in cash or liquid investments. This kind of cash reserve is necessary to meet any redemption of fund units by existing investors or to use in picking up bargains in the financial markets. The majority of mutual funds available are open-end funds.

Closed-end Funds

Closed-end funds are funds, which can sell a fixed number of units only during the NFO period. They have a set number of units issued to the public through the NFO. These funds have a stipulated maturity period – generally ranging from 3 to 15 years. The funds are open for subscription only during a specified period. You can invest in the scheme at the time of the NFO. After the closure of the NFO, purchase and redemption of units by investors directly from the fund is not allowed. Therefore, managing such funds is more economical. There is no need to deal directly with individual investors, such as sending periodic account statements. It also eliminates the need to sell shares to pay investors, who want to redeem their units, as in the case of open-end mutual funds. Consequently, a closed-end fund can be more fully invested since it does not need much cash. The money from the NFO is used to buy a specific portfolio of securities that satisfies the advertised investment objective of the fund. However, to protect the investor's interest, SEBI provides the investor of such funds two avenues to liquidate their investments.

SEBI Regulations stipulate that at least one of the two exit routes is provided to the investor – listing on stock exchanges or selling back the units to the mutual fund through periodic repurchase at NAV-related prices. Closed-end funds are listed on the stock exchanges, where the investor can buy/sell units. The trading is generally done at a discount to the NAV of the scheme. The market price of closed-end funds is determined by supply and demand and not by NAV, as is the case in open-end funds. As the fund units cannot be exchanged for the underlying securities that the units represent, there is usually a large difference between the unit price of the fund and the

NAV of the fund, which is the actual value of the securities represented by each mutual fund unit. If the fund's unit price is higher than its underlying NAV, then the units are said to be **selling at a premium over their net asset value**. If the price is lower, then the units are **selling at a discount from their net asset value**.

Closed-end funds may also offer "buyback of units" to the unit-holders. Such repurchase would reduce the unit capital of the scheme. In this case, the corpus of the fund and its outstanding units change. According to SEBI regulations, transfer of units is required to be done within thirty days from the date of lodgement of certificates with the mutual fund. It is not normal for closed-end schemes to sell new units on an ongoing basis, though they could make a rights offering to the existing investors.

SEBI has made listing mandatory for all closed-end mutual fund schemes (except equity linked schemes) that are launched on or after December 12, 2008. Since the trading of units takes place only on the exchange, NAVs will not be impacted. Investors, who remain invested in the scheme, are protected to a great extent and the fund manager is also not forced to sell securities before maturity at a huge discount, as is the case now when large investors in closed-end schemes pull out. However, there will be a listing cost involved in the form of listing fees, which may be recovered from the investors in the scheme. Listing fees will be part of the expense ratio of the fund. For closed-end schemes, the underlying assets will not have a maturity beyond the date on which the scheme expires. These norms came in the wake of a liquidity crisis faced by the mutual fund industry when investors heavily redeemed from fixed-income funds fearing their credit quality after rumours that funds had invested in commercial papers of real estate companies and NBFCs, which were unable to pay them back.

A majority of funds the Indian mutual fund industry offered until 1994 were closed-end. But their popularity suffered as they lacked some basic features. They traded at a discount to the NAV in the secondary market (the major exit route), which is illiquid due to lack of buyers.

Shortcomings of Closed-end Funds

* Relatively illiquid due to inconvenient exit options (on stock exchange where trading in these units is not very high and to the fund itself at

predetermined intervals, say every 6 months and that too at a heavy load).

* Switching and rebalancing of portfolio difficult in view of the above.
* SIP investment not possible in a closed-end structure.
* Transparency lacking with regard to portfolio disclosure and NAV declaration.

ELSS (dealt with in a subsequent chapter) is the only closed-end fund that was not edged out over the years.

Interval Funds

Interval funds combine the features of open-end and closed-end schemes. They are open for sale or redemption during predetermined intervals at NAV-related prices. Subscription to interval scheme can be made during a specific period (known as specified transaction period) and the repurchase of units is permitted on all business days subject to applicable loads (except for redemption during specified transaction period when no load is charged). So, basically it is a closed-end scheme with a peculiar feature that every year for a specified period (interval) it is made open. For instance, an interval fund might become open-end between April 1 to 15 and October 1 to 15, each year. The benefit it offers you is that, unlike in a purely closed-end scheme, you are not completely dependent on the stock exchange to be able to buy or sell units of the interval fund. However, between these intervals, the units have to be compulsorily listed on stock exchanges to allow you an exit route.

In reality, an interval fund is an enhanced version of FMP. Both invest in similar instruments. The only differentiator is that FMPs have a fixed tenure after which they shut down. On the other hand, interval funds are ongoing and reopen for purchase or sale during intervals. These intervals are predetermined and could be monthly, quarterly, or annual. The minimum duration of an interval period in an interval scheme/plan is 15 days. The specified transaction period consists of a minimum of two working days. Moreover, investments by these schemes are only made in those securities which mature on or before the opening of the immediately following specified transaction period. In addition, it is mandatory for the units of interval schemes to be listed. Interval funds are open for sale and redemptions during predetermined intervals and hence the fund houses are able to attract fresh money during these intervals without paying the filing fees. FMPs, on the other hand, have to pay filing fees at the time of launch, which happen frequently, especially in the case of short-term FMPs. Currently, active FMPs have expense ratios ranging between 0.25% and 1%. The same for interval funds is 0.02% to 2.12%. Though the difference is not very significant, it matters since it is a debt investment where every basis point counts. Basis point is one-hundredth of a percentage point (0.01%). Basis points are often used to measure changes in or differences between yields on fixed-income securities, since these often change by very small amounts. However, the one guideline, which has hit both FMPs and interval funds, is the ban on providing an indicative yield at the time of launch.

B. By Investment Strategy

Growth Funds

A number of mutual fund families use the words 'Growth Funds' to describe their equity funds. Growth funds are funds that invest in companies, which are growing at a rate faster than the rest of the economy and industry. Their aim is to capitalise on the increase in stock prices. The risk is that many growth companies are not very big and may not be able to absorb bad news as easily as the blue-chip companies. Dividends and consequently steady income are not the primary goal of these types of funds. Instead, they focus on increasing capital appreciation in a three to five-year span.

Aggressive Growth Funds

Aggressive growth funds are funds that have primarily one objective – maximum capital gains. Capital gains are simply the increase in the value of an investment. These types of mutual funds invest in many different securities, including new industry stocks, small company stocks, less researched or speculative stocks and employ investment techniques such as short selling, futures and options. Therefore, they tend to be the most volatile of funds.

Growth and Income Funds

Growth and income funds incorporate both increased capital gains and production of steady income. They are less volatile than aggressive growth funds.

Value Funds

Value funds tend to focus on safety rather than growth and often choose investments providing dividends as well as capital appreciation. They invest in companies with sound fundamentals that the market has overlooked and stocks that have fallen out of favour with mainstream investors either due to changing investor preferences, a poor quarterly earnings report, or hard times in a particular industry. Value stocks are often those of mature companies that have stopped growing and use their earnings to pay dividends. Thus, value funds produce current income (from the dividends) as well as long-term growth (from capital appreciation once the stocks become popular again). They tend to have more conservative and less volatile returns than growth funds. The portfolio of these funds comprises of shares that are trading at a low price-to-earnings ratio (market price per share/earning per share) and a low market-to-book-value ratio (fundamental value). Value funds may select companies from diversified sectors and are exposed to lower risk levels as compared to growth funds or speciality funds. Value stocks are generally from cyclical industries (such as cement, steel, sugar, etc.), which make them volatile in the short-term. Therefore, it is advisable to invest in value funds with a long-term time horizon as risk in the long-term is reduced to a large extent.

In the Indian context, so far, actively managed equity funds with a growth style have outperformed value funds. In a rising market, adhering to a value style may involve active churning of the portfolio, given that stocks can get re-rated very swiftly in the Indian context — with value picks turning to growth stories.

Value-cum-Growth Funds

Value-cum-growth funds follow a mix of the growth and value approaches.

C. By Trading Strategy

Active Funds

Active Funds are constantly active in the market. They buy and sell the securities in their portfolio very frequently. The fund manager has the flexibility to choose the investment portfolio within the broad parameters of the investment objective set forth at the time of launch of the fund. The role of the fund manager assumes paramount importance and fund expenses are amplified. Investor expectation rules high in such funds.

Passive Funds

Passive Funds normally follow a buy and hold strategy and do not trade their holdings very frequently. They invest on the basis of a specified index, whose performance they seek to track. They are otherwise known as Index funds (dealt with in the previous chapter). Since index is the deciding factor in the portfolio of such funds, the fund manager's role is insignificant and expenses are minimal.

Active-cum-Passive Funds

There are funds that follow the middle path between the active and passive funds.

D. By Security Selection

Top-down Funds

Top-down Funds are those that select stocks using the top-down approach, where the fund manager first identifies the sector in which he would like to invest and then the potential stocks within the sector.

Bottom-up Funds

Bottom-up Funds use the bottom-up approach to investing, where the fund manager focuses on the stocks, irrespective of what sector they come under.

Technical Funds

Technical Funds are those that use technical analysis to select stocks. Technical analysis refers to a method of evaluating securities by relying on the assumption that market data such as charts of price, volume, etc. can help predict future market trends usually in the short-term.

E. By Market Capitalisation

Market Capitalisation is arrived at by multiplying the number of shares of a company by its market price.

Small Cap Funds

Small Cap Funds focus on small cap stocks (companies with a market capitalisation of up to Rs. 500 crore) for their investment portfolio. Pure small cap-oriented funds are few and far between. Best examples include DSPBR Small Companies Fund, Sundaram Select Small Cap Fund, DBS Chola Small Cap Fund (now L & T Small Cap Fund), etc.

Mid-cap Funds

Mid-cap Funds invest in mid-cap stocks (companies that have a market capitalisation between Rs. 500 crore and Rs. 1,000 crore). Mid-cap companies tend to be under-researched. Thus, they present an opportunity to invest in companies that are yet to be identified by the market. Such companies offer higher growth potential going forward and, therefore, an opportunity to benefit from higher-than-average valuations. But mid-cap funds are very volatile and tend to fall like a house of cards in bad times. So, caution should be exercised while investing in mid-cap mutual funds. Examples include SBI Midcap Fund, Birla Midcap Fund, etc.

Large Cap Funds

Large Cap Funds are those that invest in large cap stocks (companies with a market capitalisation in excess of Rs. 1,000 crore). They seek capital appreciation by investing primarily in stocks of large blue-chip companies with above-average prospects for earnings growth. Investing in large caps is a low-risk-low-return proposition, because such companies are usually widely researched and information is widely available. Good examples are SBI Bluechip Fund, UTI Large Cap Fund, Franklin India Bluechip Fund, etc.

Chapter 11
Geographical Classification of Funds
The Logic Behind Logistics

Domestic Mutual Funds

Domestic mutual funds are funds launched with a view to mobilising the savings of the citizens of the country. These funds could fall under any of the categories mentioned under portfolio classification and operational classification.

Offshore Mutual Funds

Offshore mutual funds are funds launched with a view to mobilising the savings of the foreign countries for investments in local markets. These funds facilitate cross border fund flow, which is a direct route for getting foreign investment. From the investment point of view, offshore funds open up domestic capital markets to the international investors.

Regional Funds

Regional funds make it easier to focus on a specific area of the world. This may mean focusing on a region (say Latin America) or an individual country (for example, only Brazil). An advantage of these funds is that they make it easier to buy stocks in foreign countries, which is otherwise difficult and expensive. Similar to sector funds, you have to accept the high risk of loss, which occurs if the region goes into a recession. ING Latin America Equity Fund (now Birla Sun Life Latin America Equity Fund), launched in July 2008, is an excellent example.

Global Funds

Global funds are those that invest in equity securities of companies around the world and in India. These funds can change the percentage of their allocation in foreign and domestic markets, as well. For example, if there are major problems in foreign markets, global funds will allow the mutual fund company to pull out money invested there.

International Funds

International funds invest in equity securities of companies located outside India. Two-thirds of their portfolios must be invested in these companies at any time. Many of these international funds invest in the emerging markets of nations around the world. They do not offer the flexibility of global funds because of the minimum two-thirds stipulation. It is tough to classify these funds as either riskier or safer than domestic investments. They do tend to be more volatile and have unique country and/or political risks. But, on the flip side, they can, as part of a well-balanced portfolio, actually reduce risk by increasing diversification. Although the world's economies are becoming more inter-related, it is likely that another economy somewhere is outperforming the economy of your home country.

Mutual funds that invest in foreign stocks and bonds provide an excellent opportunity to diversify your portfolio. They also reduce the country risk or the risks that could affect all Indian investments – changes in the Indian economy, politics, etc. If investments are chosen carefully, an international mutual fund may be profitable when some markets are rising and others are declining. However, fund managers need to keep a close watch on foreign currencies and world markets as profitable investments in a rising market can lose money if the foreign currency rises against the dollar. The local investors invest in rupees for buying the units. The rupees are converted into foreign currency for investing abroad. They need to be re-converted into rupees when the money is to be paid back to the local investors. Since the future foreign currency rates cannot be predicted today, there is an element of foreign currency risk.

Global and international funds can invest in securities of foreign companies in accordance with the SEBI Regulations. Previously, Indian mutual funds were not allowed to invest overseas in stocks except in the case of quoted companies that had at least 10% equity holding in Indian companies. This meant that hardly 40 or 50 global corporations (such as Unilever) qualified for mutual fund investment from India, thus reducing investment options. The stringent restrictions that narrowed down the universe of stocks in which mutual funds could invest abroad have now been relaxed. Now Indian mutual funds can invest in any listed company on a foreign exchange anywhere in the world. So, technically, an Indian mutual fund can invest in Microsoft or Toyota or any listed company on any exchange. Mutual funds can make investments in ADRs/GDRs issued by Indian companies, equity of overseas companies listed on recognised stock exchanges overseas, foreign debt securities in the countries with fully convertible currencies and short-term and long-term instruments with highest rating. The Government has allowed investment of U$ 7 billion by Indian mutual funds in various instruments overseas, of which, US$ 1 billion can be in ETFs. Only Indian mutual funds, which are in existence for a minimum period of 10 years, would be eligible for investing a maximum of 10% of their net assets in ETFs abroad, subject to a maximum of US$ 50 million per mutual fund. Each fund house will be able to invest approximately US$ 125–150 million abroad.

If you are interested in investing abroad, do not just leap in the dark. International investing can be trickier than domestic investing. Most nations do not have corporate financial reporting requirements as stringent as ours and are not as stable as we are. Still, great money is being made out there. Global equity and bond markets are extremely volatile and, therefore, they signify a very high degree of risk for the uninitiated. The best option is to find top-notch Indian mutual funds focused on international investments.

Beyond Borders – One World… One Fund…

The first fund in the Indian mutual fund industry that invests exclusively in overseas equities is Principal Global Opportunities Fund. Rather than investing directly in stocks, it is a feeder fund, whereby, it invests all its assets in PGIF Emerging Markets Equity Fund, one of Principal's global offerings. The fund invests in regions such as Latin America, Asia, Eastern Europe, the Middle East and Africa, with exposure to twenty-two countries, including South Korea, Brazil, Russia, China, Taiwan and India (up to 5.1% of its portfolio). Franklin India Equity Income Fund has 20% exposure to overseas markets. Franklin India International Fund gives you access to a portfolio of US Government securities by investing in the Franklin US Government Fund, which is a gilt fund run by the AMC's US-based parent.

Snail's Pace to Rocket's Pace!

Indians wanting to globally diversify their portfolio have no dearth of options. From being permitted to invest US$ 500 million in 1999, mutual funds can now go up to US$ 7 billion. However, it is a completely different matter that fund houses have given a cold shoulder to their enhanced foreign investment limit. Even the first Indian fund with a mandate to invest abroad – Principal Global Opportunities Fund – was launched in March 2004, a good five years after Indian funds were permitted to invest abroad. There were no takers for overseas investing even when the rupee was appreciating. So, it is a relief to see a change in the attitude of asset management companies. In the Indian mutual fund industry, there are about thirty-eight funds focused on the global space covering emerging and developed equity markets, commodities such as gold, energy and agriculture and even alternative asset classes including real estate and other real assets. Total AUM of these funds stands at Rs. 2,381 crore as of October 2016. Franklin India Feeder Franklin US Opportunities Fund is the largest in terms of AUM, which stands at Rs. 678 crore. The next two largest funds are DSP BlackRock World Gold Fund (Rs. 340 crore) and ICICI Prudential US Bluechip Equity Fund (Rs 168 crore). Of the thirty-eight funds available in the industry, only 6 have a corpus of more than Rs. 100 crore.

On the Indian Investor's Menu!

When the four-year bull-run in domestic stocks faltered, Indian fund houses stepped up efforts to woo investors to 'global' funds. As many as seventeen fund houses now feature global products in their menu. While the global funds launched earlier had focused on foreign stocks, usually from the high-growth emerging markets in Asia, the recent ones promise entry into new asset classes not readily available to Indian investors – precious metals and gold mining companies, natural resources, commodities and global real estate.

What do these global funds offer that domestic funds don't? Global equity funds such as the ICICI Prudential US Bluechip Equity Fund or the

DSP Blackrock US Flexible Equity Fund tap their global research teams to buy stocks from new sectors or themes that are not well-represented in the Indian listed space. Retail, consumer electronics and natural resources are key sectors in which these funds shopped overseas for global flavour. Fund houses have to hire highly paid experts to manage international funds, which would add to the fixed costs of managing the fund, justified solely by a huge corpus.

Fund houses such as Kotak Mutual Fund have used an alternative route, the 'feeder' fund route to allow Indian investors to access a recognised global manager. Kotak Mutual Fund has tied up with the host fund, T.Rowe Price Global Emerging Markets Fund and has launched a feeder fund called Kotak's Global Emerging Markets Fund. Investors in India will invest in the feeder fund and money collected in the feeder fund will be invested in the host fund. When the host fund does well, the feeder fund will follow suit.

A feeder fund can be associated with any host fund with any investment objective in any part of the world, subject to the legal restrictions of India and the other country. Feeder funds have also been used to tap into new asset classes such as gold or property overseas. DSP BlackRock offers global funds that invest in foreign funds managed by BlackRock, a market leader in natural resources. ING Global Real Estate Fund (now Birla Sun Life Global Real Estate Fund), also a feeder fund, features investments in REITs and property developers across the globe.

Insulation in Times of Desolation!

Only 35 out of 280-plus equity funds managed to outperform their benchmark indices during 2008. The only bright spot, solely by virtue of lower losses, have been those funds investing in overseas economies (international/ offshore funds), which have fallen by 8–18%. Of the small number of funds that beat the benchmarks handsomely, a majority are those that also invest abroad. Though some international funds lost investors' money, they lost a lot less than domestically-focused funds. This demonstrates the value of true diversification by including global funds as they would limit the downside in bad times.

International Investments Over-hyped?

The case for investing abroad appears to be somewhat stronger today than it was in the past. The basic reason that has always been offered is obviously diversification. This most basic idea in investing is that different types of investments may lose or gain at different times. Therefore, it makes sense to put money in investments that are mutually dissimilar. However, a close look at the actual performance of stocks around the world indicates that the advantages offered by such diversification may not be as strong as they are supposed to be. Moreover, the argument may be getting weaker just as it is being accepted by more investors. As things have turned out, this diversification may prove to be illusory. While the market commentators' daily recitation of the 'global cues' becomes tedious after a while, the broad direction of the domestic market is interlinked to the world's stock markets. From a global perspective, investors in one emerging market, India, investing in the other emerging markets including China or Latin America does not seem to be a great idea.

Overseas investing is about diversifying risk and not always about enhancing your opportunity or returns.

Chapter 12

Speciality Funds
Speciality Genres

Speciality funds are funds with a narrow portfolio orientation that meet predefined criteria. This classification of mutual funds is more of an all-encompassing category that consists of funds that have proved to be popular but do not necessarily belong to the categories that have been described so far.

Exchange Traded Fund (ETF)

An Exchange Traded Fund (ETF) (sometimes called exchange listed portfolios, exchange index securities, exchange shares, or listed index securities) is a hybrid financial product, a cross between a stock and a mutual fund. Identical to a stock, it can be traded on a stock exchange and similar to a mutual fund, it behaves in the same manner as a diversified portfolio and invests in the stocks of an index in approximately the same proportion as held in the index.

ETFs – The Modus Operandi

This process flow diagram lucidly explains the working of an ETF.

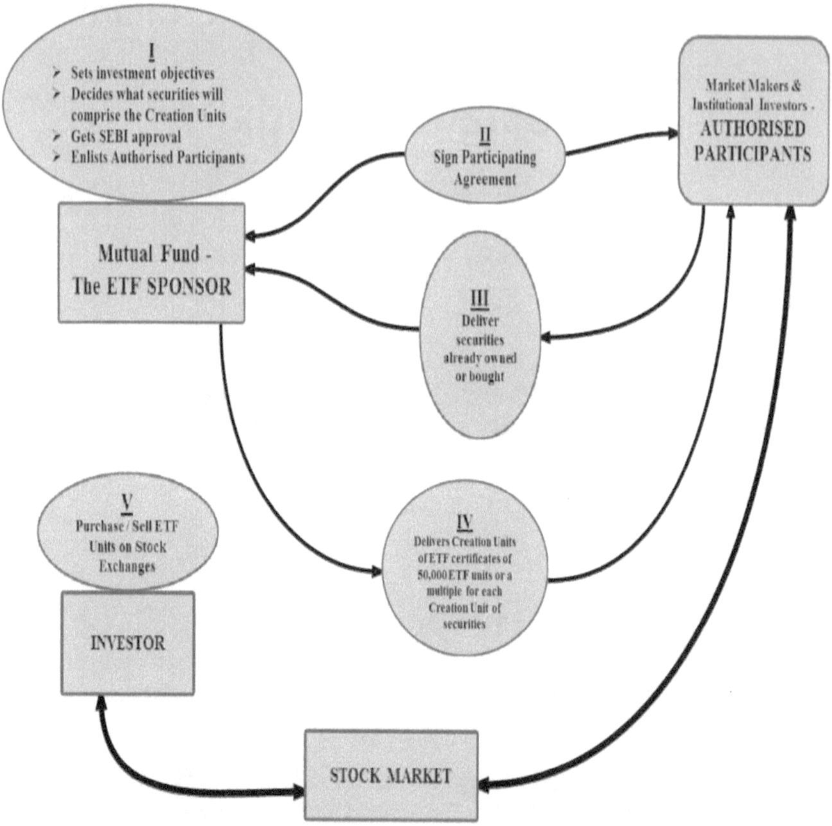

Figure 12.1   Working of the ETF

When an ETF sponsor senses a market for a new issue of ETFs, it files a prospectus with SEBI for creating an ETF fund. The ETF sponsor also enlists market makers or institutional investors (referred to as Authorised Participants or Creation Unit-holders), who sign Participating Agreements with the fund sponsor. The authorised participants deliver securities, already owned or bought, to the ETF sponsor. The sponsor creates "creation units". Usually, a "creation unit" of ETF represents a bundle of 50,000 ETF units. ETFs represent ownership in a fund. Each ETF is designed as a share. Shares are only created or redeemed by institutional investors in large blocks (typically 50,000 shares). A Creation Unit is exchanged for a number of ETF units with the authorised participants. Authorised participants, who are market makers for ETFs, sell the units on exchanges similar to a normal stock.

Investors open a demat account to hold the ETF units and a broking account to purchase and sell the ETF units. They purchase ETF units in small quantities through brokers at a small premium or discount to the net asset value through which the institutional investors make their profit.

If you want to invest in an ETF, you have to approach the broker, who, in turn, goes to the market maker, who is expected to offer a two-way quote at all times. The money collected from you would be invested in the index stocks by the market maker and this would become part of the ETF's portfolio. On exit, the ETF will release index stocks from the portfolio, which the market maker would sell to pay you. The market maker makes money based on the spread in the two-way quotes. Competition between the market makers is expected to keep the bid-ask-spread low. Bid-ask-spread is the difference in price between the highest price that a buyer is willing to pay for an asset (bid) and the lowest price for which a seller is willing to sell (ask). For instance, if there are more market makers in the market, the buyer can get the ETF for a lower price and the seller can sell the ETF for a higher price, thereby, lowering the spread. This structure ensures that the AMC need not pay commission to the market intermediaries to bring the investor into the ETF fold. Similarly, there are no loads recovered by the AMC. The investor only bears the cost that arises out of the difference between the bid price and the ask price.

When the ETF share price is significantly higher than the NAV, authorised participants can buy the basket of securities on the open market and exchange the securities for ETF shares and then sell them in the market for a profit. This is how ETF shares are created. When the NAV is significantly higher than the ETF share price, authorised participants trade their ETF shares for the basket of securities and then sell the securities in the exchanges for a profit. This is how ETF shares are destroyed. It is this process that keeps the ETF share price and NAV approximately, but not exactly, equal, because it takes a certain amount of time and expense to profit from this difference through arbitrage and the market supply and demand for both ETFs and their underlying securities, with the concomitant effect on prices, which change constantly and quickly.

The table below gives a comparative analysis of ETFs with open-end and closed-end funds.

Table 12.1 Comparison of ETFs with Open-end and Closed-end Mutual Funds

	Open-end Fund	**Closed-end Fund**	**Exchange Traded Fund**
Fund Size	Flexible	Fixed	Flexible
NAV	Daily	Daily	Real-Time
Liquidity Provider	Fund Itself	Stock Market	Stock Market/ Fund Itself
Availability	Fund Itself	Through Exchange where listed	Through Exchange where listed/Fund itself
Portfolio Disclosure	Disclosed monthly	Disclosed monthly	Daily/Real-time
Intra-Day Trading	Not possible	Expensive	Possible at low cost

Source: Benchmark (now Goldman Sachs) AMC

Exchange traded funds are akin to closed-end mutual funds in that they are based on a portfolio of securities representing a category or an index and are traded in the same way as stocks on organised stock exchanges are traded.

ETFs differ from closed-end funds in that ETFs have an arbitrage mechanism that allows market makers to exchange the basket of securities for creation units consisting of 50,000 ETF shares or a multiple thereof.

Exchange Traded Funds follow stock market indices and are traded on stock exchanges similar to a single stock at index-linked prices. Like stocks and shares of closed-end mutual funds, but unlike open-end mutual funds, ETFs can be:

* bought any time during market hours;
* ordered conditionally by setting limit orders;
* priced based on market supply and demand for the shares rather than the underlying NAV;
* shorted even on a down tick; and
* bought on margins and options with calls and puts based on them.

The pros and cons of ETF investing can be lucidly summed up as follows:

* ETFs replicate index products, although some benchmarks may be new and not have a track record;

* ETFs have lower expenses, from 0.09% to 0.65%, (institutional investors handle the majority of trades);

* ETFs are tax-efficient (ETFs do not buy and sell stocks, except to replace a stock that has been replaced on an index. The exchange of stocks for creation units involves only stocks and not cash. Minor readjustments might generate small capital gains for the investor, but generally the investor faces a tax liability only at the time of selling the ETF shares for a gain);

* ETFs trade throughout the day, giving the investor flexibility;

* ETFs can be bought on margin;

* Since transactions in ETFs are effected in kind (no portion of the portfolio needs to be maintained in cash to meet the cash flow requirements for possible redemptions), short-term investments and disinvestments have no bearing on its performance;

* Buying or selling an ETF triggers a commission since it is bought through a broker; this may be disadvantageous to someone investing every month or quarter; and

* ETFs provide the investor with combined benefits of a closed-end and an open-end mutual fund.

Small investors, used to investing in mutual fund units, need to remember that unlike mutual funds, ETFs do not necessarily trade at NAV. Similar to stocks, they may trade at a premium or at a discount. This means that even if the underlying stocks in the basket are doing well, you may still book a loss by buying the ETFs being traded at a premium. This apart, the ETFs may also be subject to a bid-ask spread. Simply explained, it means that while you may be able to buy an ETF at Rs. 16.50 per share, you may be able to sell only at Rs. 16. The 50 paise that you are unable to recover, denotes a hidden cost, which may be unknown to a novice not fully conversant with the downside of the ETF.

ETFs are also not appropriate for those investors who "rupee-cost-average" their purchases or redemptions as they would have to pay brokerages on each transaction. Generally, an index ETF will do better than an index mutual fund based on the same index because of slightly lower expenses, provided few trades are made by the ETF. Since buying an ETF must be done through a broker who charges a commission, for those investors who make frequent contributions, an index mutual fund would be much cheaper and the fund would allow automatic reinvestment of income. However, there are some brokers who charge minimum fees for buying ETFs by consolidating such purchases into one large block trade. So, it helps to shop around when you do decide to invest in an index ETF.

ETFs in India and Abroad

The first ETF, created by the American Stock Exchange in 1993, was the Standard & Poor's Depository Receipts Trust, usually called an SPDR, or spider (ticker: SPY) and is based on the S&P 500 Index. Two other major ETFs are the QQQQ (nickname: qubes) based on the NASDAQ 100 and the DIA (nickname: diamonds) based on the Dow Jones Industrial Average. As the attractiveness for investing in emerging markets gains greater awareness amongst investors, we will see more emerging market ETFs launching and those already in the market will gain significant assets. Similar to institutional investors, the US retail investors are attracted to emerging market economies because these economies are outgrowing the US economy. Since retail investors lack the sophistication and resources of financial institutions, they prefer to invest in emerging countries through US-listed products akin to ETFs and ADRs.

ETFs are becoming increasingly popular among retail investors in India. ETFs held assets worth Rs. 29,035 crore (Rs. 12,900 crore in August 2014) as on September 2016 with Rs. 6,295 crore (Rs. 7,661 crore in August 2014) coming from Gold Exchange Traded Funds (GETFs) and Rs. 22,740 crore (Rs. 5,239 crore in August 2014) coming from other ETFs. There are 64 ETFs as of September 2016 as against 42 in August 2014. ETFs are almost a decade-old in the country now. Benchmark Mutual Fund (now Goldman Sachs Mutual Fund) has been a pioneer of sorts in the Indian mutual fund industry. It was the first company to come up with exchange traded funds in India. Back in 2001, it launched Nifty BeES, which invested only in S&P CNX Nifty stocks. After that, it launched a slew of ETFs such as Nifty Junior, Banking, PSU Banking and Gold. Currently it has 12 ETFs functioning on the National Stock Exchange (NSE) with AUM of around Rs. 7,477 crore. Precious metal-based ETFs were first launched in 2007. Of the 64 ETFs launched so far, 13 are on gold.

Though ETFs *per se* are popular abroad, in India, they have not caught on as expected. These ideas have not yet materialised in view of the lingering pain looming large in the mutual fund industry, owing to the global financial crisis.

ETFs open up a world of new possibilities to investors, whose investment habits have thus far been honed only on investing in pure equity, debt and recently in derivatives. But domestic investors, still not conversant with the downside of investing in the capital market, need to first evaluate if ETFs are the best investment option going for them, before taking the plunge. While they look more attractive compared to open-end mutual funds, there are several hidden costs and charges involved in dealing with ETFs, which need to be factored in before investors "spice" up their portfolios.

Mutual Midas Touch?

"Give Me More... Gold!"

India, the world's second largest consumer of gold (surprisingly, China overtook India in 2013), consumes around 1,000 tonnes per year – a massive 26% of the global gold off-take. With the launch of GETFs by Benchmark AMC (now Goldman Sachs AMC), the pioneer of the concept of GETF, closely followed by UTI AMC, Kotak AMC, Reliance AMC, Quantum AMC, SBI AMC, Religare AMC, HDFC AMC, ICICI Prudential AMC, Axis AMC, Birla Sun Life AMC, Canara Robeco AMC, IDBI AMC and Motilal Oswal AMC, India has become the seventh country in the world that has GETFs. Canara Robeco Gold ETF, launched in March 2012, was the latest entrant and the total assets of gold ETFs amounted to Rs. 6,295 crore on September 30, 2016. However, since December, 2007, when total assets were just around Rs. 447 crore, gold ETFs have come a long way. While the rising valuation of gold has definitely added to these AUM figures, the mutual fund houses have also admitted to witnessing an increase in the number of investors for this product. **The Midas Magic is being recreated**...

A Guided Tour Through the GETF Maze

ETFs or Exchange Traded Funds are those that manage a fixed corpus representing an underlying asset – stocks, bonds, or in the case of Gold ETFs, gold. The money pooled in by retail investors are used to buy gold from **Authorised Participants (APs)**, who, in turn, are allotted **creation units** – the minimum number of units that can be bought from the fund house. Each creation unit consists of about 1,000 units (1 Kg) of GETF. The gold is stored by a **custodian** on behalf of the mutual fund. Unless the custodian certifies and confirms that the gold deposited by the AP matches their standards, the AMCs do not issue creation units. Moreover, the gold held with the custodian is fully insured and is not used for lending. Physical verification of gold underlying the GETF units should be carried out by the statutory auditors of mutual fund schemes and reported to the trustees on a half-yearly basis. The confirmation on physical verification of gold should also form part of the half-yearly report by trustees to SEBI. The norm on half-yearly reporting of statutory audits came into effect from April 2011. The units are allotted in such a way that the value of each unit corresponds to one gram of gold (half a gram in the case of Quantum Gold Fund).

All subsequent transactions are facilitated by the APs and should be routed through the NSE. The APs provide continuous two-way quotes on which you can either buy or sell the GETF units. You need to maintain a **demat account** and a **broking account**. Unlike APs, investors do not get any physical gold on sale of units. Similar to other mutual fund products, GETFs publish their NAV on a periodic basis and this would be linked to the prevailing gold price. Under the present regulations, GETFs in India track London gold prices expressed in US dollars and represent 'standard' gold of 99.5% purity.

GETFs – One Up on Other Forms of Gold Investment

Since GETFs are traded on the stock exchange, they are liquid. As they are held as electronic entry, in the investor's demat account, they are convenient; besides, the investor does not have to worry about purity, storage, or safety. The investor can use his GETF investment to take a loan from the bank by offering it as a collateral security. In contrast, gold jewellery, bars and coins are repurchased at a huge discount with purity, storage and safety being major issues of concern.

Gold ETFs allow you to invest in gold even if you have a small investible surplus. Instead of waiting until you accumulate enough funds to buy a 50 gm gold bar, you can make investments in gold ETFs with an outlay of just Rs. 5,000, to start with. You can also gradually build your exposures by buying additional units as and when you can afford them and reap the benefits of rupee-cost-averaging.

Since GETFs are being sold as non-equity schemes (there is no buying/selling of shares), **there is dividend distribution tax** (DDT). DDT is the tax levied on dividends distributed by mutual fund schemes. It is applicable on dividends distributed by debt schemes only. However, **there is no wealth tax** (since the investor is not in possession of gold in physical form) **or securities transaction tax (STT)**. STT is a tax levied on all transactions done on the stock exchanges. It is applicable on the purchase of equity shares, derivatives and equity-oriented mutual funds.

All that Glitters is not Gold!

On the returns front, while gold ETFs can add lustre over smaller periods, the returns they generate in the long-term are not very encouraging. Fund management costs further reduce returns.

If the ETF units are not actively traded in the stock market, you may not be in a position to sell your investments at the time or price of your choice.

Being low-cost products with limited marketing budgets, AMCs have to undertake awareness campaigns to market the schemes to investors.

However, these risks appear unlikely to play out in practice. Competition between different ETF products may ensure that these products generate returns that are pretty close to those generated by physical gold. The problems associated with liquidity may be sorted out if the idea of Gold ETFs really catches on with investors.

Invest in GETFs If:

* gold is one more asset class in your portfolio;
* you are comfortable with returns that are slightly better than inflation;
* you want wealth tax benefits; and
* easy entry and exit are important.

Do not Invest in GETFs If

* you need the comfort of physical gold;
* you are looking at an asset class that earns a high rate of return; and
* you are an investor looking at trading to take advantage of short-term price movements.

Granted, electronic gold is no substitute for physical gold in your possession. However, as the core foundation of a prudent portfolio, GETF is a great starting point for gold lovers. Gold should ideally not account for more than 5% of your long-term investment portfolio. The reason is that in the long-term, it is likely that other investment avenues similar to equity and property are more beckoning. Gold is a store of value and a hedge in turbulent times and not a wealth-creation investment vehicle. Given the global geopolitical risk, gold is a very good all-seasons asset. The purchasing power of gold remains constant irrespective of the situation. Gold is the only perfect destination on earth for capital to avoid inflation. HNIs took to gold ETFs initially. Now, middle class investors have started making GETFs a part of their portfolios. If you are looking to give your portfolio a defensive tilt, gold is a good choice and gold ETFs are the best way to get that exposure. Knowing Indians and their love for gold, GETFs could be a huge success story for the fund houses. A mutual MIDAS TOUCH!

Gold ETFs Versus Gold Equity Funds

While on the subject of GETF, it is imperative that we mention another innovation that beats this seemingly invincible instrument – Gold Equity Funds. These funds, however, do not invest directly in gold but in stocks of companies that are part of the global gold mining and refining industry. The World Gold Fund by DSP Merrill Lynch (now DSP BlackRock) routes all its investments through a feeder fund, BlackRock Global Funds – World Gold Fund. AIG World Gold Fund is also a feeder fund that invests in companies engaged in extracting, processing and marketing of gold through its gold fund, AIG PB Equity Gold Fund. Gold Equity Funds are susceptible to many factors – the sentiment in the equity markets, price of gold as well as a host of company and industry related issues. Gold ETFs, on the other hand, react only to the price of gold. If you invest in Gold Equity Funds, you would not need a demat account. But you would need a demat account if you want to invest in Gold ETFs.

Another variant of gold investment is Gold Fund of Funds (Gold FoFs). Reliance AMC, Kotak AMC, Quantum AMC, SBI AMC, ICICI Prudential AMC, Axis AMC, HDFC AMC, Religare AMC and Can Robeco AMC have launched Gold Fund of Funds. So, investors who were wary of opening demat accounts to invest in gold ETFs might not have to do so at all. Investors can purchase Gold FoFs similar to any other mutual fund. Unlike gold ETFs, which closely track the price of gold, Gold FoFs, apart from bearing their expenses, have to bear the expense of another fund as well. As a result of this, your investment expenses might shoot up.

What seems to be catching on is the gold equity hybrid fund popularised by UTI Mutual Fund's UTI Wealth Builder II in 2008. UTI Wealth Builder – Series II invests in a diversified portfolio of equity and equity related instruments as well as Gold ETFs. It also has a debt and money market component. AMCs including Sundaram, Axis, Canara Robeco, etc. have launched Sundaram Equity Plus, Axis Triple Advantage, Canara Robeco Indigo Fund, as they want to incorporate the best and worst, of both the worlds. There is nearly a dozen such funds in India today. Multi-asset products have gained popularity in Europe and the US since 2009 because of lack of confidence about equities. On the face of it, it does not seem to be a tax-efficient product, as it will be taxed similar to a fixed-income fund. Therefore, an informed investor would choose to put money into various assets separately, rather than club them into a single scheme.

Of Fund of Funds and Multi-Managers

As the name suggests, multi-manager funds (MoM) or fund of funds (FoFs) are funds that tap the combined skills of several fund managers in handling investors' money and pool money from various people and invest it in a select set of funds, instead of putting the money directly in stocks. The performance of the multi-manager fund is directly linked to that of the underlying funds in its portfolio. Multi-manager funds conduct their own research and analyse factors beyond performance to assess the fund managers' ability to deliver consistent results. The parent fund changes the asset allocation strategy and the weightage in any particular fund depending on the lead manager's view of the market and fund performance. The lead manager tries to identify the best funds in terms of research capabilities, internal processes, portfolio concentration, apart from consistency in performance.

While the fund of funds concept is new in the Indian markets, it has been around for years in the American and European markets. In India, FoFs were initially offered by three funds – Franklin Templeton's Franklin India Dynamic PE Ratio Fund of Funds, Birla Sun Life's Birla Asset Allocation Fund and ICICI Prudential Mutual Fund's ICICI Prudential Advisor Series Plans. Fund houses such as Birla, Franklin Templeton India, ICICI Prudential and Kotak that offer FoFs have a longer track record in the Indian market and a relatively larger universe of schemes to choose from within their respective fund houses. Birla, for instance, has over 25 open-end equity funds in its stable. Kotak Equity Fund of Fund and Fortis Multi-Manager Fund provide the flexibility to invest in other fund house schemes as well. Quantum Equity Fund of Fund and ING Five Star Multi-Manager Fund of Fund (now Birla Sun Life Five Star Multi-Manager Fund of Fund) are a few other notable fund of funds. There are seventy FoFs according to the September 2016 AMFI data. But the combined AUM of all the FoFs is a mere Rs. 7,470 crore – miniscule compared to the total AUM of the entire mutual fund universe.

Marketed as a one-stop investment shop, multi-manager funds are designed to make your life easier by bringing together a range of specialist managers into a single fund. There are two types of multi-manager funds: **Fund of funds** that invest in funds and **Manager of managers** which invest in stocks and shares through appointed investment managers.

Funds as Building Blocks

FoFs are mutual fund schemes that invest in other mutual fund schemes rather than investing directly in shares or bonds or debentures. Just as fund managers for single manager funds vary their approach to stock selection, managers of these FoFs seek the valuable inputs from a team of experienced researchers to choose the funds for their portfolio in an array of ways, with a combination of quantitative and qualitative research being used in a majority of cases. Teams of researchers will look at the ratings that funds have been awarded by reputed agencies tracking mutual funds, besides meeting the managers of the single manager funds. Fund of funds either operate as a single asset fund or as a mixed asset fund, such as a 'Balanced' fund which will invest in a range of asset classes. Mixed asset funds are particularly popular because they offer you a well-diversified portfolio, selected by an experienced fund manager, all within a single fund. Once you have decided on your risk profile (usually Aggressive, Balanced, or Cautious) all further fund choices are left to the manager in charge of running the fund of funds. The manager will then monitor and manage the portfolio on your behalf. A **Fettered FoF** limits the FoF to only include the range of funds its AMC manages (e.g. Birla Sun Life Asset Allocation – Aggressive/Moderate/Conservative, Franklin India Life Stage Fund of Funds – the 20's Plan/the 30's Plan/the 40's Plan/the 50's Plan, etc.) whereas **Unfettered FoF** includes funds from various AMCs (e.g. Kotak Equity FoF). Principal Global Opportunities Fund, Sundaram Global Advantage Fund, Kotak Global Emerging Market Fund and DSP BlackRock World Gold Fund are FoFs that invest abroad.

Managers as Building Blocks

Manager of manager (MoM) funds operate along the lines of institutional investments such as pension funds, foundations and charities. Rather than investing in funds, MoM funds employ the underlying investment managers in what are called 'segregated mandates'. Each manager is responsible for working to the instructions provided by the MoM. Usually, the managers are responsible for a specific asset class which ensures that the overall fund draws on the expertise of specialists in each field. The segregated mandates are built specifically for the MoM fund and are, therefore, tailored to their precise requirements. In addition to selecting the manager responsible for each 'segregated mandate', the role of the MoM includes monitoring the overall portfolios at a stock-by-stock, manager-by-manager level. Of significant benefit to those investing in MoM funds is the fact that the multi-manager has direct control over the assets. This level of control can be extremely important should it be necessary to change one of the underlying investment managers. In such a case, the contents of the segregated account is simply passed to a different manager negating the costs that would be incurred had the investments needed to be cashed in. The additional benefit of this arrangement is that the transition to a new manager is done quickly and efficiently, a difference which should ensure minimal disruption to the performance of the segregated mandate and, therefore, the overall fund. Multi-manager funds cherry-pick the underlying fund managers in such a way that each brings a different style to the table that dovetail seamlessly into a complete portfolio. The fund is carved into small chunks with segregated mandates and tailored to their precise requirements, with each manager responsible for his/her own segment. ING Financial Planning Multi-Manager FoF Scheme (now Birla Sun Life Active Debt Multi-Manager FoF Scheme) is a multi-manager fund.

Are more minds better than one? Or, do too many cooks spoil the broth? These are the questions you need to ask when you consider whether to invest in a FoF or multi-manager mutual fund, which is one of the greatest ideas that has tread the path of the fund industry.

"Does it Make Sense to Invest in FoFs?"

Churning Cheers!

The positive spin is that the FoF/Multi-manager approach combines the top picks from some of India's leading funds/money managers with double diversification across asset classes and investment style. A Fund of Funds diversifies across many different funds (which, in turn, diversify across securities).

Convenience in investing, monitoring and affordability with a wide reach are the fortes of FoFs and Multi-manager Funds. Suppose you wanted to invest in five equity funds and five debt funds, assuming each fund has a minimum stipulated investment of Rs. 5,000, you would need Rs. 50,000. In a FoF, Rs. 5,000 would suffice.

FoFs have access to the portfolio of various top-performing funds with just one investment. This simplicity allows for much less paperwork and easy monitoring.

Fund of funds can often invest in desirable institutional funds that are outside the purview of retail investors. They also have the ability to invest in some load funds without paying the load.

An investment manager may actively manage your investment with a view to selecting the best securities. A FoF manager will select the best performing funds to invest in based upon the performance of the managers.

This additional level of selection can provide greater stability and take on some of the risk relating to the decisions of a single manager.

The movement of the fund managers from one fund to the other does not affect the performance of FoFs or Multi-manager funds since FoFs and Multi-manager funds are not at the mercy of a single fund manager but draw expertise from a smart pool.

Asset allocation accounts for 90% of portfolio performance. Portfolio rebalancing is one of the greatest benefits that FoFs and Multi-manager Funds offer. The in-built rebalancing feature ensures that market movements do not change the desired asset allocation. The fund composition can be altered in no time in FoFs whereas this process may take a long time to complete in a balanced fund since its constituents are instruments instead of funds. It is the difference between having 10 individual roses and a bouquet of 10 roses. Rebalancing involves capital gains tax, if you do it by holding individual mutual funds. When a FoF does it, there is no long/short-term capital gains tax, which can be as high as 30% on short-term capital gains in a debt fund. You end up selling when the markets are rising and buying when the markets are falling, on account of rebalancing. This psychological benefit transcends time and the ill-effects of market timing.

Whipped While Whipping!

On the flip side, Single AMC FoFs or Fettered FoFs, which invest in different funds of the same AMC, are more prevalent and will not be truly diversified with duplication of holdings and style; unfettered FoFs result in a patchwork portfolio that lacks any clear direction or investment philosophy.

Double diversification may at times result in duplication as it is possible for the FoFs to own the same stock through several different funds and it can be difficult to keep track of the overall holdings. You may have to monitor whether the fund manager is sticking to the stated asset allocation.

Fund of Funds = Cost of Costs

The effective cost for the investor works out to be high for FoFs, which charge 0.75% as annual management fees for the underlying funds. The convenience that a FoF offers should more than make up for this marginally extra cost. Taxation of FoFs is the same as for debt funds.

A Motley Mixture!

FoFs offer off-the-shelf asset allocation. Being a ready-made asset allocation solution, as opposed to investing directly in a varying portfolio of shares, bonds and mutual funds, they save time. A critical evaluation of FoFs *vis-à-vis* equity funds have revealed that FoFs have a better standard deviation (risk) but score low on the Sharpe ratio (risk-adjusted return) front. Corpus size, investment in funds across the industry and performance *vis-à-vis* the benchmarks are other key criteria in the selection of FoFs. FoFs lag in performance in a broad-based bull market. The bull market of 2007 made it difficult to outperform the index. In the 2008 down-market, these funds managed to preserve their capital since they had allocated a lion's share to liquid and debt funds in their portfolio. Close to 75% of the FoFs outperformed the BSE Sensex. As FoFs can take asset allocation calls, funds with flexible debt and equity mix can take advantage of volatile market conditions.

In volatile and uncertain times, diversification and rebalancing of the portfolio on an ongoing basis are crucial in order to enhance returns or minimise losses. FoFs or multi-manager funds may be just what the doctor ordered as it simplifies the investment process for investors who normally have to invest in a range of mutual funds to achieve their desired asset allocation. The different options in the FoFs make them an ideal investment avenue and distributors seeking a one-stop shop for their clients' investment needs.

The onus is on the investor to assess his/her profile in the light of these factors and then take a decision as to whether a FoF fits into his/her portfolio or not.

Is the skimmed crème de la crème for you? Yes, indeed, if you are keen on savouring the rich variety, enormity, economy, churn and convenience coupled with automatic rebalancing and market timing of this concept whose time has come.

Arbitrage/Derivative Funds

Versatility in Volatility!

How would you like to invest in a fund that gives you better returns than a liquid fund, carries the same risk as a liquid fund and offers a much better tax treatment than a liquid fund? I can see you raising your eyebrows in suspicion. No, this is certainly not a 'get-rich-quick-scheme' that will fleece you of your money...

It is an equity fund that is similar to a debt fund: An Arbitrage Fund! The common unique selling proposition (USP) of this fund is to earn a virtually risk-free return of around 10% (twice as much as the conventional short-term debt funds) from an equity investment, that too on a regular basis, by doing arbitrage between the cash market and the futures market. This fund is aimed at an investor, who seeks the returns of small savings instruments, safety of bank deposits, tax benefits of Public Provident Fund (PPF) and liquidity of mutual funds!

Arbitrage is one of the most effective ways to insulate against market volatility. An arbitrage fund buys equities in the cash market and simultaneously sells in the futures market, thus ensuring market neutrality for the investment. In other words, it is a unique asset class by itself where returns are generated by capturing the pricing differential between the cash and the futures markets. It is also termed as a market-neutral fund where the returns are not going to be impacted by volatility in the market. For any arbitrage fund, the following market conditions are beneficial – a bullish market and a volatile market. While the fund performs very well in bullish markets, a volatile market gives it opportunities for early exit, thus enhancing the overall yield of the portfolio. However, a prolonged bear phase is not an ideal situation for this kind of product.

Imbalance to Combat Insecurity!

Arbitrage, in financial parlance, is the practice of taking advantage of a state of imbalance between two or more markets, i.e. it involves buying and selling of equal quantities of a security in two different markets with the expectation that a future change in price in one market will be offset by an opposite change in the other. One of the markets is usually cash or spot, while the other is derivatives.

Derivatives are instruments whose value is derived from the value of one or more underlying assets. The most common underlying assets include stocks, commodities, precious metals, market indices, etc. Some of the common derivatives are forwards, futures, options and swaps. Fundamentally, derivatives are instruments for hedging purposes, but they can be used for speculative purposes too. Arbitrage or derivative funds are recognised for modest and secured returns across the world and are comparatively safer investment options when compared with equity funds.

The Modus Operandi

Here is how an arbitrage fund works. The equity markets offer an arbitrage opportunity between the spot and futures segments. Because of the time difference, there is a price difference between the spot and futures prices of any stock. If you are able to buy into equal but opposite positions in both the spot and futures markets, these positions will offset each other on expiry, thereby, resulting in an interest differential. For example, say a share is trading in the cash market for Rs. 100 and its one month futures price is Rs. 120. You can buy the stock in cash and sell the futures. On expiry, if the share price goes up by Rs. 30, then you would earn Rs. 30 from the share and lose Rs. 10 from the futures, leaving you with a net profit of Rs. 20. However, if on expiry, the share drops to Rs. 90, then you would lose Rs. 10 from the share and make Rs. 30 from the futures. That would leave you with a total gain of Rs. 20. You should remember that on the expiry date, the spot and futures prices converge leaving you with no arbitrage opportunity. When settlement day arrives, it is irrelevant whether the share price of the company has risen or fallen. You would still make the same amount of money. This happens because on the date of expiry (settlement date), the price of the equity shares and their stock futures will tend to coincide. Now, all you have to do is to reverse the initial transaction, i.e. buy-back the contract in the futures market and sell off the equity. So, four transactions have taken place – buy stock, sell futures, sell stock, buy futures. In this manner, irrespective of the share price, you earn the spread between the purchase price of the equity shares and the sale price of futures contract.

The return of the fund is, thus, linked to the extent of arbitrage opportunity regardless of which direction and to what extent the market rises or falls.

The Fledgling Indian Market

An Arbitrage/Derivative Fund is the closest any mutual fund scheme in India can get to a hedge fund. SEBI has not allowed any AMC to float a hedge fund in India. Pioneered by Benchmark Mutual Fund (now Goldman Sachs Mutual fund) in December 2004, a little more than a dozen derivative funds have made their appearance in the Indian mutual fund scenario in the past 10 years. Presently, there are arbitrage funds from JM (JM Arbitrage Advantage Fund), Kotak (Kotak Equity Arbitrage Fund), ICICI Prudential (ICICI Prudential Equity Arbitrage Fund), UTI (UTI SPREAD Fund), SBI (SBI Arbitrage Opportunities Fund) and HDFC (HDFC Arbitrage Fund), to name a few. A variant of arbitrage funds is Enhanced Arbitrage Fund. The fund may take exposure to equity, betting on the direction the overall market is going to take, of up to 10% of the corpus in equity and equity related securities, thereby, enhancing portfolio returns.

During their heyday in 2006–2008, arbitrage funds generated better returns than debt products and this attracted large sums of money into the category. Fund houses also launched new arbitrage funds, increasing the competition. Since all arbitrage funds were fighting for the same set of opportunities, the category performance suffered and investors deserted the funds. This resulted in the average AUM of several schemes falling below Rs. 1 crore. Currently, sixteen of the seventeen arbitrage funds have an AUM of more than Rs. 100 crore, with ICICI Prudential Equity Arbitrage Fund having the largest corpus of Rs. 5,475 crore.

SEBI allows full-fledged participation of mutual funds in derivatives trading with arbitrage activity up to 75–80% of the asset size. Earlier, they were permitted to participate in the derivatives market for the purpose of hedging and rebalancing their portfolios only and the maximum derivatives position a fund could take was 50% of its asset size. In view of the liberal SEBI policy, assets under management of arbitrage funds surged more than six times over the past 6 years. The AUM of arbitrage funds skyrocketed from Rs. 1210 crore in June 2010 to Rs. 7,284 crore in September 2016.

The Attraction

An Arbitrage/Derivative Fund is virtually a risk-free product, with better post-tax returns. Liquidity is available either on a daily or an intermittent basis. It has lower fund outlay (margin on derivatives contract). It is economical with expenses ranging between 1 to 1.5%, completely hedged at all times and hardly impacted by the volatility in the markets. In terms of returns, an arbitrage fund is better than an income product. An income product has a fixed yield to maturity while in an arbitrage product, the yields are better due to lower cost of carrying (expenses incurred while an arbitrage fund is being held) and are usually in the range of 10–14%. Yield to maturity is the rate of return anticipated on a fixed-income security if it is held until the maturity date. Secondly, the risk parameters are similar or lower than an income product. An arbitrage fund does not carry any credit risk and interest rate risk, while the returns can be much higher than an income product.

The equity arbitrage fund is market-neutral; hence, it will not be affected by temporary fluctuations in the Sensex. It does sound to be a very simple and effective way of making money in the market. If only life were indeed that simple…

The Repulsion

As more and more money chases the limited amount of mispricing (arbitrage) opportunities, the occurrence of such situations tends to diminish. Arbitrage investment opportunities have become even lesser due to increase in transaction costs and portfolio turnover rate. An investor needs to be cautious with regard to redemptions. Once the derivatives contract passes its expiration date, the contract is invalid and you lose the money paid to buy the derivative. Each leg of the entire transaction, i.e. buying stock, selling futures, selling stock and buying futures, will entail the payment of brokerage and securities transaction tax (STT). These costs directly dilute the earnings.

In a period when no or few arbitrage opportunities are available, the fund will have to rely upon the fixed-income instruments, which may dampen the returns. Moreover, arbitrage activity in India is largely concentrated in some of the stocks. But, more and more stocks are being introduced in the derivatives markets, broadening the investment universe for these funds to 172. In a given period of time, the market may or may not provide any meaningful arbitrage opportunities that hold the key to the amount of money the fund will earn. If they do not find enough opportunities, they will invest in debt to achieve their objective, but in the process, they lose their tax advantage. No doubt, the fund management team has sophisticated software that flags such mispricing the moment it occurs and is extra vigilant in identifying such opportunities.

Reaching the Pinnacle

The performance of arbitrage funds during the 2008 bear run was exhilarating. These funds offered returns in the range of 6.5% to 9.7%, outperforming both the Sensex and the equity diversified category by 34% and 40% respectively. Otherwise, these funds give returns similar to that of FDs or other income schemes and are normally preferred by risk-averse investors. One of the reasons for the spectacular performance of arbitrage funds is that they cashed in during the market fall in January 2008; they unwound their position in the cash market, which was quoting at a price higher than the futures market.

In A Dry Spell

In 2009, with equity markets picking up and diversified funds once again showering generous returns, the investment appeal of arbitrage funds suffered drastically. On an average, these funds managed to return just about 3.7% in 2009. This not only pales in comparison to the 104% returns delivered by the diversified fund category during 2009, it also compares poorly against its own performance in 2008.

The Magnetism Unleashed

While a pickup in market volatility helps arbitrage funds score better, the ruling by SEBI directing mutual funds to mark-to-market short-term debt securities has helped them stage a comeback. The NAVs of liquid and short-term debt funds have become more volatile and a portion of the assets has found its way back into arbitrage funds.

It is important that you carry out basic due diligence before selecting an arbitrage fund. To begin with, you need to differentiate between pure arbitrage and arbitrage plus funds. In the former, the equity component is completely hedged while the latter can take unhedged positions and thus carry a higher risk. Only 50% of the arbitrage funds available can be considered as pure arbitrage funds. You must also ensure that your arbitrage funds maintain an equity exposure of at least 65% to enjoy the tax benefits of an equity fund.

You can park your short-term surplus with arbitrage funds – around 10% to 20% of a portfolio should be allocated to these funds. You should take a 3 to 6 months' time frame while investing in arbitrage funds. Clearly, one of the reasons is that you have an exit load ranging from 0.25% to 1% for exits varying from seven days to one year. Now it looks to be a small load, but in the overall reckoning, it eats into the total returns. Moreover, similar to any investment, there is a gestation period. For a derivative position to unfold its true potential, it takes around 3 to 6 months. This is because futures contracts are for a month. So, a strategy to roll over, hold, buy or sell requires 3 to 6 months to fructify. When the market is very volatile, arbitrage funds are an option one can consider. The market neutrality factor that we talked about earlier has ensured that wherever the markets go, these funds remain unscathed – an ideal way indeed to get a decent return with moderate amount of risk.

Quant Funds

If science fiction movies including "The Matrix" and "2001: A Space Odyssey" are any indication, homo-sapiens are not comfortable with the idea of artificial intelligence controlling their destiny. So, why ever rely on a computer model to manage your investments? Because, in the real world, it seems to pay off…

Meet Your New Fund Manager: A Computer!

Many mutual funds that make their trades based on the advice of a proprietary computer model (known as quantitative or quant funds) have outperformed their benchmarks.

The Black-Box

A quant fund is an investment fund where the managers build computer-based models to determine whether or not an investment proposition is warranted. The models have been called black boxes, while the brains that built the models have often been dubbed "quants", "quant jockeys", or "rocket scientists," with "financial engineers" being the latest preferred euphemism. It is not for nothing that they are called "black-box" funds – opaque to outsiders, the boxes contain investment magic understood by only the wizards, who conjured it up.

The Magic Unleashed

Inside these black boxes, one finds what are called factor models. Quant models use a variety of techniques such as fuzzy logic, neural networks, genetic algorithms, Markov models, clustering techniques, etc. The process begins with a fairly straight-forward stock screen that acts as a search engine. The fund manager programs it to look for stocks with variables that matter, say, high percentage growth. Once the stock screen culls out a long list of stocks, the quantitative model kicks in, measuring such things as to how those stocks performed assuming an estimated economic growth rate, interest rate, etc. These models are very early on their initial buys and very late on their sells. This can be adjusted appropriately by...the inevitable human touch.

Quant Funds in India

Quantitative techniques emerged in the early 1970s in the United States; the Vanguard Group created the first Quant fund in 1985. Quant funds slowly reached Indian shores as Religare India Mutual Fund (then called Lotus India Mutual Fund) launched India's first Quant fund called Religare India AGILE Fund in November 2007. An ELSS Fund by the same name, which worked on quantitative techniques, was also launched. AGILE means Alpha Generated from Industry Leaders Fund. Alpha is the measure of a fund's performance with respect to the performance of the index against which the fund is benchmarked (the S&P CNX Nifty in this case). The portfolio of the fund comprises of stocks that have at least a one year price history, market capitalisation and floating stock not less than that of any other stock in the benchmark index and industry representation in the benchmark index. The fund invests in 11 stocks determined by a mathematical model and the portfolio is reviewed and reset every month. Out of the total corpus, 9% is invested in each of the eleven stocks and 1% is kept in money market instruments. This fund was back-tested down to 11.5 years and the results of the back-test demonstrated that it performed extremely well in bear markets (losing less) as well as in bull markets (gaining more). The intention of the fund is to generate alpha or excess returns over significantly long time periods. Unlike its US counterparts (where leverage ripped quant funds apart), leverage is conspicuous by its absence in this fund. AGILE is not a replacement to existing funds. It is an additional asset allocation option to de-risk your portfolio.

An ode to Quants

If computers can beat world champion chess players, should they not be able to beat the traders on Dalal Street? That is the rationale behind quant funds.

* Emotions and human behaviour are too often the enemy of sound investment hygiene. Computers are not swayed by emotions and they obviously react much faster than a person ever could.

* Quantitative models can examine a much larger universe of stocks and at greater speed than human analysts, thereby ensuring that odds ultimately work in their favour.

* Quant funds follow a consistent investment strategy and do not deviate from the same resulting in higher long-term returns.

* Most models keep sector and equity picks within the benchmark attributes they are built around, thereby incorporating superior risk control.

Research by Dresdner Kleinwort's behavioural strategist James Montier demonstrates that where quant models and humans had the same information set, the quant models performed much better than humans – a hit ratio of 73.2% as against 66.5%. The evidence is clear: **returns from quant models usually serve as an upper limit from which the human analysts falter rather than a lower limit on which the human analysts build performance.**

The Woes of Quants

So, why do we not see more quant funds in the market? The answers unfold...

* Preference for human judgement to computer processing, over confidence and resistance to change.

* Reliance on historical data (quant models use extensive back-testing of past data to create their investment algorithms) and their inability to assimilate new information quickly (the efficacy of a particular factor is either not recognised by the models or gets arbitraged away over time).

* The shroud over the complex investing strategies (for fear of replication and subsequent self-destruction) makes it difficult for the investor to judge how much risk he/she is taking on.

* The high expense ratio (quant funds typically buy and sell stocks whenever their computer models tell them to) can eat into the fund's total returns and result in short-term capital gains and higher tax bills.

Computers that aid trading are fair, but using computers to search the market for arbitrages is not fair on the small investor. Further, these practices bring problems of their own similar to those witnessed during Black Monday and the Long-term Capital Management (LTCM) crisis...automated trading is neither efficient nor safe. October 19, 1987 was called Black Monday when the Dow Jones Industrial Average (a stock market index in the United States created by Wall Street Journal editor, Charles Dow) lost almost 22% in a single day. It marked the beginning of the global stock market decline. By the end of the month, most of the major exchanges had dropped more than 20%. The LTCM Crisis is the near collapse of a huge hedge fund LTCM in the United States in 1998. Markets derive their safety by refraining from allowing any person, institution, or thought process to dominate them. As markets zig and zag, discovering the truth and assimilating the news flow, the person who best anticipates the market's direction is successful. Let that be the only way to gain success in the markets...

The success of quant funds in India remains to be seen...The huge growth in the size of the Indian markets, the availability of computing prowess at low costs coupled with the penetration of internet trading, formalisation of quant investing arresting the initial inertia and the robust and dynamic models with built-in risk control and exceptional returns seem to favour quant funds. These factors herald a new era of machines meticulously managing money under the able tutelage of his majesty, MAN, of course!

Commodity Funds

Commodities, as an asset class, include food crops including rice, wheat and gram, spices such as pepper, cumin and turmeric, fibres for instance: cotton and jute, industrial metals including copper, iron and aluminium, energy products like petroleum, oil and natural gas and precious metals (bullion) such as gold and silver. The investment objective of commodity funds would specify which of these commodities it proposes to invest in. As with gold, such funds can be structured as Commodity ETF or Commodity Sector Funds. In India, mutual fund schemes are not permitted to invest in commodities other than gold. Therefore, the commodity funds in the market are in the nature of Commodity Sector Funds, i.e. funds that invest in shares of companies that are into commodities. Like Gold Sector Funds, Commodity Sector Funds too are a kind of equity fund.

SBI Magnum Comma Fund was the first commodity fund to be launched in July 2005. Eight commodity funds were launched in 2008 – Reliance Natural Resources Fund, DSP Blackrock Natural Resources and New Energy Fund, Sahara Power and Natural Resources Fund, Mirae Global Commodity Stocks Fund, ING Global Commodities Fund (now Birla Sun Life Global Commodities Fund) and Birla Sun Life Commodity Equities – Global Agriculture, Precious Metals and Multi-Commodity Funds. The latest commodity fund was DSPBR World Agriculture Fund, launched in October 2011.

Though mutual funds neither invest directly in commodities nor are they authorised to invest in commodity futures, there are some, which act as a substitute, for commodity funds. For instance, Magnum COMMA Fund invests in stocks of domestic companies engaged in the commodity business. There are some others including ING Global Commodities Fund (now Birla Sun Life Global Commodities Fund) and Mirae Asset Global Commodity Stock Fund, which put money in overseas mutual funds that invest in stocks of commodity-oriented companies abroad. But overseas, there are funds that invest directly in commodity futures in the manner of PIMCO Commodity Fund, Rydex Commodities Fund and Oppenheimer Real Asset Fund, to name a few.

Real Estate Mutual Funds and REITs

Technically, mutual funds can invest in any asset. This includes real estate, precious metals (gold and silver), other metals (aluminium, steel, etc.), oil and commodities. Real estate has often rivalled common stocks as amongst the most profitable of investments. A drawback to investing in real estate is that it is not very liquid. In other words, you cannot pick and sell and turn around and buy as quickly as you do in the case of other investments. Real Estate Mutual Funds (REMFs) provide some of this liquidity. Real Estate

Investment Trusts (REITs) are sold similar to stocks in an exchange. They are not exactly mutual funds. REITs provide more liquidity, in addition to the lucrative benefits of investing in real estate.

In September 2014, SEBI issued final guidelines for Real Estate Investment Trusts (REITs), a long-awaited move that should result in greater stability for the real estate industry in India. The idea of introducing REITs was initiated as far back as 2008. The formation of REITs – funds that own real estate but have shares that are listed on the stock market – will encourage the creation of big-ticket institutional grade projects and will give developers a ready outlet for development projects. Many institutional investors are put off investing in Indian property because it is highly fragmented.

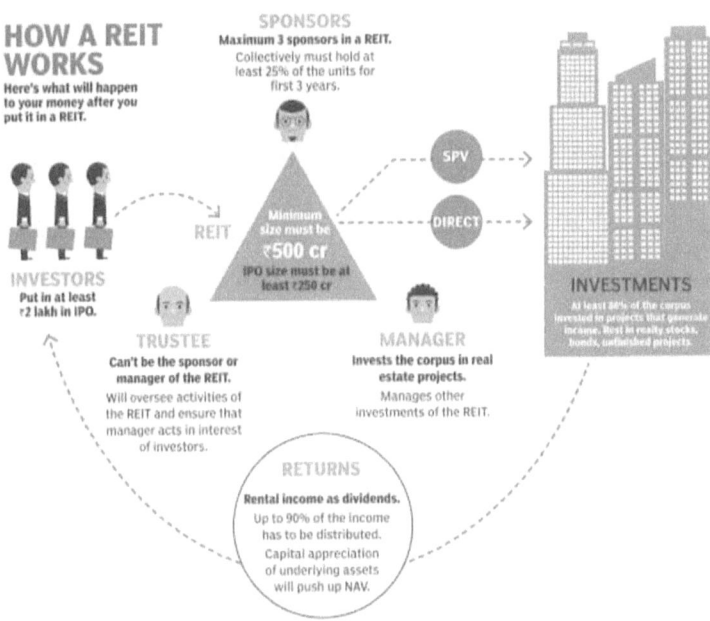

Source: www.simpleinterest.in

Figure 12.2   Structure of REIT

The SEBI (Real Estate Investment Trusts) Regulations, 2014 (REIT Regulations) provide a framework for registration and regulation of Real Estate Investment Trusts (REITs). REITs shall be set up as a trust and registered with SEBI. It shall have parties such as Trustee, Sponsor(s) and Manager.

According to SEBI, REITs will be allowed to invest only in commercial property. REITs will invest in commercial real estate through special purpose vehicles (SPVs) in which they must hold a controlling stake of more than 50%. The SPV in turn must hold at least 80% of its assets directly in income-producing properties and will not be allowed to invest in other SPVs. Only 20% of an Indian REIT's assets can be invested in development, the riskiest end of the real estate industry or in cash and cash equivalents for liquidity management with a maximum of 10% for the former. Since income-producing projects – often office buildings or shopping malls – have already been developed and have tenants, their income stream is relatively easy to predict. The buildings must have multiple tenants to reduce risk to any one company and there must be a single ownership structure for any building that is folded into a REIT. The REIT must also hold multiple projects and cannot have more than 60% of its assets in any one project. At least two projects should be held by a REIT, either directly or through the SPV. REIT is barred from investing in vacant land or agricultural land or mortgages other than mortgage backed securities. Not less than 75% of the revenues of the REIT and the SPV, other than gains arising from disposal of properties, shall be, at all times, from rental, leasing and letting real estate assets, or any other income incidental to the leasing of such assets.

Once registered, the REIT shall raise funds through an initial offer. Subsequent raising of funds may be through follow-on offer, rights issue, qualified institutional placement, etc. It must own assets worth Rs. 500 crore at the time of going public and must have an initial size of Rs. 250 crore on the stock exchange when it lists and must adhere to stringent disclosure norms. Small property developers, who do not have sufficient rent assets to float a Rs. 500 crore REIT, can combine with multiple sponsors, subject to a maximum of three, to launch a joint REIT. Each sponsor should hold a minimum of 5% of the units and overall 25% of the units for a period of not less than 3 years from the date of listing. After 3 years, the sponsors shall collectively hold a minimum of 15% of the units of REIT, throughout the life of the REIT.

In the case of REITs, the minimum public holding should be 25%. Under both the initial offer and follow-on public offer, the REIT shall not accept subscription of an amount less than 2 lakh rupees from an applicant. Trading lot will be Rs. 1 lakh. REIT, through a valuer, shall undertake full valuation on a yearly basis and update the same on a half-yearly basis and declare NAV within 15 days from the date of such valuation/updating.

SEBI has given its go ahead for Foreign Investments in REITs. Under existing rules, foreign direct investment must go into new projects under development. Now overseas investors will be able to access stable assets via REITs. This will allow insurance companies and pension funds to invest in real estate, thereby providing the much needed financial cushion for this sector.

REITs are tax-efficient as they will be taxed only once the projects are sold. REITs ensure transparency as investors know the property's current value, since the investments are not made in properties under construction. Indian REITs, akin to many others around the world, will be required to pay out 90% of their income from stable assets to investors. That will result in dividend, twice a year. It makes REITs perfect stocks since they spin off cash regularly and are relatively low-risk.

The real estate sector has been at the forefront of the Government of India's agenda on account of its potential to propel as well as support high economic growth. The Indian real estate sector's growing need for additional sources of funds and the success story of global REITs has been compelling enough to encourage the implementation of a similar regime in India with requisite adjustments, keeping in perspective the unique dynamics of the Indian economy.

Entertainment Funds – the Emerging Star

The Indian Media and Entertainment sector is a sunrise industry. The momentum of expenditure on leisure and entertainment is higher than the economic growth, owing to favourable demographics, rising disposable incomes and regulatory shifts. India's media and entertainment sector registered 11.8% growth in 2013 to reach Rs. 96,300 crore and it is expected to register a compounded aggregate growth rate (CAGR) of 14.2% by 2018, according to the FICCI-KPMG report. The media and entertainment industry landscape is undergoing a significant shift. Cable digitisation, the promise of wireless broadband, increasing DTH penetration, digitisation of film distribution, growing internet use are all prompting strategic shifts in the way companies work. Traditional business models are evolving for the better as a host of new opportunities emerge. The growth trajectory is backed by strong consumption in Tier II and III cities, continued growth of regional media and fast increasing new media business. While television continues to be the dominant medium, sectors such as animation and visual effects, digital advertising and gaming are fast increasing their share in the overall pie. There are just two dedicated mutual funds focusing on the growth opportunities in the media and entertainment sector – Reliance Media and Entertainment Fund and Sundaram Entertainment Opportunities Fund.

Equity Linked Savings Scheme

Versatility is the Name of the Game (Scheme)!

100% tax deduction, high returns, no lock-in period and full safety – seems to be more of a Utopian dream. But the ELSS comes closer to achieving this Utopian dream. It offers 100% tax deduction up to Rs. 1,50,000 per year, it delivers returns higher than traditional investment avenues and it has a moderate lock-in period of 3 years. Though equity and risk go hand in hand with each other, history has shown that most ELSS schemes have been relatively safe.

What is this versatile ELSS all about? ELSS was introduced by a special scheme notified by the Government of India in 1990 to promote investments in equity markets by giving tax concessions. As the name lucidly suggests, it is a savings scheme that is linked to equity. It invests in stocks of various companies in different sectors. It is mostly open-end in the sense that you can buy and sell units from the mutual fund anytime you desire (there are a few exceptions including TATA Tax Advantage – 1, which is a closed-end fund).

Mutual funds, by their very nature, are not tax saving instruments but investment products that may offer tax concessions. But the question is whether these can be looked at as tax saving instruments.

For an Equity Fund (for the financial year 2016–2017):

* long-term capital gains are tax-free;
* short-term capital gains are taxed at only 15% plus 15% surcharge plus 3% cess;
* dividend is not subject to dividend distribution tax; and
* redemption of units is subject to an STT.

So, is it just another diversified equity fund? In many ways, yes... but the difference lies in the tax benefit. Equity Linked Savings Schemes are special equity funds, which give a tax benefit of up to Rs. 1.5 lakh under Section 80C of the Income Tax Act. But, to get this benefit, your investment is locked-in with the fund for at least 3 years and the fund has to invest at least 65% of its corpus in equity. Section 80C covers housing loan, provident fund, pension plan, life insurance premiums, etc. So, only what is left after that can give a tax benefit if invested in ELSS. ELSS funds, in general, have been found to outperform their equity diversified counterparts. This happens essentially as the fund manager has the money at his disposal over the long term without having to cater to everyday redemptions. Therefore, regardless of the tax benefit, even investing over Rs. 1.5 lakh may be an idea to consider.

Titans of Tax Saving

In the case of a debt-oriented mutual fund scheme, short-term capital gains are taxed at the normal slab rates applicable to the individual. But long-term capital gains are taxed at 20% (with the benefit of indexation). Indexation is a factor used to adjust the impact of inflation to the cost of acquisition of mutual fund units. An equity-oriented scheme provides an added advantage, both in the case of short as well as long-term capital gains. For the financial year 2016–2017, while the short-term gains are taxed at the moderate rate of 15% plus15% surcharge and 3% cess, irrespective of the income tax slab to which the individual belongs, long-term gains are exempt from tax. ELSS has an additional feather tugged to its cap! While the exit is tax-free since it carries a lock-in period of 3 years (rendering it as a long-term investment instrument), the initial investment is also eligible for deduction under the Rs. 1.5 lakh threshold of Section 80C. ELSS schemes give twice the benefit when compared with diversified equity schemes. They give you tax sops on investments and are also exempt from long-term capital gains tax (likely to change if Direct Taxes Code comes into effect).

Monarch in the Money Game

You are in the money game. At the end of the day, you want to know what you are getting in return for your investment. Fidelity Worldwide Investment conducted a study based on the historical long-term performance of ELSS funds in the Indian mutual fund industry. As a first step, it identified all the open-end ELSS funds which have been in existence for more than 10 years (in existence since October 2001) and then calculated the CAGR of each of those funds for 2 five-year periods at every month-end starting from October 2001 to October 2006 and from October 2006 to October 2011. The results clearly showed that ELSS funds' average returns have been better than PPF/NSC in 58 out of 61 periods and average five-year annualised performance of ELSS funds was 26.43% as compared to average PPF rate of 8.32% and average NSC rate of 8.59% — an out-performance of 18.11% and 17.94% respectively. In other words, Rs. 1 lakh invested in ELSS funds on an average would have grown to Rs. 3,23,036 in a five-year time frame whereas the same amount invested in PPF or NSC would have grown to just Rs. 1,49,120 and Rs. 1,50,317 respectively. More than three times out of five, ELSS funds outperformed PPF by over 10% on an annualised basis. Besides having the potential to deliver the most lucrative returns, the lock-in period of 3 years is considerably less when compared to other tax saving avenues similar to PPF (fifteen years) and NSC (five years). Since tax planning funds have a three-year lock-in period, it gives greater room to fund managers in making flexible investment decisions and taking massive sectoral bets. Consequently, majority of these funds are relatively more volatile than their equity diversified peers. The Fidelity Worldwide Investment study revealed the range of returns from ELSS funds over different time periods and the divergence of returns (and hence the risk) that reduces with increase in investment horizon. For example, over a three-year period, the average CAGR of ELSS funds have been in the range of 9.15–76.75% but if the investment horizon is increased to 5 years, the return range narrows down to 7.03–53%. But this should not be a cause for concern as over the long term, the returns get smoothened. Moreover, they are not required to hold huge cash, as they are usually not susceptible to huge redemptions. They provide decent scope for capital appreciation with added advantage of tax-free dividends. Though they do not provide an assured return, when reviewed over a long-term horizon, they tend to give superior returns. ELSS funds invest across all sectors because of the flexicap mandate. ELSS funds can invest in all stocks across market capitalisation. Funds, which could do relatively better did so due to better stock picking capability and probably higher concentration in specific stocks.

The Ban(e) Bombarding from the Bust

The market meltdown raised a question as to whether you should opt for the ELSS of mutual funds or take a mix of fixed-income tax saving investments and diversified mutual funds that would provide you with some flexibility even while offering tax benefits. The question arose because of the steep decline in the value of equity linked savings schemes, which come with a lock-in period of 3 years, thus blocking the exit route for you in any falling market before the mandatory three-year period is served. It is true that it is not only the ELSS but also the diversified mutual funds which took the stick in the sharp fall the market witnessed – from a high of more than 21,000 points of BSE Sensex in January 2008 to its nadir of 8,160 on March 9, 2009. The sustained market volatility led to a huge fall in the NAV of ELSS of even established fund players with proven track record. The rising interest rates of bank deposits and the fact that diversified equity funds offer the flexibility of cashing out in a falling market without worrying about lock-in period further eroded the AUM of ELSS Funds.

The market turmoil and volatility lead many investors to have a re-look at their ELSS investment options. But they learnt a valuable lesson the hard way. Staying away from equities carries a greater risk than staying with it.

A Boon Blossoming from the Boom

A booming stock market coupled with relaxations in the overall investment limits for ELSS funds eligible for tax breaks prompted investors to allocate larger sums to equity linked tax saving schemes floated by mutual funds. Assets managed by ELSS mutual funds grew twenty-nine-fold between April 2005 and September 2016, from a miniscule Rs. 1,727 crore to Rs. 50,737 crore. The ELSS category has sixty schemes in all (42 open-end ELSS funds and eighteen closed-end ELSS funds), of which eighteen have a track record of 5 years and less. While there have not been too many new launches in this space, established ELSS funds, which have topped the return charts over the past 3 years, have been the ones to see substantial inflows.

A More Rewarding Option... To Help Finance Your Future

Come March 31 and you will, as is the practice every year, find people running around, looking to invest in tax saving instruments. Most choose the regular ELSS instruments that have a three-year lock-in period as it gets them tax benefits under Section 80C. Mutual fund houses offer interesting options by launching products similar to the usual ELSS, but which are closed-end with a maturity of 10 years and a lock-in of 3 years. Tata Tax Advantage Fund, SBI Tax Advantage Fund, ICICI Prudential R.I.G.H.T. Fund, etc. are notable examples.

Nuggets to Gnaw At...

By keeping a few strategies in mind, you can make the most of your ELSS investment.

Keep financial goals in mind: Every ELSS adopts different stock picking strategies. Some schemes such as Franklin India Tax Shield maintain a large cap focus and are suitable for those who have a lower risk profile. On the other hand, funds that have greater exposure to small and mid-cap stocks, such as Principal Tax Savings Fund, fit the portfolio of those willing to take a higher degree of risk. Ignoring this aspect would lead to a mismatch between the fund and your profile.

Diversify among styles: The role of the ELSS in a portfolio is restricted to providing tax benefits without compromising on the return. It cannot form part of the core portfolio. A portfolio should ideally stick to at best two schemes with varying investment styles and market focus.

ELSS and SIP – A Perfect Match: The first option gives you twin benefits of tax savings and capital gains. The next option helps you take advantage of fluctuations in the stock market and averages your cost of investment. What more do you need? However, remember that each instalment will be subject to a 3-year lock-in. So, if you enrol in a 3-year SIP and invest systematically every month for 3 years, you will get your entire proceeds only after 6 years, after your last instalment (at the end of the third year) completes 3 years.

Growth or dividend option: Choosing the growth option ensures compounding and capital appreciation in a mutual fund investment. However, in the case of an ELSS, the dividend payout option provides a degree of liquidity even during the lock-in period. The dividend paid out can be invested in other investment options, whether equity or debt, depending upon the rebalancing needs of your portfolio and, thereby, reduce the risk in the overall investment plan. From the tax perspective, both options are equally efficient.

Do not chase NFOs: A new fund does not offer a track record to bank on. Populating your portfolio with ELSS NFOs every year is a mistake.

See the Whole to Avoid The Hole...

ELSS should be treated as part of the overall portfolio and not merely as a tax saving instrument. This will ensure that all your investments are in accordance with your risk profile. Moreover, it should be goal-oriented and not for the temporary purpose of saving tax only. You get returns from the equity market only when you have a long time horizon. If you keep adding money in a disciplined manner, you create a good corpus. It is indeed a good option to save tax and create long-term wealth with ELSS.

ELSS gives you the option of saving tax while participating in the growth of the capital market. ELSS funds are evergreen funds and are ideal for:

* small investors since it is a simple way of investing in the stock market; and
* investors, who may not have a lump sum to invest in order to save tax, since open-end ELSS allows them to invest at various points of time depending on the availability of funds as well as take advantage of cost averaging.

Constant tracking is passé. Daily statistics will tell you nothing. Consider investing in ELSS through a systematic investment plan so that you can fully exploit the potential of such funds. Tax planning should never be left till the end of the financial year; it should be an ongoing process. If you commit your money at one go, you will be at the mercy of the market. But by distributing it over the months, you minimise your risk. Develop an early tax planning strategy within the broad framework of your financial plan and take advantage of this versatile scheme.

Contra Funds

Contra Funds invest in sectors that are out of favour in the market. "Go against the herd" is the key to earning superior returns. The fund manager's prowess plays a prominent role in such funds. Contra or contrarian funds seek to invest in fundamentally good stocks that are undervalued due to temporary market sentiment, in the hope that when the undervaluation is corrected, such stocks deliver superior returns.

Contra funds have been around for a while in the Indian mutual fund industry; with the first one, i.e. SBI Magnum Contra Fund launched in July, 1999. The other contra funds, Kotak Contra Fund, L&T Contra Fund, J M Contra Fund, ING Contra Fund, Religare Contra Fund, Tata Contra fund and UTI Contra fund, were launched between 2005 and 2007. JM Contra Fund has become a part of JM Multi-Strategy Fund. Another contra fund ING ATM (Against The Tide) Fund, changed its name to ING Contra Fund and was later merged with ING Dividend Yield Fund (now merged with Birla Sun Life Dividend Yield Plus Fund). So clearly, the mutual fund houses, which launched contra funds, are now washing their hands off the strategy. There are six contra funds at present with no new contra funds having been launched in the past 7 years.

Ethical Funds

Socially Responsible (Ethical) Funds or Shariah Funds invest only in companies that meet the criteria of certain guidelines or beliefs. Most socially responsible funds do not invest in industries such as tobacco, alcohol, weapons, or nuclear power. The idea is to get a competitive performance while still maintaining a healthy conscience. *Shariah* is the moral code and religious law of Islam. Shariah compliance means that companies are screened on the basis of the businesses that they undertake as well as their financial ratios. Activities prohibited under the Shariah law include drinking alcohol, consuming tobacco, gambling, eating pork, interest lending business which includes traditional banks and hotels, etc. On the other hand, financial ratios refer to leverage, cash compliance and share of revenue, which is derived from non-compliant activities. Shariah principles for stock market investment are:

* The company should not be involved in business related to banking and financial services, gambling, lottery, pornography, alcohol and tobacco.

* The interest income should not be more than 5% of the company's total income.

* Debt liability should not be more than 33% of the average market capitalisation of the trailing 12 months.

* Accounts receivable should not be more than 33% of the average market capitalisation of the trailing 12 months.

* Liquid assets (cash and interest bearing securities) should not be more than 33% of the average market capitalisation of the trailing 12 months.

In the mutual fund space, we currently have three Shariah-compliant funds, one of which is a passively managed fund, while the other two funds are actively managed. Benchmark Mutual Fund (acquired by Goldman Sachs group in July 2011) was the first to launch a Shariah based ETF called the Shariah BeES (now renamed as GS S&P Shariah BeES) in March 2009. This was followed by Taurus Mutual Fund, which launched an actively managed Shariah-Compliant fund 'Taurus Ethical Fund' in the same year. After this, there was a repositioning of a 15-year old diversified equity fund from the Tata stable called Tata Select Equity Fund, which has been renamed as 'Tata Ethical Fund' in September 2011.

Benchmark Mutual Fund launched the first ever Shariah Benchmark Exchange traded scheme in India in February 2009. The investment objective of the scheme is to provide returns that, before expenses, closely correspond to the total returns of the securities as represented by the S&P CNX Nifty Shariah Index by investing in those securities in the same proportion as in the Index. It enables millions of Muslims and other investors to participate in stock markets. To be Shariah-compliant, the fund does not invest in business activities related to pork, alcohol, gambling, financials, advertising and media (newspapers are allowed and sub-industries are analysed individually), pornography, tobacco and trading of gold and silver. The scheme is benchmarked against the S&P CNX Shariah index, an index that was launched by Standard & Poor's and India Index Services & Products. Each unit is priced at $1/10^{th}$ of the S&P CNX Nifty Shariah Index.

Launched a month later, in March, 2009, Taurus Ethical Fund, an open-end equity-oriented fund, is the first actively managed product in the Indian mutual fund space that conforms to the principles of Shariah investing. It is benchmarked to the S&P CNX 500 Shariah Index. The fund refrains from investing in sectors or companies that are not compliant with

Shariah principles – banks and finance companies, tobacco, breweries, alcohol-related chemicals and meat processing businesses. The fund also applies additional company-specific filters to weed out companies that are high on debt or interest outgo, in keeping with the Shariah principles. The three financial filters are: Total debt/total assets less than or equal to 25%, cash or receivables/total assets less than or equal to 90% and interest income/total income less than or equal to 3%. These filters make the fund's investment universe more restricted as compared to a plain vanilla diversified fund. But Shariah-compliant stocks account for roughly half of the market capitalisation and turnover on the NSE. Approximately, 260 of the CNX 500 companies and 40 of the 50 CNX Nifty companies feature in the respective Shariah indices of the NSE. This suggests that this fund has access to a sufficiently large universe to deliver good diversification. In fact, this fund's investment universe is much larger than that of most theme funds.

The scheme was certified by an independent Shariah Board, Taqwaa Advisory and Shariah Investment Solutions (TASIS). The role of this board is to regularly monitor stock picks and certify their Shariah compliance on a quarterly basis. TASIS Shariah Board has eminent Shariah Scholar Mufti Barkatuallh Abdul Kadir, who is on the Shariah Board of reputed UK-based banks.

HSBC Asset Management launched a Shariah portfolio scheme for affluent Indian investors. The HSBC Amanah India Shariah Portfolio is an actively managed open-end equity offering wherein you can invest in conformity with Islamic Shariah principles. Minimum investment amount for this customised product is Rs. 25 lakh.

An insight into the AUM of Shariah funds shows that the corpus has actually witnessed near stagnation. The AUM of Shariah BeES from Goldman Sachs increased from Rs. 1.25 crore in March 2009 to Rs. 2 crore in September 2016. The AUM of Taurus Ethical Fund is Rs. 29 crore in September 2016. However, for Tata Ethical Fund, the AUM has grown by approximately 392% from Rs. 103.61 crore in September 2011 to Rs. 510 crore in September 2016. If we look at the total AUM of all diversified equity funds, we find that the actively managed Shariah funds constitute only 0.1% of this total AUM. This is a clear indication of the fact that the investors for whom this product is actually designed are not really aware about this offering; and in this regard, the fund houses need to make a serious effort to reach out to the respective community and create awareness about this product.

Saudi Arabia is the largest market in the world for Shariah mutual funds measured in terms of number of funds or by assets. In Asia, Malaysia is also the most important market for Shariah funds. Internationally, other prominent markets for Shariah products are the Middle East countries, Indonesia, Pakistan, United States and South Africa. There were 532 Shariah-compliant stocks in the Indian bourses in February 2015 according to CMIE (Center for Monitoring Indian Economy) data. Pakistan, a favoured Islamic capital market investment destination, has only thirty Shariah-compliant stocks out of some 700-odd companies. The current share of Indian Shariah-compliant market capitalisation (at over 60%) is highest even when compared with Islamic countries including Malaysia, Pakistan and Bahrain.

The Value of Innovation

In developed countries comparable to the United States, there are funds to satisfy everybody's requirement, but in India, only the tip of the iceberg has been explored. Innovation is the key to success. So, in the universe of mutual fund schemes, new ones keep passing by but it is those that stand apart that catch the discerning investor's eye. For long, the Indian mutual fund industry has stuck to the tried-and-tested debt and equity schemes that are merely replicas of each other (though asset management companies claim otherwise). Mutual funds seeking to differentiate themselves are waking up to that fact. Not every mutual fund scheme is a "me-too product".

Tantalising Techniques

Portfolio leveraging is a method of raising easy interest loans where you leverage on your own fund portfolio to raise a loan that will be reinvested in the market, either in mutual funds or stocks. At the height of the rally, investment firms (mostly NBFCs) allowed 60–70% exposure on the pledged portfolios. You get increased exposure (pledged portfolio + loaned amount) due to the arrangement. Portfolio leveraging and super-portfolio leveraging – leveraging again on an already leveraged portfolio, also called pyramiding – is done by those investors, who have high-return funds, stocks and gilt instruments. The investor is safe till the time the portfolio yields decent returns, i.e. more than the interest payable on the leveraged portion. When the NBFCs see the value of underlying assets depleting, they simply ask the investor to meet the differential (between assessed value at the time of taking the loan and current market value of the portfolio) in hard cash. If the investor fails to do so within the deadline, the NBFC asks its broking arm to redeem the entire portfolio. The 13–14% interest on loan is acceptable for NBFCs only when the market is buoyant. When the market goes downhill, they force the investor to replenish the depleted value or sell out. Those investors who had leveraged on funds lost heavily in the deal.

These risky strategies apart, there are relatively safe and innovative ideas spreading their wings in the mutual fund market. Let us take a peek at a few important ones.

Customisation – Caring for the Customer

There is an information overload in the mutual fund industry because of the multiplicity of products. These products are generic and do not help investors meet all their investment objectives. The mutual fund industry should instead focus on custom-tailored products that can help investors achieve their time-based objectives. Such products require minimal investor education.

Take a typical young married couple with one child. Suppose their investment objective is to meet their child's university-level education 20 years hence; they will have to invest in some generic fund such as India Opportunities Fund or Long-term Equity Growth and hope that their long-term objectives are met. Fund houses can instead tailor a 20-year Education Fund. Such a fund may invest in the same universe of stocks as that of the generic fund. The difference is that the portfolio manager will design an asset allocation policy that helps the investor meet the future education costs.

There will also be good demand from investors, who are currently excluded from medical insurance coverage. These are people in their late 40s, who suffer from acute medical conditions. A custom-tailored product will consist of a portfolio of stocks and bonds that will fold at age 65. So, if a fund is targeting 40-year old group, it will have a fixed maturity of 25 years.

Of course, with the proliferation of such products, the investor will require professional advice to choose from peer funds. But that is a far cry from the problem that they currently face – generic funds that have no specific horizon objectives.

Innovation is the key to flourishing in the mutual fund business. While there are no dearth of 'innovative' schemes on the equity side, replicating the same on the debt side is difficult.

A Question Of 'Liq-uity'

Liq-uity from Bharti AXA Mutual Fund (now BOI AXA Mutual Fund), introduced in June 2009, is one such product that stands out. Liq-uity is a revolutionary concept in investing where the daily gains, if any, from BOI AXA Liquid Fund (BOILF) or BOI AXA Treasury Advantage Fund (BOITrAF) get transferred to BOI AXA Equity Fund (BOIEF)/BOI AXA Focused Infrastructure Fund (BOIFIF) on all business days. Daily transfer of such gains enables you to ride market volatility with the endeavour to optimise returns. So your capital is liquid and your daily gains keep growing! Here is how it works. You would have to invest a minimum amount of Rs. 1 lakh in BOILF or BOITrAF. If you select the dividend option, then the dividend declared on a daily basis will automatically get transferred to your diversified equity scheme – BOI AXA Equity Fund. If you select the growth option, then the daily appreciation in NAV is what gets transferred. To carry out the switch, the units in BOILF/BOITrAF will automatically get redeemed to the extent of the daily appreciated amount and the latter will be invested in the equity fund.

What is the purpose? You get to keep your capital safe and liquid while the gains can be shifted to an equity fund. The gains moving to an equity fund utilise the concept of daily systematic investing (SIP) without tapping on additional savings. It is a great option to park your short-term surplus cash.

If you had invested Rs. 1 lakh for a year, the daily dividend, which is declared only on business days, would have varied from a minimum of 0.007421% (Rs. 742.1) to 0.0743513% (Rs. 7,957.49). And over 12 months, it amounts to a tidy sum.

Small investors will not really be able to benefit from this option as the minimum amount required is Rs. 1 lakh. Under the institutional plan, the minimum amount is Rs. 1 crore, while the super-institutional plan (it exists only in BOILF) takes the amount to Rs. 25 crore. If at any point the minimum balance of the fund reduces below Rs. 1 lakh for the individual, then it will automatically become a dividend reinvestment plan. Therefore, rather than transfer the gains to the equity fund, the gains shall be reinvested in BOILF/BOITrAF till the minimum level is reached.

Tax application too would be different under this facility. Generally, you have to pay taxes on gains in a debt fund at the time of withdrawal. Now, under 'Liq-uity', that will not happen as all gains will be transferred to the equity fund on a daily basis. The AMC will deduct DDT when it pays the dividend and then transfer the gains amount to the equity fund, but beyond that no other tax would be charged. And if you hold onto your investment in equity for more than one year, then even these gains would be tax-free.

DWS Money Plus Advantage Fund from Deutsche Mutual Fund also follows the same philosophy of combining an equity opportunity with a debt investment. Here, the investment is not into another equity fund, but is into an actively managed equity portfolio. The fund maintains a minimum allocation of 90% to debt, including money market instruments, securitised debt and Government securities. The weighted average duration of the fixed-income portfolio would be less than one year. Weighted Average Duration is a time measure of the fixed-income security's interest rate sensitivity, based on the weighted average of the length of time the fixed-income security will pay out. It is the change in the value of a fixed-income security that will result from a 1% change in interest rates. Weighted Average Duration is stated in years. For example, a five-year duration means the fixed-income security will decrease in value by 5% if interest rates rise 1% and increase in value by 5% if interest rates fall 1%. The equity allocation, which will be a maximum of 10%, will be mainly restricted to open offers, de-listing opportunities and IPOs. The fund manager will also use arbitrage opportunities by buying stocks in the secondary market and tendering them in the buy-back offer. How do you gain? The debt allocation generates a stable and consistent return while the equity portion gives it that extra punch.

Triggering on Touching Targets

A trigger is an actionable facility that allows you to specify an exit target (linked to value or time) at the time of investing in a scheme, or at a subsequent date. The moment this target is achieved, the trigger gets activated. Broadly speaking, triggers are based on value and time. Value triggers set a particular value as a target. Date triggers get activated only on a day specified by you. It could also be linked to a holding period – you decide at the outset that you want to consider exiting a scheme after two years. In downside trigger, you redeem if the investment goes down by a defined level. In upside trigger, you redeem if the investment goes up by a defined level. Index-based trigger is based on Sensex/Nifty values. In dividend trigger, dividend is declared if the investment goes up by a defined level.

Trigger facilities offer you a wide variety of options that can be used to maximise gains from your investments as well as lower the risks you face. Under the automatic trigger facility, which can be based upon stock market index levels or percentage change in the NAV of the scheme, the money can be switched to another scheme of the same fund house.

The trigger facility works in two ways – automatic transfers from a debt scheme to an equity scheme, or from an equity scheme to a debt scheme. In the case of the former, entry into equity scheme is usually based upon the market index levels. So, you can decide the index levels, say of Sensex or Nifty, when you want to enter the markets. When transfers are made from an equity scheme to a debt scheme, the triggers can be based upon either the change in fund NAV, or the index levels, or even a particular date. The transfer can be of either the appreciation part of the investment or of the complete amount in one, or more than one, instalment/s. What this means is that you can take a part of your investment out, when your investment hits a point where your predefined goals are met and you are not willing to take any more risk by staying in equity.

Let us assume that you have invested Rs. 10,000 in a trigger-activated equity mutual fund scheme when its NAV is Rs. 10. You feel the market can rise 30% in the near future and would prefer to cash in. So, at the time of investing you define a trigger that gets activated when the value of your holding appreciates to Rs. 13,000, or when the scheme's NAV touches Rs. 13. Another way of defining the trigger in this case is a 30% rise (called the percentage trigger). Once the NAV reaches Rs. 13, the trigger gets activated automatically and your gains will be either redeemed or transferred to any of the debt schemes as decided by you. Thus, trigger provides a convenient and useful financial planning tool, especially for those who want to earn a sizeable profit within a period of time.

This helps you prevent losses in two ways. For example, when an equity related investment reaches a predetermined level, then the appreciation, or a part or the whole of the investment can be transferred to a debt scheme which is safer as compared to the equity scheme. On the other hand, if the equity investment falls, then at a predefined point, the automated trigger gets activated which transfers the investments to a debt scheme, thereby ensuring the investments do not lose their worth beyond a certain point.

For an inactive investor, this automated profit-booking facility is a good mechanism to follow. In fact, in the market downfall from the beginning of 2008, when a lot of investors felt that they were not able to protect their gains, this could have proved to be a very successful way of investing.

Among the fund houses offering trigger facilities are HDFC Mutual Fund, Birla Sun Life Mutual Fund, ICICI Prudential Mutual Fund, IDFC Mutual Fund, Reliance Mutual Fund, Edelweiss Mutual Fund, Tata Mutual Fund, Quantum Mutual Fund, UTI Mutual Fund, IDBI Mutual Fund and IL&FS Mutual Fund. Birla Sun Life Mutual Fund introduced this facility in its Frontline Equity Fund. HDFC came up with HDFC Flexindex Plan for investors under its debt schemes wherein investors could choose different levels of the BSE Sensex at which the trigger would be activated and investments in the debt scheme would be switched to a predefined equity scheme. IDFC introduced its trigger facility by way of an additional sub-plan, Plan D, in its Money Manager Fund – Treasury Plan. IDFC Money Manager – Treasury Plan is a debt scheme where the investor can predefine entry into an equity scheme and also an exit from the same on the BSE Sensex reaching a certain level.

While Birla Sun Life Mutual Fund, IDFC Mutual Fund and HDFC Mutual Fund have launched the facility in their existing schemes, ICICI Prudential Mutual Fund, Reliance Mutual Fund and Edelweiss Mutual Fund have launched new equity funds, i.e. ICICI Prudential Target Returns Fund, Reliance Infrastructure Fund and Edelweiss Nifty Enhancer Fund respectively, which have the automatic trigger option as their USP. IDBI Mutual Fund and IL&FS Mutual Fund tweaked the basic trigger types of value and time to suit their schemes and their investors. For instance, IDBI offers an index trigger (linked to the Sensex and the Nifty), as well as part withdrawal of investment on activation of the trigger – withdraw the gains and reinvest the principal.

However, automated index level-governed investment behaviour is not really a new thing. An existing scheme from UTI Mutual Fund, UTI Variable Investment Scheme – Index-Linked Plan launched in 2002 also offers the benefits of trigger facility, but in a different form. The investments are not shifted to another scheme upon activation of a trigger, but each time the default trigger gets activated, i.e. each time the BSE Sensex gains/loses 1,000 points, the fund's debt allocation increases/decreases by a further 10%. This works in a similar fashion as the trigger facility, but with one crucial difference, the freedom to determine the trigger facility is not available to the investor.

A fact to note regarding the automatic trigger facility is the applicable load. In most cases, transfers will attract the usual loads. This means that if the trigger is activated shortly after the date of investment, you will have to bear the exit load applicable. But the trigger facility can nonetheless be helpful in locking in the gains in a disciplined manner, without any extra effort from you. Under the trigger option, you can wait for the opportune time to make money; when the market touches a certain level, you can book the profits and switch over to another scheme with less risk and stable gains.

However, beyond the mechanics of the trigger system, you should appreciate the fact that triggers are not so much an investment technique but a technique to manage your own psychology. Similar to their simpler cousins, the SIPs and the STPs, triggers help you avoid being swayed by momentary considerations. For example, let's say that you want all gains in a liquid fund to be shifted to an equity fund. Then, the market falls and suddenly you cancel the trigger because you do not want to get into equity. That would defeat the original purpose of the trigger. Triggers are an under-used but sharp tool to manage your investments. If understood and used well, they can be very useful.

Product Structuring

Fund houses offer fixed maturity bond funds across the yield curve. The yield curve is the relation between the interest rate (or cost of borrowing) and the time to maturity of the debt for a given borrower in a given currency. Likewise, they can launch an education or health-care fund that has maturity ranging from 5 to 25 years or more. There is, however, an important difference. Bond funds can easily horizon-match their objectives. The reason is that a 10-year fixed maturity plan will invest in a residual maturity 10-year bond. Residual maturity is the remaining time until the expiration or the repayment of the instrument. The fund will redeem the bond and return the proceeds to you. There is, hence, no price risk. There is the risk that a decline in asset prices at or near maturity will prevent the fund from meeting its investment objectives in the case of bond funds. That is not true of funds that have exposure to stocks. The reason is that stocks do not have finite life as bonds do. The fund will, hence, be exposed to price risk. Nevertheless, financial engineering can help fund houses structure such products.

Equity duration and portfolio immunisation can help portfolio managers minimise the price risk at the horizon. Equity duration measures the sensitivity of equity prices to rate changes. Unlike in bonds, interest rates do not have significant explanatory power for equity returns. Equity duration is merely a measure of rate sensitivity. Immunisation refers to investment of assets in such a manner so as to enable matching of assets and liabilities regardless of changes in interest rates. It refers not only to matching the present value of assets with the present value of liabilities, but also to matching the interest rate sensitivities of assets with those of liabilities. Since the duration of any instrument varies with time and changes in rates, complete immunisation is costly or impractical. Immunisation, in practice, is often a trade-off between cost and efficiency. A common example is a pension plan that not only has to match its present value of assets with its projected obligations, but also has to ensure that the duration of assets matches those of its obligations. Since equities account for nearly half of the assets in most pension plans, an estimate of equity duration is important. Currently, only three fund houses have retirement linked pension plans – Franklin Templeton Pension Fund, UTI Retirement Benefit Pension Fund and Reliance Retirement Fund.

Axis Mutual Fund and SBI Mutual Fund, to name a few, are now gearing up to launch retirement mutual funds, with unique features including insurance coverage, annuity, etc. Axis Mutual Fund's Retirement

Planning Fund is an open-end retirement linked plan. It will invest in equity and debt. The scheme will offer two plans – compulsory lock-in and no lock-in. While compulsory lock-in can be redeemed only after an investor attains 60 years of age, no lock-in plan can be redeemed at any point of time; however, it will be subject to an exit load for 3 years. The fund house will provide term life insurance coverage to its unit-holders who have not turned 60. Interestingly, the fund house will pay premium from the fund's expense ratio. The annuity will be offered to investors who have turned 60. This is a voluntary option. The fund house will help to channel investors' money (redeemed from units) into an annuity policy. Similarly, SBI Open-end Retirement Benefit Fund seeks to provide a comprehensive retirement saving solution by investing in equity, debt, REIT and gold. There are five plans available in the scheme – opportunistic, moderate growth, balanced, protective growth and conservative. As the name suggests, opportunistic plan will have highest equity exposure and moderate exposure to securities similar to REIT, gold and debt. The other options come with varying degree of exposure to each asset class to suit the risk appetite of different investors. The scheme will charge an exit load of up to 5% for 5 years depending on the tenure of holding. Exit load will decrease as the holding tenure increases. No exit load will be charged for investors above 55 years of age. SBI's scheme will also offer life insurance coverage to its investors under a group life insurance policy. The fund house is planning to provide health insurance coverage in future. The fund house will pay the premiums from the expense ratio charged to investors. Both Axis Mutual Fund and SBI Mutual Fund have approached Central Board of Direct Taxes (CBDT) to get tax benefit under Section 80C of the Income Tax Act and have filed draft offer documents with SEBI.

The mutual fund industry should probably focus its attention on such custom-tailored funds. Such a move will also force you to think about your long-term investment objectives. Will the industry take up the initiative to launch the generation-next product?

The Risk-Return Ladder given below summarises the risk-return profile of key funds and their suitability for a diverse range of investors:

Table 12.2 Risk-Return Ladder

Fund Type	Description	Risk-Return	Expected Returns	Ideal For
Equity Sector Funds	Investing in a specific sector of Equity Share. E.g.: Infotech Fund, FMCG Fund, Pharma Fund	Very High	Variable	Investors understanding that specific sector
Equity Growth/ Diversified Funds	Investing in Equities of various sectors, so that the risk is diversified	Reasonable over a period of 3 years	15–20% over medium-long term	Long-term investors for 3 years & above
Balanced Funds	Investing 60% in Equity & 40% in Debt. Hence less volatile as compared to Equity funds & aims for higher returns as compared to Pure Debt funds	Average Risk - Returns	10–15% over medium-long term	Those who want best of both Equity & Debt
MIPs/ Income Plus	Majorly invest in Debt with 10–25% exposure in equities	Low Risk & Average Returns	9–12%	All For 1 year & above
Income/ Debt Funds	Investing majorly in high quality debentures & bonds of highly reputed corporates & institutions & also in Gilts & Money Market	Low Risk & Average Returns	7–9%	All For 1 year & above
Gilt Funds	Investing only in Government Securities	Low	7–9%	All For 1 year & above

Fund Type	Description	Risk-Return	Expected Returns	Ideal For
Short-Term Funds	Investing in Short Maturity	Very Low	7–8%	For 6–12 mths
Floating Rate Funds	Investing in Short Maturity	Very Low	4–5%	For 1–6 mths
Liquid/ Money Market Funds	Investing in call money market, treasury bills, CDs, CPs, etc. where the liquidity is very high	Very Low	4–5%	Businessmen & Corporates

Source: www.brainpointinv.com

SECTION V
FUND CHOICE

The choice of mutual funds as an investment avenue merits our attention in view of the fact that several attractive avenues exist in India today. An overview of the various investment instruments, their features, their suitability for different types of investors and comparison with mutual funds are presented on a platter to simplify the herculean task of zeroing-in on the investment avenue.

Subsequently, the edge, mutual funds enjoy juxtaposed against their drawbacks are explored in an unbiased manner with a note of caution.

Chapter 13

Comparison With Other Investment Avenues
One up on Counterparts

A comparison of mutual funds with other investment avenues would put things in the proper perspective.

Popular Small Savings Schemes

National Savings Certificate

Investing in National Savings Certificate (NSC) entails making a lump sum investment for a 5-year period. While the minimum investment amount is Rs. 100, there is no upper limit. Presently, investments in NSC earn a return of 8% p.a., compounded on a half-yearly basis.

Liquidity

NSC scores poorly on the liquidity front. Interest income is received on maturity. In addition, premature withdrawals are permitted only in specific circumstances such as death of the holder, forfeiture by the pledgee, or under court orders.

Taxation

Investments up to Rs. 1,50,000 p.a. are eligible for tax benefits under Section 80C. Furthermore, the interest accruing annually is deemed to be reinvested. Hence it qualifies for deduction under Section 80C. However, the interest income is chargeable to tax.

Apt for...

Given its nature (lump sum investments), NSC is best suited for gainfully investing one-time surpluses and to provide for needs that will arise over a corresponding (5-year) time frame. It will be apt for investors preferring higher returns over liquidity.

Public Provident Fund

Public Provident Fund (PPF) is a 15-year deposit product of the Government offered through banks and post offices. Thereafter, this can be extended further by a period of 5 years each time. Interest is fixed by the Government and is paid on monthly balances. Returns are assured but not fixed. This is because the rate of return is subject to revision, i.e. it can be revised upwards or downwards, thereby, impacting returns. The interest rate at present is 8% p.a. A minimum investment of Rs. 500 has to be made every year. Annual contributions are mandatory to keep the PPF account alive. The maximum investment has been capped at Rs. 1,50,000 per year. Any amount invested over and above the maximum limit is returned without interest.

Liquidity

Limited liquidity is available. You can withdraw up to 50% of your 4th year balances from the 7th year onwards.

Taxation

Both interest and withdrawal of principal are exempt from tax. Section 80C tax benefits are applicable for investment in PPF.

Apt for...

PPF is suitable for investors who are conservative and not in need of regular income but interested in safety and growth.

Post Office Monthly Income Scheme

As the name suggests, Post Office Monthly Income Scheme (POMIS) generates a monthly income for you. The minimum investment amount is

Rs. 1,500 and the maximum amounts have been pegged at Rs. 4,50,000 and Rs. 9,00,000 in the case of single and joint accounts respectively. Investments in POMIS earn a return of 7.7% p.a. and the investment time frame is 5 years.

Liquidity

With a monthly interest payout, POMIS fares better than all its peers on the liquidity front. Premature withdrawals are permitted after completion of one year from the date of making the investment. If the premature withdrawal is made after one year but before 3 years, then 2% of the initial amount invested is deducted as a penalty. Premature withdrawal after 3 years attracts a penalty of 1% of the initial amount invested.

Taxation

Investments in POMIS are not eligible for any tax benefit and the interest income is chargeable to tax.

Apt for...

POMIS is suited for investors including retirees and senior citizens, who seek regular and assured income.

Post Office Time Deposits

Post Office Time Deposits (POTDs) are fixed deposits from the small savings segment. While investors can opt for 1-year, 2-year, 3-year and 5-year POTDs, only the 5-year ones are eligible for tax benefits under Section 80C. A 5-year POTD earns a return of 7.8% p.a. The interest is calculated quarterly and paid annually. The minimum investment amount is Rs. 200, while there is no upper limit.

Liquidity

For accounts opened up to November 30, 2011:

Where a deposit in 1-year, 2-year, 3-year, or 5-year account is withdrawn prematurely after 6 months but before expiry of one year from the date of deposit, no interest is paid.

In the case of deposits for 2, 3, or 5 years, withdrawn prematurely after the expiry of one year from the date of deposit, interest is payable for the completed years and months at 2% lower than the rate specified for the completed period.

For Accounts opened on or after December 1, 2011:

Where a deposit in 1-year, 2-year, 3-year, or 5-year account is withdrawn prematurely after 6 months but before expiry of one year from the date of deposit, simple interest at the rate applicable to Post Office Savings Account from time to time shall be payable.

In the case of deposits for 2, 3, or 5 years, withdrawn prematurely after the expiry of one year from the date of deposit, interest is payable for the completed years and months at 1% lower than the rate specified for the completed period.

Taxation

Investments in the 5-year POTD are eligible for tax benefits under Section 80C. The interest income is chargeable to tax.

Apt for...

The 5-year POTD can be utilised for generating an annual risk-free income with tax benefits under Section 80C.

Senior Citizens Saving Scheme

Unlike the other avenues that we have discussed so far, the Senior Citizens Savings Scheme (SCSS) is open only to a section of the investor community, i.e. senior citizens. Individuals, who are 60 years of age and above, can invest in the scheme. Those who have attained 55 years of age and have retired under a voluntary retirement scheme and retired personnel of the Defence Services (excluding Civilian Defence Employees) irrespective of the age limits, can also participate in the scheme, subject to certain conditions being fulfilled. The minimum and maximum investment amounts are Rs. 1,000 and Rs. 15,00,000 respectively. The tenure of the scheme is 5 years, which can be extended by 3 more years. The rate of interest is 8.5% p.a.

Liquidity

Given that SCSS is targeted at senior citizens, the liquidity aspect has been adequately addressed; interest payouts are made on a quarterly basis, i.e. on March 31, June 30, September 30 and December 31 every year. One can opt for annual interest payouts also. Premature withdrawals are permitted after the expiry of one year from the date of opening of the account. In the case of withdrawals made after one year but before the completion of 2 years, an amount equal to 1.5% of the initial amount invested is deducted. In the case of withdrawals made on or after the expiry of 2 years, an amount equal to 1% of the initial amount is deducted.

Taxation

Investments in SCSS are eligible for tax benefits under Section 80C during the year of investment. The interest income is chargeable to tax and subject to tax deduction at source as well. Investors whose tax liability on the estimated income for the financial year is 'nil', can avoid tax deducted at source (TDS) by furnishing a declaration in Form 15-H or Form 15-G as applicable.

Apt for...

Expectedly, SCSS is meant for senior citizens, who wish to receive an assured income at regular time intervals. The tax benefits only add to the allure of the scheme.

How They Compare...

The returns from the small savings schemes are comparable to those of the debt schemes of mutual funds. Unlike debt schemes which carry a certain amount of risk, these small savings offer assured returns and safety of investment. From the point of view of liquidity, mutual fund debt schemes score over these small savings schemes.

Equity funds have been left out of this comparison in view of the fact that they are outside the ambit of these small savings schemes.

Company Fixed Deposits

Fixed deposits are unsecured borrowings by the company accepting deposits. Credit rating of the fixed deposit programme is an indication of the inherent default risk in the investment. Returns under fixed deposits are certain, subject only to default risk on the part of the company. There is no certainty of yield in a mutual fund scheme, where gains and losses flow in totality to the investor. The money mobilised by a mutual fund scheme is invested by the AMC in specific instruments according to the stated objectives of the scheme. There is no such direct correlation between the company fixed deposit mobilisation and the avenues in which they are deployed.

Liquidity is offered by both the instruments, subject to the following differences:

* The liquidity provider is the scheme itself (in the case of open-end schemes) or the stock market (in the case of closed-end schemes), whereas it is the borrowing company in the case of fixed deposits.

* The basic value at which fixed deposits are encashed is not subject to market risk. The redemption value of a mutual fund is high or low depending on the market scenario.

* Early encashment of both fixed deposits and mutual funds are subject to penalty. In the case of mutual funds, it entails 'exit load'. A capital gain is possible if the appreciation in NAV is over and above the exit load.

Bank Fixed Deposits

Similar in many respects to company fixed deposits, what makes bank FDs stand apart are the rather stringent regulations with respect to Statutory Liquidity Ratio (SLR) and Cash Reserve Ratio (CRR). But bank FDs are also subject to default risk. The Government and the RBI try to steer clear of such defaults, given the adverse political and economic ramifications of such an eventuality. Besides, the Deposit Insurance and Credit Guarantee Corporation (DICGC) protects bank deposits up to Rs. 1,00,000. Each depositor in a bank is insured up to a maximum of Rs. one lakh for both principal and interest amount held by him in the bank. DICGC insures all deposits such as savings, fixed, current, recurring, etc. held in commercial banks and co-operative banks. All funds held in the same type of ownership (as an individual, or as a joint holder with another individual, or as a guardian for a minor, or as a partner in a partnership firm, or as a director in a company) at the same bank are added together before deposit insurance is determined. If an individual opens more than one deposit account in one or more branches of a bank, the balances in all these accounts are aggregated and insurance cover is available up to a maximum of Rs. one lakh. If he has deposits with more than one bank, deposit insurance coverage limit is applied separately to the deposits in each bank.

Bonds and Debentures

Credit rating of bonds and debentures is an indication of the inherent default risk in the investment as in the case of FDs. But, unlike FDs, bonds and debentures are transferable securities.

While an early encashment option is possible in the case of bonds and debentures when the investor has a put option (right to sell at a certain price within a certain time period) or if the security is listed and traded (which is not always the case), liquidity is always present in the case of mutual funds.

The value realised by the investor in the case of both mutual funds and bonds and debentures is subject to market risk.

Active management of a debt portfolio in the Indian scenario is similar to a tight rope walk. Investment in debt schemes of mutual funds is without such difficulties.

While debt securities such as secured bonds may be hypothecated or mortgaged to identified assets, unsecured bonds (though debt securities) cannot be. The latter is, for all practical purposes, a fixed deposit. But the securities of a mutual fund scheme are held by a custodian for the investors' benefit in a scheme.

Equities

Investment in both equities and mutual funds are subject to market risks.

If you hold an equity share not traded in the market, you encounter a problem in encashing it. However, such illiquid securities are likely to be a miniscule portion of a mutual fund scheme's portfolio.

Portfolio diversification through a small investment is possible in the case of mutual funds and not equities.

The following table is a lucid summary of the distinction between mutual funds and equities:

Table 13.1 Comparative Analysis between Equities and Mutual Funds

Transactions	Nature of expense	Equities	Equity-oriented MFs	
			Traded on Stock Exchanges	Not traded on Stock Exchanges
Purchase/Sale (delivery based)	Brokerage	Around 0.5%	Around 0.5%	Nil
	STT	0.10%	Nil	Nil
	Entry Load	Nil	Nil	Nil
Sale (non-delivery based)	Brokerage	Around 0.5%	Around 0.5%	Nil
	STT	0.03%	0.03%	Nil
	Income Tax	Nil	Nil	Nil
Dividend	Dividend Distribution Tax	17.304% (15% + 12% SC + 3% EC)	Nil	Nil
Capital Gains	Short-Term	17.7675% (15% + 15% SC + 3% EC)	17.7675% (15% + 15% SC +3% EC)	17.7675% (15% + 15% SC + 3% EC)
	Long-Term	Nil	Nil	Nil
Exit Load	--	Nil	Load on Early Exit	Load on Early Exit
Effect of Dividend on Price/NAV	--	Small	Full Reduction	Full Reduction
Annual Management Fee of AMC	--	Nil	Full Reduction	Full Reduction
Risk	--	High	Medium	Medium

All tax rates are applicable for the financial year 2016–17.

On comparing, it appears that equity-based mutual funds are superior to direct investment in equities because of the following:

1. No brokerage is payable for mutual funds (not traded on stock exchanges) either at the time of purchase or sale. This, however, is offset by the exit loads and AMC fees.
2. No Dividend Distribution Tax is levied on dividends of equity-oriented mutual funds.
3. No STT is payable for mutual funds (not traded on stock exchanges) at the time of purchase. This is compensated by levy of STT at the time of switch out and redemption of mutual funds.

Portfolio Management Scheme

India's neo-rich and upwardly mobile investors are increasingly looking at portfolio managers to handle their wealth as money managers are perceived to be professionals with requisite expertise and knowledge to make the right financial decisions on their behalf.

Mutual fund is a pool of small sums of money from a large group of investors, whereas Portfolio Management Services (PMS) collects large sums of money from a smaller group of investors. Technically, PMS is almost similar to a variant of mutual funds with the main difference being the threshold limit of entry, which is Rs. 25 lakh in the case of PMS. It is the lure of higher returns that prompts investors to opt for PMS. However, in most cases the actual gain falls far short of expectation primarily due to high charges.

Unlike mutual funds, which have clearly laid down norms, portfolio management services are fuzzy. The cost structure is very arbitrary. People opt for such services without knowing how they function. PMS would have been very useful if the fee structure was rational. There ought to be either profit sharing or fixed fee and obviously not both. There are essentially 3 fee components in a PMS, namely fund management fees, which is around 1 to 2 %; performance fee or profit sharing at 15–20%; and brokerage fee, which can vary between 0.15% and 0.60% and miscellaneous expenses on the lines of custodian fee, demat account opening charges, audit charges, etc. According to SEBI, profit sharing/performance related fees shall be charged on the basis of high water mark principle over the life of the investment in

PMS. The high water mark principle means that if the portfolio value goes down and then recovers, the manager does not earn a fee till all losses have been made up. Once the portfolio rises to a certain peak and the portfolio manager charges a fee for it, the next time he could charge a fee only if the portfolio value is above the previous peak and the frequency of charging performance fee should not be less than quarterly. For example, consider that frequency of charging performance fees is annual. A client's initial contribution is Rs. 30,00,000, which then rises to Rs. 35,00,000 in its first year, a performance fee/profit sharing would be payable on the Rs. 5,00,000 return. In the next year, the base value of the portfolio becomes Rs. 35,00,000 and the portfolio manager can charge fee only if the portfolio rises above Rs. 35,00,000. If in the second year, the portfolio drops to Rs. 27,00,000, no performance fee would be payable. If in the third year the portfolio rises to Rs. 37,00,000, a performance fee/profit sharing would be payable only on the Rs. 2,00,000 profit which is portfolio value in excess of the previously achieved high water mark of Rs. 35,00,000. In the case of partial withdrawal of funds by investors, all fees and charges should be charged proportionately and the high watermark should be adjusted accordingly. Mutual funds, on the other hand, charge lesser fees. Mutual funds are well-regulated and less complicated.

In order to ensure transparency and adequate disclosure regarding fees and charges, the client agreement contains a separate annexure that should list all fees and charges payable to the portfolio manager. The client is required to separately sign the annexure on fees and charges and add in his own handwriting that he has understood the charge structure. Most brokers or investment bankers including Religare, TATA AMC, Emkay, HSBC, Kotak, Sundaram, etc. provide PMS. Different schemes are floated to suit customers with different risk appetites. For instance, Religare has schemes such as Panther – an aggressive one, Tortoise – a moderate one and the like. Each of the schemes is customised to suit the needs of individual investors. With close to 200 service providers, PMS is increasingly gaining popularity in India. However, proper knowledge is crucial before investing in PMS.

There should be a lot of interaction between the manager and the client so that the latter understands the functioning of such a scheme and a client should zero in on a particular scheme only after proper consultations.

Customisation, the forte of PMS, is conspicuous by its absence in the case of mutual funds. PMS is a rich man's pie since each portfolio has to be separately managed and pooling of resources is not allowed. The small investor cannot enter the PMS in view of the paucity of funds. Besides, more administrative work is involved in the operation of PMS since a separate portfolio has to be maintained for each client. On the other hand, a common portfolio is maintained for all investors in the mutual fund. Performance data is publicly available in the case of mutual funds, whereas, in the case of PMS, it is given by the fund manager to the individual investor. Transparency, the watch-word of mutual fund investments, is lacking in PMS.

Unit Linked Insurance Plans

Unit Linked Insurance Plan (ULIP) is an investment option provided by insurance companies. It is a single contract comprising of insurance cover with an investment benefit. Out of the premium paid in ULIP, a certain portion goes for life cover and the remaining portion goes for investment. Though both mutual funds and ULIPs expose investors to market risks and have professional fund managers to manage the assets, these products differ on several critical aspects such as insurance cover, returns potential, liquidity, taxation, charges, etc.

The basic difference between ULIPs and mutual funds is in terms of insurance cover. ULIPs provide an insurance component along with investment whereas a mutual fund is a pure investment product.

Since ULIPs invest in relatively low-risk products, the potential of returns is also low. The reason is that they have to promise sum assured irrespective of whether the plan makes money or not. Mutual funds are of different varieties investing in various instruments and they do not offer assured returns. Equity-oriented mutual funds give higher returns than the hybrid ones. Hybrid mutual funds offer better returns than debt funds.

Liquidity is defined as the time taken and the ease with which investors can redeem their investment. Needless to say, mutual funds are more liquid since you can buy and sell mutual funds anytime. Generally, mutual funds do not have lock-in period at all. There is a certain type of mutual fund, known as ELSS, which has a lock-in period of 3 years. ULIPs, in comparison, have a higher lock-in of 5 years. However, partial withdrawals are allowed subject to rules. There is no tax on such withdrawals.

Any investment made in ULIP qualifies for deduction under Section 80C of the Income Tax Act, where an investor can save tax on Rs. 1,50,000. In the case of mutual funds, only investment in ELSS, a specific type of mutual fund scheme, qualifies for tax benefits under section 80C. Both, ELSS and ULIP, will stand to lose the 80C benefit if DTC (Discussed under the Chapter on Taxes) comes into effect.

A major advantage mutual funds have over ULIPs is their history. Mutual funds are in the market for quite a number of years and hence you can look at the history of returns. Moreover, mutual funds have very stringent transparency requirements compared to ULIPs. This ensures that you have more information about mutual funds when compared to ULIPs. Insurance Regulatory and Development Authority (IRDA) only mandates insurers to issue the policyholder a certificate at maturity showing year-wise contributions, charges deducted, fund value and final payment made to the policyholder taking into account partial withdrawals, if any.

SEBI (Securities and Exchange Board of India) and IRDA (Insurance Regulatory and Development Authority) have been trying to make the respective products more cost effective. While the former has abolished entry load, the latter has capped charges on ULIPs (the Swarup Committee has recommended the abolition of commission to agents). The decision by the insurance regulator to cap the charges on insurance products may level the playing field, in terms of effective returns, between mutual funds and ULIPs. The management fee of mutual funds is typically 1% to 2%. ULIP charges are higher in spite of the changed rules. IRDA has capped overall charges at 3% of net yield in the case of ULIPs with a tenure of 10 years or below and fund management charge shall not exceed 1.5%. Net yield is the return that an investor gets on maturity minus charges. In the case of insurance policies of above 10 years, IRDA has capped the total charges at 2.25%, of which the fund management charges shall not exceed 1.25%. In a ULIP, the mortality charges keep rising as the policy holder gets older. Even though recurring charges of ULIPs are low, the upfront charges have always been higher than those for mutual funds. ULIPs have always been a bone of contention between IRDA and SEBI, with the market regulator feeling that they are being pushed by insurance companies more as an investment, rather than an insurance product.

ULIPs lack flexibility inherent in a mutual fund investment. You have to pay the premium for the entire term. If the premium is stopped, the plan is discontinued.

However, mutual funds and ULIPs are both competing for the same money from the same investor for almost the same purpose. ULIP is actually a high commission, low transparency version of mutual funds. ULIPs are mutual funds with a little seasoning of insurance added to circumvent the law. While deciding between the two, however, you should weigh in the lower costs, higher liquidity and transparency offered by mutual funds and the safety of the sum assured offered by insurance products and make the choice based on need.

Basically a plan that seeks to combine insurance and investment more often than not tends to be sub-optimal. It is always better to keep insurance and investments separate. All endowment policies, whole life policies and ULIPs are examples of combination insurance plans. On the other hand, a term insurance plan has no cash payout at the end of the term. This means if the policy holder were to pass away during the term of the policy, his family will get the sum assured. However, were he to survive he will not get a single rupee. In other words, term cover is pure life insurance and has no cash or surrender value. If this is indeed the case, why favour term insurance as against ULIPs which, at least pay, at the end of the day, no matter what, either the sum assured or the maturity value?

The reason is because basically insurance is a cost. It is a contract (policy) in which you purchase financial protection or reimbursement against a loss or an unanticipated expense. The price paid to purchase such protection is also called premium in insurance parlance. Such premium is payable every year till you desire protection from the loss. A term plan gives life cover, with no maturity or interim benefits. Premiums are the lowest for this type of policy and for this low premium, your family will get the highest benefit. A Rs. 10 lakh term plan for a 35 year old with a 20-year policy tenure will cost around Rs. 5,000 per year.

Now, take for instance car insurance. You pay the insurance premium every year to protect yourself against the financial damage an accident can cause. If you are a safe driver and manage not to damage your car during the year, the premium paid is lost – you don't get anything out of it. And you are perfectly happy to have done so, so long as you and your car are safe. You do not mind this, do you? Then why should life insurance be any different? But it is. It always has been. The reason for this is mainly because life insurance premiums come bundled with the pure premium part combined with the part that gets invested on your behalf. The policy is sold more as an investment where the insurance just comes along. However, understand that insurance never comes along. It always has to be paid for. In the case of life insurance, the premium is known as mortality premium. Such mortality premium is applicable for all policies every year, without any exception, till such time that the life is insured. Even in the case of single premium plans or policies where the premium is payable only for a part of the policy term, the mortality premium keeps getting deducted every year from the fund value. So, you buy insurance directly or indirectly each year.

Of course and understandably so, brokers earn a far greater commission if they sell you policies other than the term cover. And it is an easy sell too since the logical sounding argument given against buying a term cover is, "why opt for the same when you don't get anything back in the end?"

You should understand the difference between investment and insurance. Never mix these two important aspects of your financial life. The purpose of insurance is to protect your family in case of any exigencies. The purpose of investment is to build wealth over time. Pure term policies serve the need for protection. Mutual funds are great products to earn higher returns and build wealth over time. You should stay with mutual funds for longer time to earn higher returns. The optimum strategy would be – buy a term policy and invest the difference in mutual funds.

Chapter 14

Raison d'etre

Ingenious Investment

If you are looking for a good investment "story", buy a stock. If you are looking for a smart investment, buy mutual funds. Strange as it may seem (since mutual funds are primarily composed of stocks) such a distinction succinctly underlines the fact that there are some notable advantages in opting for mutual funds.

Professional Management: Mutual funds are managed by investment managers, who are appointed by trustees and are bound by an investment management agreement. Investment managers and funds are bound by the AMFI code of ethics. When you buy a mutual fund, you are enlisting professional help at an extremely affordable price. Mutual fund managers choose securities to buy or sell based on their years of experience in the markets and on research specific to individual stocks, in keeping with a mutual fund's objective as stated in the prospectus. Therefore, instead of you taking decisions based on gut-feeling or what someone told you, simply leave your investments in the expert hands of professional fund managers, who invest your money on the basis of minute analysis and astute investment strategies.

Convenience: The convenience of mutual funds is undeniable – you do not have to micromanage the portfolio yourself. It reduces paperwork and helps you avoid many problems such as bad deliveries, delayed payments and follow-up with brokers and companies. You save your time, besides not having to time the market.

Diversification: To achieve a truly diversified portfolio, you may have to buy stocks with different capitalisations from different industries and bonds having varying maturities from different issuers. For an individual investor, besides being cumbersome and time-consuming, this can be quite costly. This is where mutual funds pitch in. Spreading fund assets among different investment vehicles and different stocks in a variety of industries with different rates of return helps offset losses in one investment with gains in another. To diffuse your risk while increasing your potential for return, choose a variety of well-performing funds with different objectives and different investments.

Economies of Scale: Mutual funds are able to take advantage of their buying and selling size and negotiate better terms with brokers, bankers and other service providers, thereby reducing transaction costs for you. In addition, the low cost per individual can be attributed to the cost of trades and fixed costs such as costs related to infrastructure including office space, investment research, etc. being spread over all investors in the fund.

Affordability – a better portfolio for less money: The minimum initial investment for a mutual fund is fairly low for most funds (as low as Rs. 500 for some schemes). Investors individually may lack sufficient funds to invest in high-grade stocks. Say, you want to invest Rs. 500 in a top-notch software company. You find that it is not enough to buy even one share! If you invest that same Rs. 500 in an IT mutual fund, you get yourself a proportionate share in a large number of premium software stocks!

Impartiality: Wealthy stock investors get special treatment from brokers and wealthy bank account holders get special treatment from the banks, but mutual funds are non-discriminatory. It does not matter whether you have Rs. 500 or Rs. 5,00,000; you are getting the same manager, the same account access and the same investment portfolio.

Liquidity: There are times when you remain stranded with a security, unable to find buyers, or face an even more alarming situation – you are unable to stumble on the security you invested in the market! Such investments, whose value cannot be realised in the market by you, are termed illiquid investments. You are doomed to lose money on such investments. But, mutual funds can provide liquidity even if the underlying market may not have the liquidity. You can sell your mutual funds on any business day and receive your current market value of investments within a short period of time (3 to 5 days), thus maintaining immediate access to capital.

Tax Advantages: The interest income from the traditional investment options such as bank FDs, NSCs, etc. (except PPF) are fully taxable. Therefore, if you are in the highest tax bracket, even the seemingly attractive interest rate of 9–10% actually means a net return of just 6–7%. But, in the case of mutual funds, you would have to pay a much lower tax (in the case of debt mutual funds) or no tax (in the case of investments for more than one year in equity mutual funds).

Mutual funds offer options, whereby you can let your money grow in the fund for several years. By selecting such options, it is possible for you to overcome tax liability. This helps you to legally build your wealth faster than if you were to pay tax on the income each year.

Specific schemes of mutual funds such as ELSS allow you to avail of tax benefits. This will be dealt with elaborately in the chapter on taxation.

Transparency: Two key documents – the prospectus and shareholder reports – highlight the fund's strategy and performance. You get regular information on the value of your investment in addition to disclosures on the specific investments made by your scheme, the proportion invested in each class of assets and the fund manager's investment strategy and outlook.

Choice of Schemes and Flexibility: Mutual funds offer a family of schemes to suit your varying needs over a lifetime. You determine your own needs and risk tolerance and then choose a mutual fund that fits your financial goals. You can build your portfolio by investing across equity, hybrid and debt funds and thus aspire to meet your financial goals. Through features such as systematic investment plans, systematic withdrawal plans and systematic transfer plans you can systematically invest or withdraw funds according to your needs and convenience. You can switch a part or all of your investment from one fund to another when your goals change over time.

Return Potential: Over the medium to long-term, mutual funds have the potential to provide a higher return as they invest in a diversified basket of selected securities.

Well-Regulated: All mutual funds are registered with SEBI and they function within the provisions of strict regulations designed to protect your interests as investors.

There is always the other side to the coin and mutual funds are no exception.

Risky: As with any investment, there are risks involved in investments in mutual funds. These investment vehicles can experience market fluctuations and sometimes provide returns below the overall market. Mutual fund returns are not guaranteed.

No free lunch: The services of mutual funds are not free. Most of them carry loads, annual expense fees and penalties for early withdrawal. Mutual funds do not exist solely to make your life easier – all funds are in it for a profit. The mutual fund industry is skilful at burying costs under layers of jargon. These costs are so complicated that in this book, we have devoted two chapters to the subject.

Idle Cash: To maintain liquidity and the capacity to accommodate withdrawals, funds typically have to keep a large portion of their portfolio as cash. Having ample cash is great for liquidity, but money lying idle as cash is not working for you and, therefore, is not very advantageous.

Dilution: It is possible to have too much diversification. Since funds have small holdings in so many different companies, high returns from a few investments often do not make much difference on the overall return. Dilution is also the result of a successful fund getting too large. When money pours into funds that have had strong success, the manager often has trouble finding a good investment for all the new money.

Taxes: When making decisions about your money, fund managers do not consider your personal tax situation. For example, when a fund manager sells a security, a capital gains tax is triggered, which affects the profits of the individual from the sale. It might have been more advantageous for you to defer the capital gains liability.

Lack of Control: You typically cannot ascertain the exact make up of a fund's portfolio at any given time, nor can you directly influence as to which securities the fund manager buys or sells or the timing of those trades.

Price Uncertainty: With an individual stock, you can obtain real-time (or close to real-time) pricing information with relative ease by checking financial websites or by calling your broker. You can also monitor how a stock's price changes from hour to hour – or even second to second. By contrast, with a mutual fund, the price at which you purchase or redeem units will typically depend on the fund's NAV, which the fund might not calculate until many hours after you have placed your order. In general, mutual funds must calculate their NAV at least once every business day. The portfolio of securities in which a fund invests is a decision taken by the fund manager. You have no right to interfere in the decision-making process of a fund manager, which some of you may find to be a constraint in achieving your financial objectives.

Too many Options: Many investors find it difficult to select one option from the plethora of funds/schemes/plans available. For this, the investor may have to take advice from financial planners in order to invest in the right fund to achieve their objectives.

Tailor-made portfolios not possible: In mutual fund schemes, your money is invested by the AMC in various securities. The AMC, thus, builds a portfolio that is common for all the investors in the scheme. Tailor-made portfolio that is possible in direct investing or PMS is not possible in a mutual fund.

Lack of Infrastructure: Most fund houses do not have the necessary infrastructure and you may be daunted at the thought of facing a long queue at the mutual fund office or customer service centre.

If we cautiously approach these caveats, the advantages far outweigh the disadvantages and elevate mutual funds to the status of a preferred investment vehicle. The investor, who is able to accentuate the positive and eliminate the negative, is the one who has accepted the challenge to garner more advantages and will be richly rewarded.

SECTION VI
FUND PERFORMANCE

> "Where is the wisdom we have lost in knowledge? Where is the knowledge we have lost in information?"
>
> — T. S. Eliot

Wisdom is knowledge guided by understanding. Investors need information before they can develop knowledge and knowledge before they can develop wisdom and wisdom before they can develop a common sense financial plan.

On an opening note, this section introduces the reader to the ground rules of successful investing, i.e. the process of developing a common sense financial plan. Subsequently, it delves at length on the information needed, their sources, how they can effectively be transformed into knowledge by evaluating relevant parameters and viewing mutual funds from the various dimensions – returns, risks and costs (only the tax aspect is dealt with in this section). Eventually, it facilitates development of wisdom by honing up your decision-making skills in narrowing down your choices of funds.

The discussion from a three-dimensional point of view leads to a proper framework within which you can sift the grain from the chaff and create an optimal fund portfolio suited to your needs.

Chapter 15

Becoming an Informed Investor
Right Use of Knowledge

Having demystified the concept of mutual funds, let us now traverse the investment jungle!

How can you tell whether a particular mutual fund is right for you? The only sure way is to become familiar with the language used in the fund industry (discussed under the section on Fund Concepts), be aware of the various categories of funds (dealt with in detail in the section on Fund Flavour), apprise yourself of the performance parameters of mutual funds (covered in the following chapter) and scheme options available (discussed in a subsequent chapter) and to have a sound investment strategy. Investing your money haphazardly without knowledge or a strategy is the fastest way to lose it quickly. Does this mean that you should keep your money safe by putting it under the bed or keeping it in the bank? No, all you need to do is to set the ground rules for successful investing.

Define Your Investment Objective(s)

Successful investing is a journey – not a one-time event – and you need to prepare yourself. What is your destination? How long will it take you to get there? What resources will you need? These are questions you must first ask yourself. The plan that you come up with will depend on your investment goals. Nobody knows you and your situation better than you do. Your financial goals will vary, based on your age, lifestyle, financial independence, family commitments, level of income and expenses and a whole host of factors. Therefore, the first step should be to assess your needs. You can begin by defining the investment objectives, which could be regular income, buying a home, or financing a wedding, or educating your children, or a combination of some or all of these needs.

Define Your Cash Flow Requirements

A careful assessment of your investment objectives will enable you to estimate the amount of money you require for satisfying your various needs at different points of time in your life.

Determine Your Risk Appetite

Your objectives should be realistic and move in tandem with your risk tolerance. How much, or how little of risk can you take? If you are unable to stomach the constant volatility of the market, your objective is likely to be safety or income-focused. However, if you are willing to take on volatility, then a growth objective may suit you. Taking on more risk means you are increasing your chances of realising a loss on investments as well as creating an opportunity for greater profits.

Identify Funds with Matching Investment Objectives

Finally, zero in on the mutual funds, which meet your risk tolerance (needs) and risk capacity (budget) levels. If your aim is to increase the value of a portfolio through mutual funds, look for growth funds which focus on capital appreciation. If you are income-oriented, you will want to choose funds with dividend paying stocks or bond funds that provide regular income. You have already been exposed to the various types of mutual funds. This will come in handy here.

Making informed investment decisions entails not only researching individual funds but also understanding your own finances and risk profile. To get an estimate of the schemes suitable for certain levels of risk tolerance and to maximise returns, you should have an idea of how much time and money you have to invest and the returns you are looking for. What you achieve as an investor will depend on your goals, but sticking to these simple steps will help in keeping you on the right path.

Jason Zweig, in his commentary on Benjamin Graham's *The Intelligent Investor* aptly sums up this point thus: "After all, the whole point of investing is not to earn more money than average, but to earn enough money to meet your own needs. The best way to measure your investing success is not by whether you're beating the market but by whether you've put in place a financial plan and a behavioural discipline that are likely to get you where you want to go. In the end, what matters isn't crossing the finish line before anybody else but just making sure that you do cross it." Bon voyage!

You can make money from a mutual fund in three ways:

Income is earned from dividends on shares and interest on debentures held by the mutual fund. A fund pays out nearly all the income it receives after meeting all the operating expenses, over the year on a prorated basis as dividends. Say for instance, a fund earns Rs. 3 crore in dividends and interest in a given year and if the fund has 10 lakh units outstanding, each unit will receive an annual dividend payment of Rs. 3.

If the fund sells securities that have increased in price, the fund has earned a capital gain. Most funds also pass on these gains (minus any capital losses) to investors through dividend distribution. Suppose the fund bought some share a year ago for Rs. 30 and sells that share now for Rs. 70 per share. Clearly, the fund has earned capital gains of Rs. 40 per share. If it holds 1,00,000 shares of this security, it will realise a total capital gain of Rs. 40,00,000 (Rs. 40 × 1,00,000 = Rs. 40,00,000). Given that the fund has 10 lakh units outstanding, each unit is entitled to Rs. 4 in the form of capital gains distribution. Note that this capital gains distribution applies only to realised capital gains, i.e. the security holdings are actually sold and the capital gains actually earned.

If the market value of a fund's portfolio increases after deduction of expenses and liabilities, then the value of the fund (NAV) increases resulting in the investor seeing a rise in the value of his investment. Unrealised capital gains (or paper profits) are what make up the third and final element of a mutual fund's return. When the fund's holdings go up or down in price, the net asset value of the fund moves accordingly. Suppose you buy into a fund at Rs. 10 per share and sometime later the fund is quoted at Rs. 15. The difference of Rs. 5 per share is the unrealised capital gains. It represents the profit that you would receive (and are entitled to) if the fund were to sell its holdings.

In the case of closed-end funds, there is a fourth source as well: changes in price discounts or premiums. But because discount or premium is already embedded in the unit price of a fund, it follows that, for a closed-end fund, the third element of return, i.e. change in unit price, is made up not only of change in net asset value but also of change in price discount or premium.

Is Investing in Mutual Funds Safe?

The mutual fund industry is well-regulated in India. The market regulator, the SEBI, has ensured that investors do not experience the problem of vanishing companies as they did in the past. While the AMC manages the investments of the scheme, the assets of the scheme are held by the custodian, who is independent of the sponsor and the AMC. This ensures structural protection of the scheme assets for the benefit of investors. The AMC and the custodian operate under the overall control of the trustees. This system of checks and balances protects the investors from misappropriation of funds, fraud, etc. Even if some sponsors wish to move out of the business, they need to bring in a suitable replacement, acceptable to SEBI, before they can exit. The new sponsor would need to put in place the entire framework of trustees, AMC, etc. Further, if an investor is not comfortable with the new sponsor, he can avail of the option of exiting from the scheme with the full NAV, which is available for a 30-day period. These structural requirements ensure that the investor is fully protected from most of the contingencies that can be envisaged. Therefore, mutual funds in India are in the form of a Trust. This means that the money belongs to investors and is only held in the name of the Trust. The investment arm, the AMC, acts as an investment manager which earns a fee but does not own the money. This does not mean that the investments are risk-free. Mutual fund investors need to take the risk of volatility or bad management and money can grow or lose value depending on the market and investment decisions. However, sensible mutual fund investing is a good way to include equity and debt in your portfolios to see realistic growth.

Mutual funds are proven winners and investment in mutual funds is one of the best ways for you to build wealth while managing risk. As already discussed, a firm foundation can be laid by defining and articulating your investment goals and identifying the types of funds you need to achieve your goals. But the key to finding the right mutual fund is to research the available resources.

Research Your Resources

Every financial daily offers daily NAVs of all mutual fund schemes. Magazines and periodicals also come out with annual surveys of mutual funds. There are even magazines including "Mutual Fund Insight" (www.valueresearchonline.com) dedicated entirely to the mutual fund industry. The internet is indeed a great source for information. There are dedicated sites as well as financial sites, which offer information on mutual funds. Mutual funds themselves maintain websites, which are a veritable treasure trove of information. Fund information can also be found on the sites of AMFI and SEBI. But none can replace the omnipotent offer document.

Prospecting the prospectus seems to be the key to catapulting yourself to the winning position with precision.

The Prospectus or the Offer Document (OD) explains the financials, performance, objectives, fees, risks associated with a fund and legal issues. This document is as comprehensive as an encyclopaedia. It is not feasible to distribute it to every prospective investor. It runs into eighty pages or more. However, funds also offer an abridged version of the offer document, a simplified "fund profile" known as the Key Information Memorandum (KIM) that covers the highlights in a few pages. SEBI regulation makes it mandatory to attach KIM along with every application form.

Mutual Fund Prospectus and Shareholder Reports

To protect investors, all mutual funds are highly regulated by the Securities and Exchange Board of India. SEBI requires that all funds provide two types of documents to current and potential investors free of charge: a prospectus and a shareholder report.

A mutual fund's **prospectus** or offer document describes in plain English the fund's goals, fees and expenses, investment strategies and risks, as well as information on how to buy and sell units. You can get a copy of a fund's current prospectus from the fund or your broker or financial planner. Many funds also make prospectuses available on their websites.

Shareholder reports typically include two main types of information:

* the fund's financial statements and performance; and
* a list of securities the fund held in its portfolio at the end of the most recent accounting period.

For most of you, the KIM should suffice. But, you should also be aware of the offer document.

The Offer Document

Nobody wants to read the Offer Document. It is a document that describes a mutual fund, often in legal and financial terms that may sound awfully technical. But the language is precise for a reason. SEBI has strict guidelines about what the fund can say about itself and how it must present information. Remember, SEBI's approval of a prospectus is only that. It is not an endorsement of any particular investment. Simplifying a prospectus is never easy because it is a document that is trying to serve two purposes. Its stated objective is disclosure: informing you how a fund invests and operates. It is also a document that lawyers of the mutual fund design as a litigation shield, making sure that the fund managers will be able to run the fund without inviting lawsuits.

Do not let the offer document unnerve you. The financial matters and investment policies may be unique. But much of the other material is boilerplate and does not vary much from fund to fund. And not all of it is pertinent to every investor. When thumbing through the offer document, look for important statistical nuggets including the fund's condensed financial history, fund performance (showing the average annual total returns and cumulative total returns for the fund over various fiscal-year periods) and the investment policy section (outlining the overall strategy, the permitted investments in the broadest of terms and restrictions, if any). Pay careful attention to the investment objective and how the fund managers plan to achieve it, especially the kind of risk they might undertake (with your money). Be forewarned. Most fund prospectuses are written in a way that gives fund managers the widest latitude and discretion. The information in this section helps to describe the fund's character. The document plainly lists all sales charges, deferred sales charges, redemption fees, exchange fees, management fees and other pertinent expenses. It also outlines the various options available to you including growth, dividend reinvestment and dividend payout. (These options will be explained and analysed in the context of tax implications shortly). Last but not the least, the risk factors will be stated in no uncertain terms.

A draft offer document is to be prepared by the AMC at the time of launching the fund. It needs to be approved by the trustees and the board of directors of the AMC. The offer document is filed with SEBI and the observations made by SEBI on the offer document need to be incorporated in the offer document. Typically, the offer document pre-specifies the investment objectives of the fund, asset allocation, sale and repurchase procedure, load and expense structure of the scheme, accounting and valuation policies, structure of the mutual fund, its constituents, operational details as to how to apply and the rights and duties of the investor. Whenever a new scheme's offer document is made, a certificate is given by the Compliance Officer of the mutual fund that proper care has been taken in structuring the scheme and drafting the offer document.

Simplification of the Offer Document

SEBI, on the recommendation of the Committee set up by AMFI, has simplified the offer document and key information memorandum to be filed by mutual funds, to make them reader friendly. To reduce bulkiness, the OD has been split into two parts – Statement of Additional Information (SAI) and Scheme Information Document (SID). The revised format for the OD and KIM has been effective from June 1, 2008. Both documents are prepared in the format prescribed by SEBI and submitted to SEBI. The contents need to flow in the same sequence as in the prescribed format. The mutual fund is permitted to add any disclosure, which it feels, is material for the investor.

Statement of Additional Information

SAI is common for all schemes from the mutual fund house and has to be filed with SEBI as a one-time filing. SAI contains information about the mutual fund, its promoters, sponsors, trustees and the AMC, among others. It is a kind of permanent document about the fund. Information includes contact information, share holding pattern, responsibilities, names of directors and their contact information, profiles of key personnel and contact information of service providers.

SAI contains condensed financial information for schemes launched in the last 3 financial years, instructions on how to apply, rights of unit-holders, investment valuation norms, tax, legal and general information (investor grievance redressal mechanism, data on number of complaints received and cleared and opening and closing number of complaints for the previous 3 financial years and for the current year to date).

Regular update of SAI is to be done by the end of 3 months of every financial year. Any material changes in SAI should be made on an ongoing basis by updating them on the mutual fund and AMFI websites. SEBI should be intimated of the changes made in SAI within 7 days. The effective date for such changes should be mentioned in the updated SAI. Every mutual fund, in its website, provides for download of its SAI. Investors have the right to ask for a printed copy of the SAI. Investors can access the SAI of all the mutual funds through the AMFI website (www.amfiindia.com).

Scheme Information Document

SID, which contains complete information about the scheme in question, is valid for 6 months from the date of issuance of the final observation by SEBI. If the AMC intends to launch the scheme at a date later than 6 months, a fresh SID along with filing fees has to be filed with SEBI. The front page of the SID should compulsorily mention the name of the mutual fund, name of the scheme, type of the scheme, name of the AMC, classes of units offered for sale, price of the units, name of the guarantor in case of assured return schemes, the opening, closing and the earliest closing date of the scheme and the mandatory statements as required by SEBI. The SID mentions the proposed asset allocation mix and nature of investments in which the money of the scheme will be deployed. However, names of specific securities where the scheme will invest are obviously not mentioned.

SEBI's format of SID is produced below for your perusal.

SEBI's Format of Scheme Information Document
Preliminary Information
Summary Information
Mandatory Disclosure Clauses
I. INTRODUCTION
• Risk Disclosures
• Requirement of Minimum Investors in the Scheme
• Special Considerations, if any
• Glossary of Defined Terms
• Due Diligence by the AMC

II. FUND-SPECIFIC INFORMATION

- Type of the Scheme
- Investment Objective of the Scheme
- Allocation of Assets by the Scheme
- Types of Instruments in which the Scheme will invest
- Investment Strategies of the Scheme
- Fundamental Attributes of the Scheme*
- Benchmark Index to compare Scheme Performance
- Fund Manager details
- Investment Restrictions
- Scheme Performance

III. UNITS AND OFFER

Details of the Scheme Being Offered

- NFO Offer Period and Price
- Minimum Subscription
- Minimum Target Amount
- Dividend Policy, Allotment and Refund
- Special facilities to investors and plans being offered
- Eligibility for investing and documentation period
- Procedure for applying and subsequent operations relating to transfer, redemption, nomination, pledge and mode of holding units
- Listing

Ongoing Offer Details

- Ongoing Offer Period and Price
- Cut-off timing
- Place of Submission of Application
- Minimum amount for Purchase/Redemption/Switches
- Minimum balance to be maintained
- Availability of Special products like SIP, SWP and STP
- Account Statements
- Dividend Warrants and Redemption/Repurchase Proceeds

Periodic Disclosures

- Net Asset Value daily
- Half-yearly Disclosure of Portfolio and Financial Results
- Monthly Portfolio Disclosure [along with International Securities Identification Number (ISIN)]
- Scheme-wise Annual Report or Abridged Summary every year
- Associate Transactions (refer SAI)

Computation of NAV

Taxation

Investor Services

Name, address and telephone number and e-mail of the contact person/grievances officer who would take care of investor queries and complaints.

IV. LOADS, FEE STRUCTURE and EXPENSES

- NFO Expenses
- Annual Scheme Recurring Expenses
- Load Structure
- Waiver of Load for Direct Application

V. UNIT-HOLDER RIGHTS (refer SAI)

VI. DETAILS OF PENDING LITIGATION AND PENALTIES

Penalties, pending litigation or proceedings, findings of inspections or investigations for which action may have been taken or is in the process of being taken by any regulatory authority.

*The fundamental attributes of the scheme are the basic features of the scheme and they are of paramount importance to investors. **The type of scheme, investment objective and pattern of the scheme, terms of the scheme with regard to liquidity, fees and expenses, valuation norms and accounting policies and investment restrictions are the fundamental attributes of the scheme.** The first 5 attributes are very important and differ from scheme to scheme, whereas SEBI has issued common regulations for the last two.

Draft SID is a public document, available for viewing in SEBI's website (www.sebi.gov.in) for 21 working days. The final SID (after incorporating SEBI's observations) has to be hosted on AMFI's website (www.amfiindia.com) two days before the issue opens.

Every mutual fund, in its website, provides for download of the SID for all its current schemes. If a scheme is launched in the first 6 months of the financial year, say, April 2016, then the first update of the SID is due within 3 months of the end of the financial year (i.e. by June 30, 2017). If a scheme is launched in the second 6 months of the financial year, say, October 2015, then the first update of the SID is due within 3 months of the end of the next financial year (i.e. by June 30, 2017). Thereafter, SID is to be updated once every financial year.

In the case of change in fundamental attributes, SID should be revised and updated immediately after the deadline stipulated for investors who want to exit from the scheme. In the case of other changes, the AMC is required to issue an addendum and display it on the website. The addendum should be circulated to the distributors/brokers/Investor Service Centres (ISCs) so that the same can be attached to KIM and SID already in stock till they are updated. For instance, in the case of changes in load structure, the addendum carrying the latest applicable load structure should be attached to the KIM and SID already in stock till they are updated. A public notice should be given in respect of such changes in an English language daily having nationwide circulation as well as in a newspaper published in the language of the region where the head office of the mutual fund is situated. A copy of all changes made to the scheme should be filed with SEBI within 7 days of the change.

Key Information Memorandum

The KIM, an abridged version of SAI and SID, should accompany every application form. Hence, KIM is more widely circulated in the market and is easily accessible to the investor. The key details contained in KIM include name of the AMC, mutual fund, trustee, fund manager and scheme, dates of issue opening, issue closing and re-opening for sale and repurchase, plans and options under the scheme, risk profile of the scheme, price at which units are being issued and minimum amount/units for initial purchase, additional purchase and repurchase, benchmark, dividend policy, performance of the scheme and benchmark over the last one year, three years, five years and since inception, loads and expenses and contact information of registrar for taking up investor grievances.

KIM should be updated at least once a year and should be filed with SEBI forthwith. Just like SID, KIM has to be revised in the case of change in fundamental attributes. Other changes can be disclosed through addenda attached to the KIM.

How Can a Prospectus Help You?

Consider these hypothetical situations in which the information found in a prospectus could have been very useful:

* An investor sells his mutual fund units and is surprised to learn that a portion of the sale price is paid to the fund company in the form of a back end load.

* An investor exchanges his investment in one fund for another fund in the same fund family. He did not know that fees were charged for the exchange.

* A retiree in search of income invests in a high-yield bond fund but does not know that it is also high risk and is disturbed by its fluctuating value.

All the necessary information to prevent these situations is contained in every mutual fund's prospectus. Take a look at the following key elements:

Date of issue: First, verify that you have received an up-to-date edition of the prospectus. A prospectus must be updated regularly.

Minimum investments: Mutual funds differ both in the minimum initial investment required and the minimum for subsequent investments. All mutual funds specify the minimum amount that has to be invested and the multiples thereof. These restrictions are usually not applicable to inter-scheme and inter-option switches.

Investment objectives: This explains the mandate and scope of investment. It includes – whether the fund is equity or debt-oriented, whether the fund is multi-cap, large cap, mid-cap, or small cap specific, the level of diversification, the option to the fund manager to invest overseas and other such issues. The goal of each fund should be clearly defined – from income with preservation of principal to long-term capital appreciation. Be sure the fund's objective matches your objective.

Type of fund: Is the fund open ended or close ended? In the case of a closed-end fund, look at the lock-in period, liquidity window and repurchase options.

Investment strategies: A prospectus outlines the general strategies the fund managers can adopt. You learn what types of investments are to be included, such as Government bonds or common stock. The prospectus may also include information on minimum bond ratings and types of companies considered appropriate for a fund. Be sure to consider whether the fund offers adequate diversification.

Risk factors: Every investment involves some level of risk. In a prospectus, you can find a description of the risks associated with investments in the fund. Refer to your own objectives and decide if the risks associated with the fund's investments match your own risk tolerance.

Performance data: You can find selected per unit net asset value and total return for different time periods as prescribed by SEBI guidelines. Performance data listed in a prospectus is based on standard formula established by SEBI. It enables you to make comparisons with other funds. Remember that past results do not guarantee future performance. When evaluating performance, look at the track record of a fund over a time period and check whether it matches with your own investment goals.

Fees and expenses: Sales and management fees associated with a mutual fund must be clearly listed. The prospectus also displays the impact these fees and expenses would have on a hypothetical investment over time.

Tax information: A prospectus includes information on the tax status and implications on a fund's distributions – whether they are treated as dividend income or capital gains.

Investor services: You may have access to certain services, such as automatic investment of dividends and systematic withdrawal plans. This section of the prospectus, usually near the back of the publication, describes these services and how you can take advantage of them.

While the rest of the material can appear in any order, you will generally have no trouble finding the information you need – prospectuses generally run into eighty pages or more and include a table of contents. After reviewing a few prospectuses, you will become accustomed to the language and be able to reduce the time it takes to find the information you need to make a sound investment decision.

Here are some key factors that you need to keep an eye out for:

Investment: Minimum initial investment, methods of purchasing, redeeming and making additional investments, the time taken for redemption, etc.

Investment Team: Name of the fund manager, number of fund managers managing the fund and information on each. This information is useful for those who would check the antecedents of the manager.

Closed-end schemes issue the offer document during the NFO. The offer document prepared for open-end funds is valid through the life of the scheme but it is updated every year.

The major changes that have to be notified to the investors are:

* change in the AMC or sponsor of the mutual fund;
* changes in the load structure;
* changes in the fundamental attributes of the scheme; and
* changes in the investment options to investors (inclusion or deletion of options).

Think of the prospectus as your travel guide to the world of mutual funds – it provides all the details you need to map out a successful investment plan. At first glance, of course, a prospectus may not look as reader-friendly as you would hope. It is, after all, a legal document that must adhere to rigorous standards set forth by SEBI. But with a little basic knowledge of the information contained in a prospectus, you can make effective use of this valuable investment planning tool.

Product Labelling System

AMCs were following different methods to classify their schemes. To end this confusion, SEBI had asked AMFI to standardise the methodology for uniform application of product labelling across industry. SEBI had instituted a product labelling system to provide investors an easy understanding of the kind of product/scheme they were investing in and its suitability to them. All mutual funds had to label their schemes on the following parameters:

- Nature of the scheme such as to create wealth or provide regular income in an indicative time horizon (short/ medium/ long term).
- A brief about the investment objective (in a single line sentence) followed by the kind of product in which the investor is investing (Equity/Debt).

- Level of risk, depicted by the colour code boxes as under:
  - Blue – principal at low risk.
  - Yellow – principal at medium risk.
  - Brown – principal at high risk.

Therefore, with effect from July 1, 2014, all debt-oriented schemes, comparatively lower in risk, were denoted with 'Blue' colour. All diversified/blended schemes, with a mix of debt and equity into the portfolio construct, were assigned 'yellow' colour to indicate moderate risk. All equity-oriented schemes had 'brown' colour to show higher risk. All static allocations domestic feeder funds which have a predominant equity allocation were colour-coded as 'brown' and which have a predominant debt allocation were colour-coded as 'yellow'. All active allocations domestic feeder funds (i.e. where the allocation is based on a model or parameter, etc.) were colour-coded as 'brown'. All foreign feeder funds were colour-coded as 'brown'.

The colour codes had to be described in the text beside the colour code box. A disclaimer had to be included, that investors should consult their financial advisers if they are not clear about the suitability of the product. The product labels were to be disclosed in the front page of the initial offering application forms, Key Information Memorandum (KIM) and Scheme Information Documents (SIDs). The product label was to be placed in proximity to the caption of the scheme and should be prominently visible.

Effective July 1, 2015, SEBI had replaced the product labelling system using "colour codes" by a "pictorial meter" known as Riskometer comprising 5 levels of risk – low, moderately low, moderate, moderately high and high.

1. **Low:** Principal at low risk. Liquid funds and ultra-short-term bond funds having average maturity of less than 90 days should be listed under this category.
2. **Moderately Low:** Principal at moderately low risk. Short to medium-term funds having average maturity between 91 days and 3 years should be listed under this category.
3. **Moderate:** Principal at moderate risk. Income funds and gilt funds having average maturity of more than 3 years; Arbitrage funds and debt-oriented hybrid funds having an exposure of up to 20% to equity components in the portfolio will fall under this risk category.
4. **Moderately High:** Principal at moderately high risk. Diversified equity funds, balanced funds, indexed ETFs and gold ETFs will come under this category.

5. **High:** Principal at high risk. Sectoral funds/Thematic funds, international funds and sectoral ETF come under this category.

Say, for instance, a long-term income fund having moderate risk would be depicted as follows:

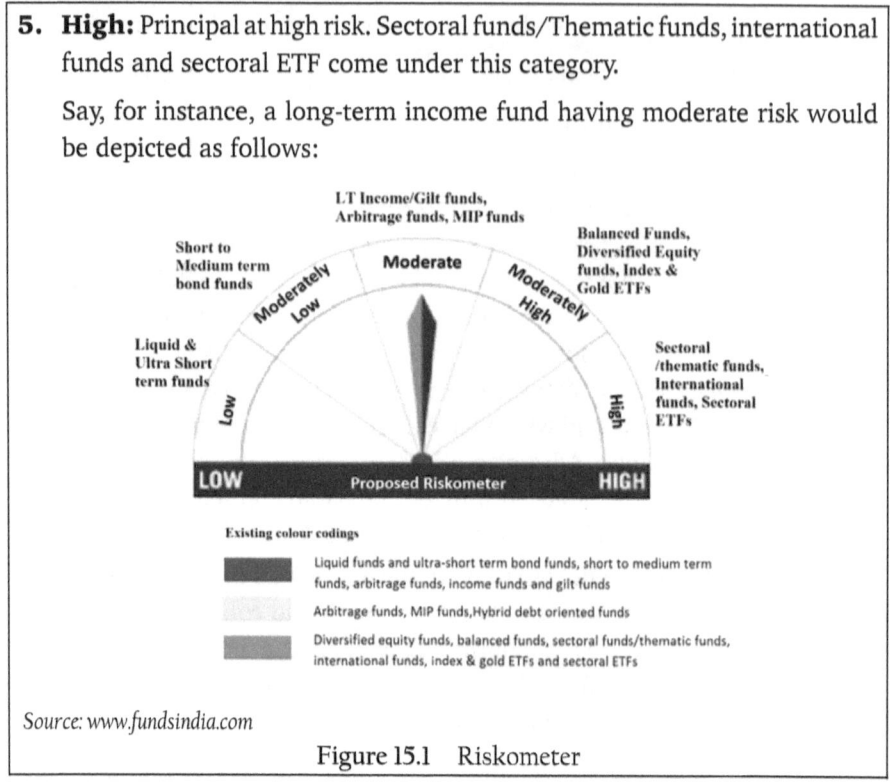

Source: www.fundsindia.com

Figure 15.1   Riskometer

Shareholder Report

Mutual Fund Fact Sheets

Most Asset Management Companies usually publish monthly reports (also called fact sheets) that contain critical information related to the portfolios, at times a round-up on debt and equity markets from the fund manager and performance details of the schemes managed by the AMC. The idea is to help investors (both existing and potential) to track the performance of the mutual fund schemes so as to take an informed decision. To that end, fact sheets serve as an investor's guide.

Fact sheets are always meant to be the investor's guide. However, in many cases, they are not up to the mark leaving much scope for improvement and even standardisation. Let us highlight the most critical reference points for the benefit of the uninformed investor based on data that is more or less standardised across AMCs. For ease of reference, the first part discusses how to assess the equity fund fact sheet and the second part discusses the debt fund fact sheet.

A. Equity Fund Fact Sheets

1. Stock Allocation

Thankfully, fact sheets of most AMCs highlight the portfolio composition and offer some critical insight into the fund management style/approach.

To begin with, **consider the top 10 stocks in the portfolio to determine the level of diversification.** A diversified equity fund should have no more than 40% of net assets in the top 10 stocks. This should help the fund in negotiating volatility more effectively than its concentrated peers. For instance, Sundaram Growth Fund is known for its disciplined investment approach (no more than 5% of assets in a single stock) that ensures that its top 10 stocks are well-diversified. Sometimes, a fund could be well-diversified across the top 10 stocks, but investments in a single stock could be high enough to offset an otherwise diversified portfolio. A case in point is HDFC Capital Builder (a well-managed value fund), which was in trouble during the market crash in May 2007 due to unduly high investments in a single stock Hindustan Zinc.

In addition, **look at the fund's portfolio over several months to get a sense of the consistency in the fund manager's stock picks.** Too much churn in the stock picks (new names every other month) indicates that the fund manager could be punting rather than investing, thereby, adding to the trading cost, which ultimately eats into the returns.

2. Sectoral Allocation

Just as you evaluate the stock allocation, it is important to consider the sectoral allocation of the equity fund. Diversified equity funds should be well-diversified across stocks and sectors. A fund could be well-diversified across stocks, but may pay the price for not diversifying well enough across sectors. For instance, Sundaram Growth Fund, admired for superior diversification across stocks, learnt the hard way during May 2007 that diversification across sectors is as important as diversification across stocks. The fund had unduly high investments in infrastructure-related stocks.

The crash proved particularly harsh for the fund, as it had failed to diversify across other sectors. So, similar to stocks, being diversified across sectors is just as important. Unfortunately, it often takes a sharp dip in the stock markets to highlight the importance.

However, funds such as HSBC Equity Fund, which pursue the top-down investment approach, have concentrated sectoral allocations, which suit their investment style. These funds need to be evaluated differently from funds that pursue the bottom-up investment style.

While calculating the sectoral allocation, you **must combine like-natured sectors to understand the level of sectoral diversification**. For instance, most equity funds list Auto and Auto-ancillaries as distinct sectors. Given the similar nature of these sectors, their allocation must be combined.

Another problem relates to **the categorisation of companies across sectors**. Different equity funds categorise the same company across different sectors. There is no standardisation. While AMFI has introduced certain standardisation processes in this regard, the same is not adhered to across the industry.

3. Asset Allocation

Stocks and sectors apart, there is another detail that must catch your attention – the asset allocation. The asset allocation table tells you how the fund's net assets are diversified across stocks and current assets/cash. An equity fund's allocation to cash should be noted. Among other reasons, this could be because the fund manager is not comfortable with market levels at that point of time. This fact can be established easily by browsing through the fact sheets of the previous months.

4. Other Points to Be Considered

In addition to the points listed above, there are some more points that must be marked by you.

a) Portfolio Turnover Ratio

Portfolio Turnover Ratio is the frequency at which assets (stocks in the case of equity mutual funds) are bought and sold by a mutual fund.

Simply put, this ratio tells you how much churn the portfolio has witnessed. This ratio is calculated based on the value of shares bought and sold by the equity fund over the review period. To calculate this, you take either the total value of stocks bought or the total value of stocks sold, whichever is lower, for 12 months and divide it by the average corpus of the fund less expenses. For example, if the fund has bought assets/stocks worth Rs. 1200 crore and has sold assets/stocks worth Rs. 900 crore in a year and at the end of the year the fund has an average corpus less expenses of Rs. 3,000 crore, the portfolio turnover ratio is 30% (900x100/3,000). So, on an average, 30% of the portfolio is churned in a year.

When mutual fund managers buy and sell a high number of stocks, frequently, within a fund, it will have a high turnover rate, causing a higher capital gains tax and *vice versa*. The high turnover rate lowers tax-efficiency, increases transaction costs and lowers returns. A lower turnover rate lowers capital gains and transaction costs, thereby, improving returns. Check the fund reports for the turnover rate. A rate of eighty or less is usually considered low.

A high turnover ratio (*vis-à-vis* peers or other equity funds from the same fund house) indicates that the portfolio has seen above-average churn. A high churn by itself does not necessarily imply that the fund is good or bad; however, it must be in line with the fund's investment philosophy. A growth fund or a liquid fund can have a high turnover ratio (although that is not necessarily a good thing as it adds to the trading costs and, therefore, eats into your returns). However, a value fund or an index fund should typically have a lower churn as the fund manager would usually be investing in the stocks over the long term.

Important as it is, the portfolio turnover ratio is yet to be given due importance by the fund houses (maybe they are afraid of 'exposing' their fund managers). How else do you explain the fact that fund houses either do not reveal the portfolio turnover ratios or when they do reveal them, it is not standardised, thereby, robbing you of the opportunity to compare them across fund houses? All said and done, sites like www.valueresearchonline.com clearly state this information.

b) Expense Ratio

This ratio underscores how expensive your equity fund really is. A high expense ratio (regulations cap this at 2.5% for equity funds and 2.25% for debt funds) indicates that your mutual fund investment is expensive.

Again, fund houses are not very enthusiastic about sharing this important detail with you. However, they do declare this ratio every 6 months, which is only because regulations demand that they do so.

c) Fund Manager Information

It always helps to know who is managing your fund. You should not get infatuated by any fund manager in particular; instead look for investment teams. Over the long term, it pays to have your money managed by a good investment team rather than one star fund manager, who could quit the fund house any time and take the fund's performance with him.

So, keep an eye on the fund manager details. Ideally, there should not be many changes in the fund management team. When the same names manage your money, over a period of time there is stability in the fund management process. Thankfully for you, majority of the fund houses do provide the fund manager details.

B. Debt fund Fact Sheets

Such as their equity fund counterparts, debt fund fact sheets offer enough insight to the debt fund investor. For this, you have to keep an eye on at least three aspects:

a) Average Maturity

For debt fund investors, this is, perhaps, the most significant detail to look out for in a debt fund fact sheet. Average maturity (explained in detail under 'bond funds' in Chapter 9) is the average age of debt securities in a fund portfolio. Since the average maturity of a portfolio for a particular month in isolation does not tell you much, you must go back several months to see how the average maturity of the portfolio has moved in order to understand the fund manager's view on debt markets.

To give you an idea – if the fund manager has been maintaining a higher average maturity for some time, it means that he expects interest rates to fall over time. On the other hand, if the average maturity of the portfolio is lower, it means that the fund manager is cautious about interest rates. Ideally, you must read peer fact sheets to understand the consensus on interest rates and if your fund manager has a differing view, you must try to understand why.

b) **Credit Rating Profile**

Debt funds invest in securities with varying credit ratings. In the Indian context, most debt funds do not take on undue credit risk, i.e. they invest primarily in securities that are highly rated. You should mark the credit rating profile of the debt fund. A large chunk in AAA/Sovereign paper (which is the highest rating) implies that the fund is taking lower credit risk. On the other hand, a higher allocation to AA+/AA paper underlines the fact that the fund manager is taking higher credit risk.

c) **Asset Allocation**

The asset allocation of the fund under review should help you understand the investment approach of the fund manager and the risk he is taking. Debt funds invest mainly in corporate bonds and Government securities, both of which carry varying risk. You must make a note of the assets invested across both these segments. Then there are floating rate funds that invest predominantly in floating rate paper. In practice, however, many are predominantly invested in cash/current assets for lack of adequate floating rate instruments. Likewise, MIPs invest a portion of assets in equities (the maximum limit of which is predetermined). You must check the equity allocation over the last several months to understand the kind of risk the fund manager is taking (on the equity side) and whether he is adhering to the ceiling on equity investments.

You are not going to have trouble finding out details about any fund. So, you need to know what to concentrate on rather than risk information overload. **Look out for the signs of a well-managed fund. You should focus on a fund's performance, consistency and management.**

Chapter 16

Performance Evaluation

Returns – the First Dimension

Mirror, Mirror on the Wall, Which is the Best Fund of Them All?

This seems to be the daunting question in the minds of all investors planning to park their money in mutual funds. The answer lies in systematically scouting for consistent performers with sound credentials.

In a Nutshell

The performance of a scheme is reflected in its net asset value, which is disclosed on a daily basis in the case of open-end schemes and on a weekly basis in the case of closed-end schemes. NAV of mutual funds are required to be published in newspapers.

Objective Parameters

The NAV of the scheme reflects the performance of the scheme. The fund also gives you returns for various periods such as one month, 3 months, 6 months, one year, 3 years, 5 years, since inception, etc. This will give you an idea about the performance of the fund. Funds also provide comparison with relevant benchmarks. This should tell you whether the fund manager has performed better than the benchmark. However, financial experts believe that these returns do not give the complete picture. They believe that the returns should be risk-adjusted. Various publications and internet sites provide such returns, whose computation is complicated.

Subjective Parameters

Performance alone does not make a fund house a winner. Equally important is the service standards and transparency in action. It is also essential that the fund house offers speedy solutions to your grievances. The reputation of the fund house among investors at large indicates how well the fund scores on this front.

Key Parameters in the Evaluation of Equity Funds

Fund age (existing funds with more than a 5-year track record should be preferred)

Fund size (small size means higher expenses)

Market capitalisation of the fund (indicates liquidity and level of risk – small cap is highly risky and less liquid)

NAV growth (consistent returns over a period of time)

Analysis of risk and returns

Expense ratio

Portfolio character (too much of cash means more idle funds and unnecessary management expenses)

Portfolio turnover rate (higher the portfolio turnover ratio, higher the transaction costs and *vice versa*)

Portfolio statistics like ex-marks of the portfolio (extent of sensitivity to the market), beta (extent of volatility of the fund relative to the benchmark, whose beta is always one) and gross dividend yield (a measure of the amount received by investors as dividend as a portion of their total investment expressed as a percentage)

Portfolio composition (diversified or concentrated)

Fund manager's style of investment, track record and experience

> **Key Parameters in the Evaluation of Debt Funds**
>
> Fund age (immaterial)
>
> Fund size (small size means higher expenses)
>
> NAV growth
>
> Consistency of returns
>
> Total return
>
> Relative yield (If income is needed, a fund with high current yield should be chosen and if total return is important, a fund with high Yield to Maturity (YTM) should be chosen. [YTM is the rate of return on a bond if it is held till maturity. Yield net of expenses should be compared in the case of liquid funds]).
>
> Expense ratio (is more important as it operates in narrow income margins, more so in the case of liquid funds.)
>
> Rating profile (Better the rating of the bonds better the fund; low rating may be justified in long-term liquid funds but unacceptable in short-term liquid funds.)
>
> Maturity profile (Higher the average maturity or average age of the instruments in the portfolio, higher the interest rate risk since interest rate volatility is high in the case of instruments with long maturity.)
>
> Ideal mix of corporate debt and gilt fund (Corporate debt or debt instruments issued by companies offer higher returns with moderate safety when compared to the highly safe gilt funds or instruments issued by the Government, which offer lower returns.)
>
> Industry exposures and concentrations (High exposure to certain industries leads to a concentrated portfolio which increases the risk of investors losing a major portion of their investment in the event of those sectors not performing well.)
>
> Management quality is quite important in money market mutual funds since a lot of trading skills are required.

Evaluation Parameters

The following are the evaluation parameters on the basis of which the analysis and comparison of various equity schemes is done.

Assets Under Management: It is used to gauge how much money a fund is managing. Mutual funds use this as a measure of success and comparison against their competitors. In lieu of revenue or total revenue, they use total 'assets under management (AUM)'. The difference between two AUM balances reflects market performance, gains/losses, foreign exchange movements, net new assets (NNA) and inflow/outflow. You should mainly be interested in the NNA, which indicates how much money has been received from investors for investment. Furthermore, it is common to calculate the key figure 'NNA growth', which shows the NNA in relation to the previous AUM balance (annualised).

Net Asset Value: NAV is the value of the collective investment of a fund based on the market price of securities held in its portfolio. NAV per unit is calculated by dividing net assets of the scheme by the number of units outstanding.

Expense Ratio: Expense ratio states how much you pay a fund in percentage terms every year to manage your money. For example, if you invest Rs. 10,000 in a fund with an expense ratio of 1.5%, then you are paying the fund Rs. 150 to manage your money. NAVs of funds are reported net of fees and expenses. It is, therefore, necessary to know how much the fund is deducting. Since this is charged every year, a high expense ratio over the long term may eat into your returns massively through the power of compounding. Different funds have different expense ratios. But SEBI has stipulated a limit that a fund can charge. Equity funds can charge a maximum of 2.5%, whereas a debt fund can charge 2.25% of the average weekly net assets. Net assets are the total amount of assets held by the fund. It refers to the market value of the unit capital of a mutual fund scheme after charging expenses related to the scheme. The weekly average of the net assets is calculated. The largest component of the expense ratio is management and advisory fees. The management fee is an AMC's income. Then there are marketing and distribution expenses. All those involved in the operations of a fund such as the custodian and auditors also get a share of the pie. Interestingly, brokerage paid by a fund on the purchase and sale of securities was not reflected in the expense ratio. Funds used to state their buying and selling price after taking the transaction cost into account. Funds used to launch institutional plans for big-ticket investors, where the expense ratio is relatively lower than normal funds. This is because the cost of servicing is low due to larger investment amount, which means lower expenses. According to SEBI, since October 2012, brokerage is reflected in the expense ratio and all categories of investors, retail as well as institutional, have been subjected to a uniform expense structure under a single plan. A lower expense ratio does not necessarily mean that it is a better-managed fund. A good fund is one that delivers a good return with minimal expenses.

Portfolio Turnover: Each buy or sell transaction in the stock market involves a brokerage cost. The scheme's investors have to bear this cost. Obviously, higher the volume of trading, greater will be the associated costs. Greater trading costs can definitely reduce returns. So, how do you know how much the fund manager is trading? The answer to this question is provided by the turnover ratio. The turnover ratio represents the percentage of a fund's holdings that changes every year. To put it simply, a turnover rate of 100% implies that the fund manager has replaced his entire portfolio during the given period. Higher the turnover ratio, greater is the volume of trading carried out by the fund. Is a high turnover bad? Well, that depends on what it achieves. If high turnover can generate high returns, then there should be no problem. The problem arises when a fund is trading heavily and not generating commensurate returns. The turnover ratio is more important for equity funds where the trading cost of equities is substantial. So, each time a fund manager buys or sells, he has to keep in mind that the cost of buying or selling will eat into the fund's returns.

Reputation of the Asset Management Company: Reputation of the AMC and that of the fund manager/fund management team is of paramount importance in evaluating a fund. Selection of the right fund can be quite challenging. There are two reasons for this: one is the large number of funds in India today, which makes selection very confusing; and the other reason stems from the first – more funds imply more homework on your part. To identify the right fund, you need to see how the fund measures up on the following parameters:

Fund's background: Check out whether the sponsors have adequate fund management experience, are conservative and innovative and have a clean slate untainted by scams and financial irregularities.

The fund house's overall performance: Even if you wish to invest in just one scheme of the fund house, you must check to see how the fund house is performing as a whole.

Fund manager's track record: The following factors will aid you in gauging the ability of the fund manager to demonstrate sterling performance:

History of managing funds: You can determine how effective a fund manager has been in earning superior returns at lower risk after studying the previous funds managed by him either in the same or a previous AMC. Rely on their professionalism, experience and steadfastness rather than on their stardom.

Adherence to mandate: It is common knowledge that every mutual fund scheme has an investment objective, which becomes the fund manager's mandate. But the million-dollar question is – does he abide by the mandate?

Investment by the fund manager in his own schemes: It is one thing to systematically plan how to invest other people's money and totally another to actually apply the same plan to one's own money. In India, unlike in the USA, it is not mandatory to report whether the fund manager invests his own money in the schemes he manages.

Process-driven or Fund Manager-driven: Is the fund manager driven by his own individualistic style while taking investment decisions or are there processes and systems in place to make investments? Looking at the fund's trailing 6–12 months' portfolios will allow you to understand the fund manager's style of investment over a period of time. A fund manager's investment philosophy (concentrated bets, diversified portfolio, large caps, mid-caps, etc.) gives the fund a particular risk profile. It is always 'safer' to select an AMC that has a strong, process-driven investment style and the fund manager's role is to perform within the parameters defined by the AMC. The fund manager should be able to seamlessly enter and exit from the AMC without disturbing the process. It is advisable to check the number of schemes your fund manager is handling. If the fund manager has a team of analysts in place, then even a large number of schemes under him would seem fine. While there is no definite number for ideal team size, it helps if there are enough members in the fund management team so that no individual is indispensable.

Risk mitigation is a very critical part of fund management and is its primary objective. Delivering growth comes after that and is, therefore, the secondary objective. Both these objectives are tested vigorously across bull and bear phases. And more often than not, you will find process-driven funds redeeming themselves on both these criteria more than fund manager-driven funds. From your perspective, the moot point is – how does one identify a strong process-driven mutual fund? You can do that by looking at consistency in the fund's performance across a longer time frame of 3 to 5 years. More importantly, within this period, try to see how the fund has done across bullish and bearish phases. In a strong process-driven mutual fund, you will find that even if a fund has not done exceedingly well in a bull-run, it would have mitigated losses in a bearish phase. The reason behind this is **disciplined fund management**, a rare trait in the industry.

Measurement of Performance

Percentage change in NAV is a rough method that considers only the change in NAV. It is not useful for calculating returns in the long term or on a compounded basis.

Yield is the measure of net income (dividends and interest less expenses) earned by the securities in the fund's portfolio during a specified period. Yield is expressed as a percentage of the fund's NAV (including the highest applicable sales charge, if any). Yield does not include the change, if any, in the investment's value over a given period. It does not consider the increase in the market value of the mutual fund portfolio. Yield is the income returned on the mutual fund investment. A simple example will make it clear. Let us say for instance, a mutual fund sells 200 lakh units at an NAV of Rs. 10 per unit for a total of Rs. 2,000 lakh. If the mutual fund invests in stocks that have higher market value and the market value of the stocks in the portfolio increases to Rs. 3,000 lakh after 5 years, then the NAV would be Rs. 15 (Rs. 3,000 lakh/200 lakh units). Having derived the NAV, we can calculate the yield of the mutual fund. Assuming an NAV of Rs. 15, according to our example and a dividend paid to unit-holders of Rs. 2 per unit then, yield of the fund works out to 13.33% (Rs. 2/Rs. 15 *100).

Total Return is generally regarded as the best measure of fund performance because it is the most comprehensive. Total return is absolute returns and includes dividend and capital gain distributions along with any changes in the fund's NAV. A dividend distribution comes from the interest and dividends earned by the securities held by a fund. A capital gain distribution represents any net gains resulting from the sale of the securities held by a fund. Total return, expressed as a percentage of an initial investment in a fund, represents the change in that investment's value over a given period, assuming that dividend distributions were reinvested in the fund.

Let us continue with our earlier example cited to explain yield. To calculate total returns, we have to consider the market value of the mutual fund portfolio at present. This is the current NAV of Rs. 15. Adding the dividend to it, we arrive at a total of [(Rs. 15/unit + Rs. 2/unit)/Rs. 10/unit] 1.70 or 70% (by subtracting the initial investment of Rs. 10 per unit). 1.0 represents the principal value and must be subtracted. The major disadvantage of total returns is that it does not take into account the time factor. The total return of 70% is for 5 years and not one year.

Compounded Annual Growth Rate (CAGR) overpowers all the other methods of calculating returns over the long term, since it is all-encompassing. The returns for the subsequent years include the returns accumulated thus far (interest is earned on the interest). Let us extend our example further. In order to calculate CAGR, you must begin with the total return. In our above example, the total return was 1.70 (70%). We also know that the investment was held for 5 years. Multiply the total return (1.7) by the x root (x being the number of years the investment was held). This can be simplified by taking the inverse of the root and using it as the exponent. In our example, 1/5 or 0.2 (had the number of years been 2, you should have taken ½ or 0.5 as the exponent, for three years 1/3 or 0.33 would be the exponent, for 4 years the exponent would be ¼ or 0.25, etc.). In our example, CAGR would be calculated as follows:

$1.7 \wedge (0.2) = 1.1119$ or 11.19% CAGR

Again, recall that 1.0 represents the principal value which must be subtracted.

1.1119 -1 = 0.1119 or 11.19% CAGR expressed as a percentage.

In other words, if the gains of the mutual fund investment were smoothened at $(1.7.) \wedge 1/5$, the investment grew at 11.19% compounded annually.

SEBI has formulated guidelines regarding calculation and publication of returns by mutual funds in scheme information documents, advertisements, etc. For returns of periods less than a year, returns can be shown only on an absolute basis. The returns cannot be annualised. However, liquid funds can annualise returns, provided the returns are not misleading. For periods more than a year, CAGR has to be used. Every mutual fund should highlight CAGR for the past one, three and five years of the scheme, or since inception.

Past Performance of the Fund

Though past performance alone cannot be indicative of future performance, it is, frankly, the only quantitative way to judge how good a fund is at present. By looking at the performance of mutual funds over different periods, you can select consistent performers.

Compare returns of diverse funds at appropriate time periods: Choice of an appropriate time period is of paramount importance while measuring or comparing returns. The time period over which returns have to be compared and evaluated has to be the same over which that fund type is meant to be invested in. If you are comparing equity funds, you should use 3 to 5-year returns. This should not be the case with all the funds. Liquid funds are fixed-income instruments of very short maturities. So, it makes sense to compare these funds on the basis of their six-month returns.

Compare returns across funds within the same category: Compare apples with apples and not with oranges, i.e. compare funds within a category. For instance, if you are evaluating Sundaram Select Midcap Fund for investment, you should compare its returns with other predominantly mid-cap diversified equity funds. Comparing it with large cap funds will deliver erroneous results because the risk-reward relationship between mid-cap and large cap funds is not comparable. Peer group comparison includes a careful study of the investment objective, investment pattern, risk profile, size of the fund, credit profile, average maturity and expense ratios.

Compare returns against those of the benchmark index: Regulations demand that every fund mentions a benchmark index in the offer document. Benchmarks are independent portfolios not managed by any fund manager, but are representative of the behaviour of returns from the markets. The benchmark index serves the dual purpose of being a guide-post for both the fund manager and the investing community. All eyes must be on the benchmark index and how the fund has fared against it. During market turbulence, similar to the one witnessed during the first half of 2008, you will find many equity funds trailing (or underperforming) their benchmark indices. The funds that can outperform their benchmark indices during stock market volatility must be marked closely. The concept of benchmarking for performance evaluation is of paramount importance.

Compare active equity fund performance against market indices as benchmarks. Diversified funds need to have a diversified index, such as BSE Sensex or S&P CNX Nifty or BSE 200 or BSE 500 or CNX 100 or S&P CNX 500 as a benchmark. Sectoral funds select sectoral indices such as BSE Bankex, BSE FMCG Index, CNX Infrastructure Index and CNX Energy Index. BSE Sensex and S&P CNX Nifty are calculated based on 30 (in the case of Sensex) and 50 (in the case of Nifty) large companies. Thus, these indices are appropriate benchmarks for diversified equity funds that invest in large companies. A diversified equity fund that has chosen mid-cap stocks as its investment universe, would find mid cap indices such as CNX Midcap or Nifty Midcap 50 or BSE Midcap to be better benchmarks. Some diversified equity funds prefer to have fewer stocks in their portfolio. For such schemes, appropriate benchmarks are narrow indices similar to BSE Sensex and NSE Nifty, which are calculated based on fewer stocks. Schemes that propose to invest in more number of companies will prefer broader indices such as BSE 100 (based on 100 stocks), BSE 200 (based on 200 stocks) and S&P CNX 500 (based on 500 stocks). Arbitrage funds invest in equities, but their underlying exposure is not to the equity market. The reason for this seemingly contradictory statement is that arbitrage funds take opposite positions in the cash and Futures and Options (F&O) markets. Apart from various technical factors, funding cost drives the spread between the 2 markets. Therefore, the benchmark for an arbitrage fund is generally a short-term money market index, although these are categorised as equity schemes.

In the case of debt funds, interest rates on alternative investments serve as benchmarks whereas interest rates of short-term Government instruments serve as benchmarks in the case of liquid funds. According to SEBI guidelines, the benchmark for debt (and balanced schemes) should be developed by research and rating agencies recommended by AMFI. CRISIL, ICICI Securities and NSE have developed various such indices. NSE's MIBOR is based on short-term money market. NSE similarly has indices for the Government securities market. These are available for different variations such as Composite, 1–3 years, 3–8 years, 8+ years, Treasury Bills index, etc. ICICI Securities' Sovereign Bond Index (I-Bex) is again calculated based on Government securities. It consists of an umbrella index covering the entire market and sub-indices catering to 3 contiguous maturity buckets. The 3 sub-indices are Si-Bex (1 to 3 years), Mi-Bex (3 to 7 years) and Li-Bex (more than 7 years). CRISIL gives out the values of CRISIL Gilt Bond Index and the AAA Corporate Bond Index. Some of its other debt indices are CRISIL CompBEX – Composite Bond Index, CRISIL LiquiFEX – Liquid Fund Index, CRISIL STBEX – Short-Term Bond Index, CRISIL Debt Hybrid Index – 60:40 and CRISIL Debt Hybrid Index – 75:25. Certain aspects of the investment objective drive the choice of benchmark in debt schemes. Liquid schemes invest in securities of less than 61 days maturity. Therefore, a short-term money market benchmark like NSE's MIBOR or CRISIL LiquiFEX is suitable. Non-liquid schemes can use one of the other indices mentioned above, depending on the nature of their portfolio. Gilt funds invest only in Government securities. Therefore, indices based on Government securities are appropriate. Debt funds that invest in a wide range of Government and non-government securities need to choose benchmarks that are calculated based on a diverse mix of debt securities. In the absence of a vibrant market for non-government securities, related indices are not so widely available. CRISIL's AAA corporate bond index is one such non-government securities based index.

Hybrid funds invest in a mix of debt and equity. Therefore, a blend of an equity and debt index can be considered. For instance, a hybrid scheme with asset allocation of about 65% in equity and balance in debt can use a synthetic index that is calculated as 65% of BSE Sensex and 35% of I-Bex. CRISIL has also created some blended indices. CRISIL MIPEX is suitable for Monthly Income Plans; CRISIL BalanCEX can be considered by balanced funds. However, it should be noted that, considering the prevailing tax laws, the balanced funds, in general maintain allocation of more than 65% of the NAV in equity shares. This helps them to maintain tax status as equity-oriented funds with incidental tax benefits to investors.

Gold price would be the benchmark for Gold ETFs. A few real estate services companies have developed real estate indices. These have shorter histories and are yet to earn the wider acceptance that the equity indices enjoy. For international funds, the benchmark would depend on where the scheme proposes to invest. Thus, a scheme seeking to invest in China might have the Chinese index, Hang Seng, as a benchmark. S&P 500 may be appropriate for a scheme that would invest largely in the US market.

A scheme that seeks to invest across a number of countries, can structure a synthetic index that would be a blend of the indices relevant to the countries where it proposes to invest.

According to SEBI regulations, at least one of the benchmarks for equity schemes has to be either the Nifty or Sensex. The other benchmark could be the one disclosed by the fund house in the scheme information document (SID). Similarly, the benchmark for debt schemes should be either the 364-day T-bill rate or the 10-year G-Sec rate depending on the maturity profile of the scheme. There could be a separate benchmark for the scheme disclosed in the SID. While disclosing the performance of balanced schemes, one of the benchmarks should be a composite of Nifty and G-Sec, apart from the benchmark disclosed in the SID.

Compare against the fund's own performance: Besides comparing a fund with its peers and benchmark index, you should evaluate its historical performance. Not all funds show stability in performance over the years. Many of them slip up. Only a few manage to sustain the good work they have done year after year and market cycle after market cycle. As equities are best equipped to deliver returns over longer time frames (3 to 5 years or even more), investments in diversified equity funds should be made with a long-term perspective. Comparing a fund over a longer time frame will also give you a good idea about how the fund has fared over a stock market cycle (boom and bust). Therefore, it is important to see whether the fund's return history is long enough for it to have seen all kinds of market cycles.

Do not overrate past fund performance: One of the most common ways of selecting a mutual fund is to invest with the crowd in today's hot funds. Unfortunately, jumping from one winning fund to another is a recipe for disaster. Buying the equity fund that was yesterday's best-seller is not a strategy that produces excellent returns. At the same time, you do not have to go fully in the opposite direction and ignore these hot funds; instead, you should understand their limitations and strengths. They became best-selling funds because they have merit, but you have to assess that merit in the context of your own well-diversified portfolio and not the crowd's current rush for it. There is an important role that past performance can play in helping you to make your fund selections. Returns for mutual fund schemes are displayed on a compounded annualised basis, especially for periods in excess of one year. While the need to present the returns in the given form is a statutory requirement, you should realise that returns computed using the CAGR can present a distorted picture. CAGR provides a smoothed return, i.e. the steady rate of growth. A strong surge at the end of the period can have a positive impact on the historic returns as well. While you should disregard a single aggregate number showing a fund's past long-term return, you can learn a great deal by studying the nature of its past returns. Above all, look for consistent performance.

All said and done, you must accept the fact that over time, any fund, irrespective of past performance, will inevitably revert towards the mean. Mean refers to the market mean (returns of the market as a whole) reduced by the costs the fund incurs. Never think you know more than the market. No one does.

Key Considerations about Performance

Past performance cannot predict future results: This year's top-performing funds are not necessarily going to be next year's winners.

Short-term returns may not tell the whole story: Looking at fund performance over a longer period, such as 10 years, can give you a better picture of how the fund has performed during market fluctuations and how it compares to funds with similar objectives. In the words of John Bogle, "money invested for the long-term, like the proverbial plodding tortoise, wins the race over speculative money, analogous to the fits and starts of the hare"

The Risk of Inflation: It may seem logical that the safest investment is one that seeks to preserve your money, such as certificates of deposit (bank CDs) or money market funds. While these instruments may play an important role in your overall financial plan, you need to be aware that they may not protect your assets against an easy-to-overlook risk – inflation. Think of inflation as an invisible tax that erodes the purchasing power of any investment. To maintain an investment's purchasing power, its total return must keep pace with the inflation rate.

The Quarterly Review: It is a good idea to review your investment plan at least once a quarter. In view of the fact that different investments grow at different paces, your current distribution of money among stocks, bonds and money market funds may no longer correspond with your original allocations. If this happens with your investments, you will probably want to consider whether to redistribute some money to bring your allocations back in line with your plan.

Changing Lifestyles: In addition to the quarterly review, whenever you make a major life change, it is time to reassess your overall financial situation. Some common examples of life changes are:

* getting married or divorced;
* having a child;
* buying a house;
* starting your own business;
* meeting educational expenses of children;
* switching careers; and
* retirement.

Most of these events are likely to affect your ability to invest, your time horizon and your overall financial picture, both short-term and long-term. It is never easy to find the time to review your investment plan when you are in the midst of any of these life changes, but it is worth making the effort. You do not want to enter a new phase of your life with a plan that was designed for different circumstances. By staying on course with your asset allocations, you will help ensure that your overall portfolio continues to work effectively towards achieving your investment goals.

The use of the word performance does not mean that you should limit your interest solely to return. Risk is a crucial element in investing and the subject matter of the next chapter.

Chapter 17

Understanding the Risks

Risk – the Second Dimension

"There is little certainty in investing. As long-term investors, however, we cannot afford to let the apocalyptic possibilities frighten us away from the markets. For without risk there is no return."

— John Bogle

That 'risk and return are two sides of the same coin' is an old cliché but highly relevant in the context of mutual fund performance. Investors should be aware of the effect the general market has on the investment performance of a mutual fund. The performance assessment of mutual funds should be based not only on how much a fund gains in a bull market, but also on how gradually it falls in a bear market. This throws light on the importance of reducing risks in a falling market. But the task of the fund manager to add value cannot be underplayed. A fund manager, who reduces risks by booking profits, has also to be careful in reinvesting. If the reinvestment is badly managed, the returns may not be superior.

Another important risk consideration revolves around the management practices of the fund itself. If the portfolio is managed conservatively, the risk of a loss in capital is likely to be much less than for aggressively managed funds. But, a conservatively managed portfolio does not necessarily eliminate all price volatility. The securities in the portfolio are still subject to inflation, interest rate and general market risks.

In general, mutual funds are not considered to be too risky because they invest in dozens or, in some cases, even hundreds of stocks. But, mutual funds, being market-linked, are prime candidates for stock market related risks. The 5 aspects that you should take into account while analysing risks in investing in mutual funds are volatility of the fund as indicated by the Standard Deviation and risk-adjusted returns as calculated by the Sharpe Ratio, Treynor Ratio, Beta and Alpha. While **Standard Deviation** shows the degree of risk taken on by the fund, **Sharpe Ratio** shows the return generated by the fund per unit of total risk taken. **Treynor Ratio** shows the return generated by the fund per unit of systematic risk taken. **Beta** shows how much a fund moves when compared to an appropriate index. **Alpha** represents the difference between a mutual fund's actual performance and the performance that would be expected based on the level of risk taken by the manager.

Standard Determinants of Risk

Standard Deviation

Standard deviation is a measure of total risks of a fund. In other words, it measures the volatility of returns of a fund. It indicates the tendency of the fund's NAV to rise and fall in a short period. It measures the extent to which the NAV fluctuates as compared to the average returns during a period.

A fund that has a consistent four-year return of 3%, for example, would have a mean or average return of 3%. The standard deviation for this fund would then be zero because the fund's return in any given year does not differ from its four-year mean of 3%. On the other hand, a fund, which in each of the last 4 years returned -5%, 17%, 2% and 30% would have a mean return of 11%. The fund would also exhibit a high standard deviation because each year the return of the fund differs from the mean return. The fund is, therefore, more risky because it fluctuates widely between negative and positive returns within a short period. A higher standard deviation means that the returns of the fund have been more volatile than a fund having low standard deviation. **In other words, high standard deviation means high risk.**

For a Sharper Picture

Sharpe Ratio

Information, when not put in the right perspective, can be misleading at times. It is generally assumed that high returns mean better performance. While this may be true in some cases, the real picture of a portfolio's performance can be gauged when the returns it generates are assessed with respect to the risk it assumes.

This is where the Sharpe ratio comes in handy. The downside risk of investing is one aspect that needs to be given due importance. High returns are generally associated with a high degree of volatility, which is not always the case. Hence, to get the right analysis of a portfolio, its returns must be viewed in tune with its risk factor. **The Sharpe ratio assesses the returns generated by a portfolio against per unit of risk undertaken.**

Mathematically, the Sharpe ratio is the difference between the portfolio's returns over and above the returns earned on a risk-free investment divided by the standard deviation of the portfolio. It is the reward-to-volatility ratio. A higher Sharpe ratio represents a higher return generated per unit of risk. This process of comparing the risk-adjusted returns of two portfolios gives us an insight into the efficiency of fund management as well. A portfolio could deliver superlative returns by assuming significant risk, but a superior portfolio is constructed when the manager is able to rationalise the amount of risk taken to deliver high returns.

However, while looking at the Sharpe ratio, you have to keep in mind that in isolation, it has no meaning. It can only be used as a comparative tool. Thus, the Sharpe ratio should be used to compare the performance of a number of portfolios or funds. In the case of mutual funds, you can compare the Sharpe ratio of a fund with that of its benchmark index. If the only information available is that the Sharpe ratio of a fund is 1.2, no meaningful inference can be drawn as nothing is known about the peer group performance. Another aspect to look out for is that the ratio can be misleading at times. For example, a low standard deviation can unduly influence results. A fund with low returns but with a relatively mild standard deviation can end up with a high Sharpe ratio. Such a fund will have a very tranquil portfolio and not generate high returns.

Hence, a Sharpe ratio will invariably tell you which of the portfolios under comparison is performing to the best of its abilities. The Sharpe ratio represents the trade-off between risk and returns. At the same time, it also factors in the desire to generate returns, which are higher than those from risk-free returns. Sharpe ratio is the returns generated per unit of risk over the risk-free rate. Risk, in this case, is taken to be the fund's standard deviation. As standard deviation represents the total risk experienced by a fund, the Sharpe ratio reflects the returns generated by undertaking all possible risks. It is thus one single number, which represents the trade-off between risks and returns. **A higher Sharpe ratio is, therefore, better as it represents a higher return generated per unit of risk.**

Treynor Ratio

Similar to the Sharpe ratio, the Treynor ratio (sometimes called reward-to-variability-ratio) also relates excess returns to risk. Systematic risk instead of total risk is used. Identical to Sharpe ratio, Treynor ratio does not quantify the value-added due to active portfolio management. It is a ranking criterion only. A ranking of portfolios based on Treynor ratio is only useful if the funds under consideration are sub-funds of the broader, fully diversified portfolio.

Sharpe ratio and Treynor ratio are unbiased indicators of a fund's performance. This is because it is based solely on quantitative measures. However, it does not account for any risks inherent in a fund's portfolio. For example, if a fund is loaded with technology stocks and the sector is performing well, then all quantitative measures will give such a fund high marks. But the possibility of the sector crashing and with it the fund sinking is not calculated. In view of these possibilities, quantitative tools should be used along with information on the nature of the fund's strategies, its fund management style and risk inherent in the portfolio. **Quantitative tools can be used for screening but they should not be taken as the only indicator of a fund's performance.**

Of Alphas and Betas...

Alpha

Alpha refers to the excess returns over the benchmark index that is generated due to the portfolio manager's skill. It is a statistical measure that helps to measure the risk-reward profile of a mutual fund. **It is a measure of the fund's performance with respect to the performance of the index against which the fund is benchmarked.** In layman's terms, it tells us whether or not the fund has earned returns above or below what it was expected to earn.

A positive alpha indicates that a portfolio has produced returns above the expected level at the same level of risk and a negative alpha suggests that the portfolio underperformed given the same level of risk assumed. For example, if the alpha value of the fund is 1%, it means that the fund has outperformed its benchmark index by 1%. Conversely, the negative value of alpha, say -1% indicates that the fund has underperformed its benchmark index by 1%.

Beta

Beta is a statistical measure that shows how sensitive a fund is to market moves. Let's say, the Sensex moves by 25%; a fund's beta number will tell you whether the fund's returns will be more than or less than this. The beta value for an index itself is taken as one. Equity funds can have beta values, which can be above one, less than one, or equal to one. By multiplying the beta value of a fund with the expected percentage movement of an index, the expected movement in the fund can be determined. Thus, if a fund has a beta of 1.2 and the market is expected to move up by 10%, the fund should move by 12% (obtained by multiplying 1.2 by 10). Similarly, if the market loses 10%, the fund should lose 12%.

A low-beta fund will rise less than the market on the way up and lose less on the way down. When safety of investment is important, a fund with a beta of less than one is a better option. Such a fund may not gain much more than the market on the upside. It will protect returns better when the market falls.

Essentially, beta expresses the fundamental trade-off between minimising risk and maximising return. A fund with a beta of 1 will historically move in the same direction of the market. A beta above 1 is more volatile than the overall market, while a beta below 1 is less volatile. So, while you can expect a high return from a fund that has a beta of 2, you will have to expect it to drop much more when the market falls. The effectiveness of the beta depends on the index used to calculate it. It can happen that the index bears no correlation with the movements in the fund.

R-squared

If beta is calculated for a large cap fund against a mid-cap index, the resulting value will have no meaning. This is because the fund will not move in tandem with the index. Due to this reason, it is essential to take a look at a statistical value called 'R-squared' (or ex-marks of the portfolio) along with beta. **The 'R-squared' value shows how reliable the beta number is.** 'R-squared' values range between 0 and 1, where '0' represents the least correlation and '1' represents complete correlation. If a fund's beta has an 'R-squared' value that is close to 1, the beta of the fund should be trusted. On the other hand, an 'R-squared' value that is close to 0 indicates that the beta is not particularly useful because the fund is being compared against an inappropriate benchmark.

Thus, an index fund investing in the Sensex should have an 'R-squared' value of 1 when compared to the Sensex. For equity diversified funds, an 'R-squared' value greater than 0.8 is generally accepted to mean that the underlying beta value is reliable and can be used for the fund.

Diversification

Diversification can reduce risk. Depending on your risk tolerance and how long you plan to stay invested, it may be advisable to own some equity funds and some debt funds. Select funds in each asset allocation category and spread your investment. You might not get as much diversification as you think if all your funds are with the same AMC, since they may share research and recommendations. The same is true if you have multiple funds with the same profile or investment strategy. Their returns will most likely be similar. Too many funds, on the other hand, will give you about the same effect as an index fund, except that your expenses will be higher. Do not underestimate the value of diversification by putting all your money into one single fund. An investor who puts all his eggs in one basket may come home to find someone has been making scrambled eggs in his kitchen.

Risk Appetite

It is equally important to understand your risk appetite. The concept of risk is multifaceted having different meanings for different investors. Risk appetite varies from investor to investor. Different investors have quite different and legitimate perceptions and concerns about risk, depending upon, among other things, their time horizon, goals, financial situations, other investments in their portfolio and basic attitude. In the case of an investor concerned about potential short-term loss, money market funds may rightly be characterised as low-risk and aggressive growth stocks as just the opposite. Conversely, for an investor defining risk as the potential long-term loss of purchasing power (inflation) aggressive growth stocks could be considered low-risk and money market funds as high risk. Short-term fluctuations are not relevant for long-term investors who have the discipline, patience and understanding to deal with them. Equity funds are actually less risky than money market funds for those with long-term horizons. For an 85-year old, fearful of near-term losses, money market mutual funds and short-term bond funds are low-risk avenues and aggressive growth funds are highly risky ones. Conversely, for a 30-year old, mainly concerned about loss of purchasing power, the opposite is true.

Similar to any other investment, mutual fund investment also has a lot of risks involved. Though the funds are managed by professionals and fund houses have adequate risk management policies in place, understanding the various risks involved in investment strategies adopted by fund managers will help you in choosing the right scheme depending on your risk appetite.

Risk Hierarchy of Different Mutual Funds

Different mutual fund schemes are exposed to different levels of risk, which flow from the uniqueness of the markets they invest in. You should know the level of risks associated with these schemes before investing.

Equity markets seek to reflect the value in the real economy. In performing this role, certain significant risks come up. The real economy goes through cycles. In the long run, equity markets are a good barometer of the real economy – but in the short run, markets tend to get over-optimistic or over-pessimistic, leading to spells of greed and fear. Equity markets, therefore, tend to be volatile. But the nature of the mutual fund portfolio influences scheme risk to varying degrees. While the sector funds are the most risky by virtue of their concentration risk, thematic funds are a tad better and diversified funds are relatively less risky. Midcap funds are more risky than large cap funds on account of their low liquidity while contra funds suffer from high risk of misjudgement. Dividend yield funds invest in shares whose prices fluctuate less, but offer attractive returns in the form of dividend. Such funds offer equity exposure with lower downside. In arbitrage funds, the risks are arbitraged, i.e. cancelled out, normally between the cash market and the F&O market. Therefore, the risk in this category of funds turns out to be the lowest among equity funds – even lower than diversified equity funds. The returns too are lower – more in line with money market returns, rather than equity market returns. However, one should not forget the **basis risk** in an arbitrage fund – the risk that both cash and F&O position on a company cannot be reversed at the same time. During the time gap between unwinding of the two positions, the market can move adverse to the scheme.

Unlike equity, debt securities are repayable on maturity. Thus, whatever the imperfections in the market, a solvent issuer will still repay the amount promised, on maturity. This assured value on maturity makes debt a lot safer than equity. Despite the assured value on maturity, debt securities fluctuate in value, with changes in yield in the overall market. The interest rates in the economy are influenced by factors beyond the control of any single entity. Policies of the Government and RBI influence interest rates and are unpredictable. A fund manager taking a wrong call on the direction of interest rates can seriously affect the fund performance. The debt market, especially the non-government segment, is not as vibrant and liquid as the equity market. Therefore, there is the possibility of not finding a buyer for the securities held. Similarly, when securities are not traded in the market, an element of subjectivity creeps into their valuation and therefore the NAV. In the past, when the markets turned illiquid, RBI has stepped in to make it easier for mutual funds to operate. Further, SEBI has laid down detailed portfolio valuation guidelines to enhance the transparency of NAV. Short maturity securities suffer lesser fluctuation in value, as compared to the ones with longer tenor. Therefore, liquid schemes, which invest in securities of up to 61 days maturity, have the lowest risk amongst all kinds of schemes. Even gilt schemes, which invest in only Government securities, have higher risk than liquid schemes because their NAV can fluctuate a lot more, on account of changes in yield in the market. Greater the proportion of longer maturity securities in the portfolio, higher would be the fluctuation in NAV. Since Fixed Maturity Plans align the maturity of their portfolio to the maturity of the scheme, the yield is relatively more predictable. However, such predictability is only on maturity, when the investee company will repay the principal to the scheme. In the interim, the value of these securities will fluctuate in line with the market and, therefore, the scheme's NAV too will fluctuate. If the FMP is structured on the basis of investment in non-government paper, then the credit risk is an issue. A particularly risky category of debt funds is junk bond schemes. Also called high-yield bond schemes, they invest in securities of poor credit quality. SEBI regulations, however, limit the exposure that mutual fund schemes can take to unrated debt securities and debt securities that are below investment grade. Therefore, this risky category of mutual fund scheme is not offered by Indian mutual funds.

Hybrid funds invest in a mix of debt and equity. It is rare for both debt and equity markets to fare poorly at the same time. Since the performance of the scheme is linked to the performance of these 2 distinct asset classes, the risk in the scheme is reduced. But, in a Monthly Income Plan, it is possible that losses in the equity component eat into the profits in the debt component of the portfolio. If the scheme has no profits to distribute, then no dividend will be declared. Thus, the investor may not get the monthly income implicit in the name Monthly Income Plan. Some hybrid schemes offer significant asset allocation flexibility to the fund manager. These are risky for investors, because there is always the risk that the fund manager may take a wrong asset allocation call. Further, investors do not know whether they are investing in a debt scheme or an equity scheme. Therefore, investors do not have clarity on whether to treat it as equity or debt, in the asset allocation for their financial plan.

The graphical representation hereunder provides a clear picture of the relationship between mutual funds and the levels of risk associated with these funds:

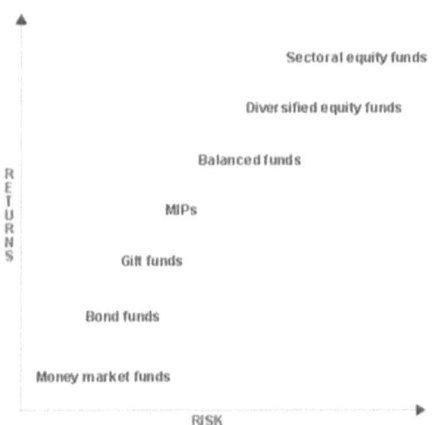

Source: www.hsbc.co.in

Figure 17.1   Risk Hierarchy of Different Mutual Funds

A fund with low risk is the one with the lowest standard deviation, the highest Sharpe ratio and Treynor ratio within its peer group, beta closer to one and alpha above one. It is advisable for you to evaluate these measures on a historical basis so as to identify the most consistent performers. Such rigorous research is done by some mutual fund sites like www.valueresearchonline.com which rate the risk profile of funds on a five-point scale.

While no amount of research can guarantee future fund performance, it certainly can reduce the likelihood of unintended risk by carefully analysing and interpreting risk statistics. In a declining market, sometimes this understanding may just provide the marginal comfort that separates those who ride out storms from those who do not.

Chapter 18
Delving Deep for Debt Funds
Returns Revisited – the First Dimension

The process of performance evaluation of mutual funds discussed so far applies to debt funds as well. But you need to familiarise yourself with certain aspects unique to debt funds. Let us outline some critical points you should consider to make an educated choice while selecting a debt fund. A broad overview was provided in the course of our discussion on debt fund fact sheets. Now, we shall delve a little deeper.

Asset allocation: A debt fund invests primarily in corporate debt, Government securities and money market instruments. You need to evaluate the asset allocation of the fund to gauge its volatility. For example, prices of Government securities (gilts) can be volatile in times of economic and political turbulence and this leads to higher uncertainty, i.e. more risk. A well-diversified portfolio is a strong positive. The ideal debt fund has 25% in gilts, 70% in corporate debt (including financial institutions) and 5% in cash/call.

Rating profile: The quality of the portfolio is of paramount importance. Look out for securities with 'AAA' rating, as this reduces the credit or default risk. The ideal debt fund has 60% exposure to AAA-rated securities and 25% exposure to gilts, which have a sovereign rating.

Maturity profile: Yield curve is the relation between the interest rate (or cost of borrowing) and the time to maturity of the debt for a given borrower. You need to find out the maturity of the various securities in which the mutual fund has invested. Then, identify the securities with low maturity. This is because an instrument having low maturity carries a low coupon rate and *vice versa*. So any change in the interest rate has a lesser effect on the price of the instrument of low maturity than the higher one. Moreover, there is an inverse relationship between the bond prices and the interest rate. When the interest rate falls, the bond prices move up and *vice versa*. A fund does not have a fixed maturity since the fund varies the composition of its portfolio in order to adjust its maturity in accordance with the interest rate scenario. Depending on the interest rate view of the fund house, the fund manager increases the fund's average maturity or shortens it mainly through the gilt route. Maturity is normally controlled through investments in gilts (normally at the longer end) and in corporate debt (normally at the short to medium end). The ideal debt fund has about 40% in less than 3-year paper and 35% in 4 to 6-year paper. Debt funds come with various options – short-term plans, long-term plans and so on. You should invest in debt schemes looking at your investment horizon. For short-term horizons, you should look at investing in liquid funds (for a one month horizon) or short-term debt plans (for 1 to 6 months). For horizons above 6 months, you should look at debt schemes or long-term gilt schemes. A good debt fund has an exit load of 0.25% to 0.5% if redeemed within 3 or 6 months. You should avoid a debt fund having a higher load structure. As far as performance is concerned, look at the returns given by the fund over a period of time – at least over 12 months – to get a fairly good idea and 36 months to judge consistency in performance. If you want to evaluate its dividend paying track record, then look at the dividend history for consistency.

Disclosure Norms for Debt Funds

In a move to enable investors to take more informed decisions, SEBI tightened disclosure norms for closed-end debt-oriented mutual fund schemes in August 2011. The regulator had barred communication pertaining to indicative portfolio and indicative yields by fund houses and distributors on mutual fund products in January 2009. From August 2011, fund houses are required to disclose their credit evaluation policy for investments in debt securities and also the list of sectors they would not be investing in. Further, fund managers need to disclose the type of instruments their schemes propose to invest in, including commercial papers, certificates of deposits and treasury bills. Mutual funds disclose the floors and ceilings within a range of 5% of the intended allocation against each sub-asset class/credit rating. For instance, if fund houses are investing 2–3% in a AAA-rated bank certificate of deposit, the same has to be disclosed. Once the new fund offer closes, asset management companies report the percentage allocation and the final portfolio. Variations between indicative portfolio allocation and final portfolio are not permissible.

Valuation Methodology for Debt Funds

The methodology of valuing debt instruments was arbitrary and many funds used it to their advantage. From August 1, 2010, it is more standardised and there are independent agencies monitoring this. Debt securities, where the residual maturity is up to 91 days (60 days w.e.f. September 30, 2012), are valued at the average price at which they are traded on a particular day or MTM basis. In case they are not traded, the valuation is on an amortisation basis, which means writing off the difference between the face value of a security and its cost over the life of the instrument.

For the securities with a residual maturity of more than 91 days (60 days w.e.f. September 30, 2012) the valuation is at the average price for that particular valuation date. In case the securities are not traded, they are valued on a mark-to-model basis of valuation provided by an independent third party. Rating agencies, CRISIL and ICRA provide a matrix of spread adjustments over the benchmark yields or simply spread that is to be added to the yield of a widely traded benchmark security to arrive at yield and valuation of a less-traded one. At the heart of this matrix lie the coupon rates of G-secs that mature at different points in time. But since your liquid fund holds other scrips such as certificates of deposit (short-term securities issued by banks) and/or commercial papers (short-term securities issued by firms), the matrix gives out a mark-up—over and above the Government security rates—across all these tenors and across credit ratings. For instance, if the matrix says that the one to two-year G-sec coupon rate is 10% and the mark-up of a "AAA" rated scrip is 0.5%, then your debt fund manager values its AAA-rated security at 10.50%. Fund houses use this rate to arrive at the price of the security that gets reflected in your debt fund's net asset value (NAV). Valuers basically provide a mathematical and statistical matrix from which fund houses derive NAVs. The CRISIL Bond Valuation service is being used by mutual funds so as to ensure the best practice of consistency in their valuation of debt securities. The methodology for CRISIL's Bond Valuation service is based on the SEBI guidelines for valuation of debt securities. In the case of banks, valuation of bonds – which is done by Fixed-Income Money

Market and Derivatives Association – is governed by the RBI. Pension funds are getting valuations for debt instruments done on an in-house basis.

Interestingly, SEBI has also brought under its purview debt schemes investing in unlisted securities. At the time of investment, asset management companies ensure that the total exposure in such unlisted securities does not exceed 5% of the total AUM of the scheme. There might also be holdings or securities held by the mutual fund that are not covered under any existing valuation guidelines. In such a situation, the mutual fund has to inform AMFI that such a situation has arisen. All mutual funds provide transaction details, including inter-scheme transfers of money market and debt securities on a daily basis to CRISIL and ICRA, the agencies entrusted for providing the benchmark yield/matrix of spread over risk-free benchmark yield. Submission of data helps in preparation of valuation matrix by these agencies and improvement of uniformity and accuracy of valuation in the mutual funds industry.

The AMC provides for the periodic review of the valuation policies and procedures to ensure the appropriateness and accuracy of the methodologies used and its effective implementation in valuing the securities/assets. The Board of Trustees and the Board of AMC are updated of these developments at appropriate intervals. The valuation policies and procedures are regularly reviewed (at least once in a financial year) by an independent auditor to ensure their continued appropriateness.

Chapter 19

The Taxing Question – Which Option to Opt For?

Keep All Options Open

The choice is endless. You decided what type of fund to invest in and that was a mammoth task in itself. But it did not stop there. Arrays of questions were then hurled at you. "Would you choose the dividend option or the growth option?" "Would you opt for a dividend payout or dividend reinvestment?" Do not get bogged down by these questions.

An illustration will aid you in finding answers to these questions. Let us say you own 100 units of a mutual fund whose current NAV is Rs. 20. Your investment value is Rs. 2,000 (100 × 20). Now, the scheme declares a dividend of 10%. It is pertinent to note that dividend is always a percentage of the face value. Face value is the price of one unit of a fund and is Rs. 10. So, 10% of face value would be Re. 1 per unit. For the bonus plan, the scheme declares a bonus of 1:10. This means an additional unit for every 10 units held.

This is what will happen under the various options:

Growth Option: The fund reinvests the money it would otherwise pay out in the form of a dividend. This money increases the NAV of growth option of the fund. That is why the NAV of the growth option is higher than that of the dividend option. You can realise a higher capital gain on the same number of units you originally purchased. The onus of booking profits (by way of redemption) lies solely on you. Sale of units results in a decrease in the number of units held by you with the NAV remaining unchanged.

Dividend Payout Option: You will get Rs. 100 as dividend while the NAV falls to Rs. 19. Effectively, the dividend received from the fund house is set off by a reduction in the fund's NAV. Moreover, your investment value falls to Rs. 1,900 (unlike all other options where the investment value remains unchanged).

Dividend Reinvestment Option: The dividend of Rs. 100 is not paid to you. Instead, 5.263 (100/19) more units are purchased at the revised NAV of Rs. 19. Consequently, you have more units to your credit every time a dividend is declared, but the NAV declines.

Bonus Option: It is similar to the dividend reinvestment option, except that the fund announces the bonus ratio instead of dividend. You get 10 more units, because of which the NAV falls to Rs. 18.1818 (2000/110). Earlier, long-term capital gains were taxed at a lower rate than dividends. This option is no longer offered since dividends do not attract tax.

Switch Option: It provides you with a simple and speedy way to shift investments from one scheme/option to another. You can opt to switch units between dividend plan and growth plan at NAV-based prices. Switching is also allowed into/from other select open-end schemes within a fund family. This option involves STT (Securities Transaction Tax).

Clearly, there is very little difference between the various options in terms of returns. If you are keen on receiving an income at various intervals, go for the **dividend option**. But the dividend is not guaranteed. Declaration of dividend is done at the fund's discretion. This means funds can decide to skip declaring a dividend one year, or vary the quantum of dividend from year to year. Choosing the dividend option is not for those of you, who seek regular income from equity funds. Rather, it is for those of you, who are not sure how to time your investments in funds. History suggests that funds often pay hefty dividends when they sense they are nearing a market peak. For instance, many top-performing funds declared huge dividends before the tech meltdown in 2000. With the dividend option, you are able to cash in on your investments in a timely manner. Moreover, you get tax benefits for dividend payout. For people falling in high tax slab, getting income by way of dividends may offer an avenue to save tax.

In the case of a **dividend reinvestment option**, you can keep the amount invested to be the same but still save a bit on the tax front. You can take advantage of the tax benefits that come in the form of dividends while maintaining your total overall investment. Under this, when a dividend is declared, you are entitled to the payout. However, this will not be received in cash but would be reinvested back into the scheme at the then prevailing NAV. Due to this, the number of units held will go on increasing with each dividend payout, although no amount will be received. At any time up to maturity, you can have these units redeemed. The benefit is that there is a dividend being received, which is then being invested back into the fund automatically, so that you do not have to bother about looking for investment avenues.

In the case of a long-term investment (which is the norm for equity investments) the **growth option** enables you to enjoy the benefits of compounding. If you are looking at a long-term investment and are not interested in money being given to you at various intervals, the growth option is meant for you. In the growth option, the decision to exit is solely at your discretion. You run the risk of exiting too early and missing out on potential returns, or exiting too late and witnessing sharp erosion of your portfolio returns. But this dilemma of timing is faced only by short-term investors – those with a time horizon of less than 5 years. If you are willing to stay with the market over a 10-year time frame through its ups and downs, the growth option is better. If you hold on, returns from the investment will eventually be healthy, after the temporary fluctuations. There is a reinvestment risk associated with opting for the dividend option. You typically reinvest dividend income in bank deposits or liquid funds, which may under-perform equities over the long term. In case you opt for the growth plan, the gains accumulate in the NAV of the fund. Here, whenever you sell the units, there will be a capital gain or loss. In the case of funds other than equity funds, this will be short-term if the units are sold before 36 months and long-term if sold after 36 months. In the case of long-term gains, there is a concessional tax treatment of a flat 20% (plus 15% surcharge and 3% cess) with indexation benefits. In the case of equity-oriented mutual funds held for one year or more, long-term capital gains are exempt from tax.

Choose between the various options based solely on your need for liquidity and tax planning. In the light of this, you should:

Opt for the dividend option if you are a conservative investor having a short time frame and uncertain as to when you will need cash. You can also opt for the dividend option for riskier funds such as mid-cap funds or theme/sector funds.

Opt for the growth option if you are a long-term investor and do not need the funds you have committed to equity any time soon. But remember to periodically rebalance your equity portfolio in tune with your changing requirements and risk profile.

Chapter 20

Turn to Towering Taxes
The Third Dimension

Costs form the crux of the third dimension of mutual fund investment. Loads and expense ratio were elucidated in Section III on concepts. The towering tax questions, an integral part of costs, are being answered in this chapter since a clear understanding of the various types of funds (elaborated in Section IV) is a prerequisite for analysing their tax implications.

There are essentially **2 kinds of incomes that you would earn from mutual funds – Dividends and Capital Gains.** If you hold on to your mutual fund investment in funds other than equity funds for more than 3 years (it was one year till July 10, 2014), it is considered to be a long-term capital asset. Sale of a long-term capital asset attracts long-term capital gains or losses and sale of a short-term capital asset attracts short-term capital gains or losses. However, in the case of equity-oriented mutual funds held for one year or more, long-term capital gains are exempt from tax. Tax treatment differs according to the kind of income and the tenure of investment besides the type of mutual fund. *The tax rates given in the book are for the financial year 2016–17.*

Dividends from mutual funds are completely tax-free in your hands. The NAV of the fund falls more than the dividend declared. This is due to the fact that the **DDT** paid by the mutual fund is deducted from the dividend itself. Dividend Distribution Tax @28.84% (including cess and surcharge) for liquid and money market funds as well as for other debt-oriented funds and 5.768% in the case of Infrastructure Debt Funds for Non-Resident Indians (NRIs) is payable by the mutual fund directly to the exchequer, before dividend is distributed to the investors. So, in effect, the investors would stand to receive lesser dividend to the extent of DDT. The Finance Bill, 2014, had changed the way in which DDT is computed. This impacts companies, mutual fund houses, as well as investors. Earlier DDT was calculated on the amount of net dividend to be distributed. However, companies and mutual funds used to compute DDT on the net distributable profits, i.e. after reducing the amount of tax, by tweaking the formula to reduce the tax outgo. Hence, DDT was calculated on a lower base, reducing the effective payout. The amount of distributable income or dividend by the unit-holder of a mutual fund or shareholder of a domestic company would now be grossed up for the purpose of computing DDT, thereby leading to a higher DDT outgo. This tax impact will be adjusted through the NAV of the fund and the investor will end up earning less. **Equity-oriented schemes are exempted from this tax.** For this purpose, equity-oriented schemes have been defined as those schemes that have more than 65% of their assets in the form of equity. The equity allocation is calculated based on the weekly average net assets in equities. If this average is below 65%, the fund stands to forfeit its equity-oriented status.

Long-Term Capital Gain (LTCG) is completely tax-free in the case of investments in equity-oriented mutual funds held for more than 12 months. In the case of debt-oriented funds, long-term capital gain attracted tax at 20% with indexation benefit or 10% without indexation benefit, whichever is lower for the period up to July 10, 2014. In the case of NRIs, it was 10% without indexation for unlisted units. Indexation is simply using the cost inflation index tables published by the Government once a year to increase the investor's investment cost to the extent of inflation. This is good because it reduces the amount of capital gain and as a result, the amount of tax payable by the investor. With effect from July 11, 2014, long-term capital gain is 20% with indexation for individuals, corporates and NRIs (for listed units only). For unlisted units held by NRIs, long-term capital gain is 10% without indexation.

Short-Term Capital Gain (STCG) is taxable at 17.7675% (15% including 15% surcharge and 3% cess) in the case of equity-oriented funds provided such transactions are subject to STT. In the case of debt-oriented funds, short-term capital gain is taxed at the tax rate applicable to the individual's total income. Since long-term capital gain is tax-free in the case of equity-oriented funds, long-term capital loss will not be available for set off against capital gain. Short-term capital loss will, however, be available for set off against short-term capital gain. While long-term capital losses can only be set-off against long-term capital gains, short-term capital losses can be set-off against both short-term capital gains as well as long-term capital gains. Unadjusted short-term or long-term capital loss can be carried forward for 8 subsequent assessment years.

Tax deducted at source (TDS) is not applicable on capital gains in the case of resident Indians. However, in the case of non-residents, tax will be deducted at source.

Securities Transaction Tax (STT) is being levied on all redemptions (including switch-outs) in equity-oriented mutual funds. STT on sale of units of equity-oriented mutual funds both delivery based through the stock exchange and to the mutual fund is 0.001%. STT on sale of units of equity-oriented mutual funds that is non-delivery based is 0.025%. There is no STT on debt-oriented funds.

The following table gives details of tax on both Long-term and Short-term Capital Gains in respect of equity-oriented as well as debt-oriented mutual funds:

Table 20.1   Long-term and Short-term Capital Gains Tax on Mutual Fund Returns

Long-term capital gains tax	Equity	Debt
Individual	Nil	20 % with indexation (plus surcharge and cess)
Corporate	Nil	20 % with indexation (plus surcharge and cess)
Short-term capital gains tax	**Equity**	**Debt**
Individual	15%*	Taxable at slab rate applicable
Corporate	15%*	30%

Plus 15% surcharge and 3% cess

The table below clearly highlights the tax rates applicable to various types of funds in debt and debt-oriented category:

Table 20.2 Current Tax Rules for Debt and Debt-Related Funds

Category of Assessee	Short-Term Capital Gains Tax	Long-Term Capital Gains Tax	Dividend Income	DDT for Liquid Funds	DDT for Other Funds	TDS
Resident Individual/ Hindu Undivided Families (HUF)	As per slab	20 % with indexation (plus surcharge and cess)	Tax-Free	28.84%*	28.84%*	Nil
Domestic Companies	30%	20 % with indexation (plus surcharge and cess)	Tax-Free	34.608%**	34.608%**	Nil

Category of Assessee	Short-Term Capital Gains Tax	Long-Term Capital Gains Tax	Dividend Income	DDT for Liquid Funds	DDT for Other Funds	TDS
		Listed 20 % with indexation (plus surcharge and cess)		28.84%*	28.84%*	STCG Equity-15% Debt - 30% LTCG
		Unlisted				
NRIs	As per slab	10% without indexation and foreign currency fluctuation benefits (plus surcharge and cess)	Tax-Free			Equity - Nil Debt - 10%@ 20%@@

*25%+12% surcharge+3% cess
**30%+12%surcharge+3% cess
@10% without indexation for unlisted units
@@20% with indexation for listed units
Surcharge at 15% to be levied in the case of individual/ Hindu Undivided Families (HUF) unit-holders where their income exceeds Rs. 1 crore.
Surcharge at 7% to be levied for domestic corporate unit-holders where income exceeds Rs. 1 crore but is less than Rs. 10 crore and at 12%, where income exceeds Rs. 10 crore
Education Cess at 3% will continue to apply on tax plus surcharge.

Tax Benefits on Investment in Mutual Funds

Mutual funds, as an investment vehicle, are one of the most tax-efficient ones. Besides, they offer a variety of products in this category to suit the needs of different investors depending on their time horizon such as ELSS, liquid, floating rate, short and medium-term debt funds, fixed maturity plans and arbitrage funds.

Let us understand what each one of these offers and how tax-efficient they are:

Equity Linked Savings Scheme (ELSS): The amount invested in ELSS would be eligible for deduction up to a maximum of Rs. 1,50,000 under Section 80C.

Liquid Funds: Liquid funds seek to maximise current income commensurate with low levels of risk and high liquidity. These funds primarily invest in low duration and liquid investments such as debt instruments. Liquid funds are ideal for those of you looking to park your short-term funds yielding higher post-tax returns compared to banks as well as for those looking for current income and preservation of capital. Liquid funds as well as the other debt funds currently pay a dividend distribution tax of 28.84% for individual investors and 34.608% for corporate investors.

Floating rate Funds: Floating rate funds invest in instruments whose interest rate changes according to the market conditions. Simply put, in a floating rate instrument, the coupon rate is not fixed. Instead, it is benchmarked against a market-driven rate such as MIBOR. As the coupon rate is adjusted to the benchmark rate, the NAVs of these funds do not react much to the changes in the interest rate environment. Floating rate funds can also be good options in a scenario where the interest rates are expected to rise. Besides, they are more tax-efficient than liquid funds. Floating rate funds are ideal for those of you looking to park short-term funds and that too without any risk of losing capital due to interest rate volatility.

Short and Medium-Term Debt Funds: Short as well as medium-term debt funds aim to generate income and capital appreciation through a portfolio of debt as well as money market instruments. Short-term debt funds, however, are less volatile compared to medium-term debt funds as they have relatively lower average maturity of the portfolio. Besides, short-term debt funds have a favourable risk-return profile as they have lower standard deviation compared to medium-term debt funds. These funds are appropriate for investors who have a short-term investment horizon and look for an option that is less volatile but has the potential to perform better than liquid or floating rate funds. Medium-term debt funds or income funds, as they are popularly known, invest in corporate and sovereign debt with maturities ranging from 2 to 5 years. While these funds have the potential to give better returns and are more tax-efficient compared to liquid or short-term debt funds, they can be much more volatile during changing interest rate scenario.

Fixed Maturity Plans: Fixed Maturity Plans invest in various types of debt instruments such as corporate bonds, debentures, Government securities, commercial papers, call money, etc. The key point in the investment strategy followed by these plans is that investments are made in instruments whose maturity will coincide with a specific time period indicated in advance by the mutual fund. As a result, FMPs carry least interest rate risk. In other words, the objective is to lock-in the investments at a specified rate of return for a specific period and thereby immunising the scheme against market fluctuations. FMPs have maturities ranging from one month to 2 years or even more. Therefore, for investors, who are sure about the time periods for which they can keep the money invested, FMPs are an ideal option as they offer not only predictable returns but are also more tax-efficient than bank deposits. The key, however, is to select an appropriate option, i.e. dividend or growth. For those who invest in a short-term FMP, i.e. say 3 months or 6 months or even one or 2 years and are in a higher tax bracket, the dividend option would be ideal. On the other hand, for those who invest in three-year FMP, growth option would be better.

Arbitrage Funds: Arbitrage funds are essentially equity funds that aim to provide capital appreciation and income through arbitrage opportunities that exist between the spot market and derivative market. It is important for you to know that though these are termed as equity funds, they are suitable for investors, who are looking to get better and tax-efficient returns compared to debt funds. That is possible because these are market-neutral funds and enjoy the tax benefits of an equity fund, i.e. tax-free dividends and zero tax on long-term capital gains. Being an equity fund, for tax purposes, even the fund is not required to pay any dividend distribution tax. However, for investors in arbitrage funds, which invest less than 65% in equities, the applicable tax rules will be that of debt funds.

On the negative side, these funds, at times, might struggle to find enough arbitrage opportunities in the market.

As is evident, the tax-efficiency of the investment vehicle plays an important role in improving the post-tax returns of those investing in conservative options. Clearly, being more tax-efficient, mutual funds can play an important role in the decision-making process even for conservative investors. There is no wealth tax or gift tax applicable to mutual fund investments.

You want your money to grow but do not give much thought to taxes while making investments. The fact that millions in our country still rely on traditional instruments similar to bank deposits and small savings schemes to invest their money testifies this point. These instruments not only give low returns but are also fully taxable. Clearly, the main attraction is the "safety" provided by these instruments. Though, it is quite natural to be concerned about the safety of your hard-earned money, by giving too much importance to this aspect, you do not allow your savings to grow at a meaningful rate.

While tax-efficiency alone should not drive the investment strategy, it can make a substantial difference to your portfolio's ultimate size. In other words, tax-efficiency has to be an essential element of any investment plan along with portfolio mix, investment philosophy and management. While paying taxes, when necessary, is understandable, paying more taxes than necessary is not! The ultimate objective of investing should be to fund your current and future requirements by maximising your returns in a manner consistent with your means, future needs and risk tolerance.

Back to the Taxing Question With a Bang – Which Option to Opt For?

Asset allocation is a method by which you decide the percentage of total investments to be made in different asset classes such as equity and debt. So, when the value of your equity fund grows over a period of time, your exposure to that asset class increases. The key to success in equity investing is to book profits periodically, even if you are a long-term investor. Undoubtedly, the **growth option** can be described as the best as it advocates long-term investing. However, you might have had mixed experiences over a period of time. There might have been occasions when you have sold your units only to see the NAV scale greater heights. Or, you might have exited in panic when you saw the NAV spiral downwards. Therefore, deciding the right time to rebalance is a challenge for those who opt for the growth option.

The **dividend payout option** allows you to book a profit at different levels without having to worry about the right or wrong time to do so. If you are nearing your retirement, have a low investible surplus, or are uncomfortable with volatility, you are better off opting for the dividend option. In doing so, you get to book profit periodically and divert the dividend amount into safer investment avenues. A dividend payout option may also be a good idea in the case of mid-cap funds or theme funds where the bulk of the returns are earned in short periods. But do not rely on the dividends as a source of income, as declaring dividends is completely at the fund's discretion.

Mutual funds can declare dividends only out of realised profits (less unrealised depreciation in the portfolio, if any). Therefore, the advantage of **dividend reinvestment option** is that, effectively, you would be booking profits and reinvesting it without paying either capital gains tax or STT at the time of investment (assuming the investment is made in an equity-oriented fund). On reinvestment, no entry load (abolished w.e.f. August 1, 2009) is payable and, therefore, there is no additional cost to you. Capital gains taxation on the dividend reinvestment portion arises only if it is sold within 12 months in the case of equity-oriented funds and irrespective of the time of sale in the case of debt-oriented funds. Your cost of acquisition is higher than what it was at the time you entered the scheme, thereby, lowering the gains. This lowering of gains also applies to the gains that you made on the units you had purchased initially. This happens because your initial gains were paid out in the form of dividends. Basically, what a dividend reinvestment option does is to convert your capital gains into tax-free dividends and then allow the capital gains to generate gains again. It is only when you book profits or exit a scheme that the gains are subject to tax. So, in effect, although you have made gains twice, you end up paying taxes just once. But the point to be noted is that the entire tax-free dividend amount is reinvested on a particular day, which in a way is timing the market. Considering that timing the market is not a strategy that works all the time, reinvestment option may not prove effective at all times. The time it takes to receive dividends and redeploy them, can be better spent by keeping the funds invested through dividend reinvestment option. Added to this is the dilemma of finding good opportunities to invest in. It is against this backdrop that we intend to lead you to the option that will enhance your post-tax returns.

The Final Call

The option you select will be a function of your income requirement (although dividend income is not a guaranteed income), time horizon as well as the tax bracket that you are in. The option of whether to go for an equity fund or debt fund is a function of your risk appetite and asset allocation.

If you want to invest in an equity-oriented fund for less than a year, it is better to go for dividend payout or reinvestment option as equity-oriented funds are exempt from DDT. The growth option would be ideal if it is for more than 12 months since only short-term capital gains are taxed in the case of an equity-oriented fund.

Debt-oriented funds are not so simple, as you have to balance out between the capital gains tax and the dividend distribution tax. If your total income falls below the minimum taxable limits, the growth option remains the more tax-efficient option across horizons because in the dividend option, you would suffer the incidence of DDT irrespective of your tax status. If you are a tax payer and plan to hold a debt fund for less than 3 years and fall under the 10% or 20% tax slab, then go for the growth option as this will save you from the 28.84% dividend distribution tax, while your capital gains tax will be 11.845% or 23.690%. However, if you fall in a higher tax slab of 30%, then it would make more sense to go for the dividend payout or reinvestment option, which will save you more on the capital gains tax of 35.5350%, even after factoring in the dividend distribution tax of 28.84%.

As regards the long-term investment in a debt-oriented fund, it would be advisable to go for the growth option. This is because the capital gains tax liability on such an investment will be the long-term capital gains tax rate of not more than 23.690% (with indexation) and you will not shell out the dividend distribution tax of 28.84%.

The following tables provide a lucid illustration of the tax implications of dividend and growth options in mutual funds both in the short-term as well as the long-term:

Post-Tax Returns of Dividend and Growth Options

Table 20.3 Short-term Tax Implications of various Options

Short-Term	Equity		Debt		Liquid	
	Growth	Dividend	Growth	Dividend	Growth	Dividend
Investment	100,000	100,000	100,000	100,000	100,000	100,000
Return @ 10% (a)	10,000	10,000	10,000	10,000	10,000	10,000
Dividend @ 4% (b)	Nil	4,000	Nil	4,000	Nil	4,000
Capital Appreciation (c)	10,000	6,000	10,000	6,000	10,000	6,000
DDT (d)	Nil	Nil	Nil	1154	Nil	1154
Tax on STCG* (e)	1,777	1,066	3,554	2,132	3,554	2,132
Post-Tax Return**	8,223	8,934	6,446	6,714	6,446	6,714

Table 20.4 Long-term Tax Implications of various Options

Long-Term	Equity		Debt		Liquid	
	Growth	Dividend	Growth	Dividend	Growth	Dividend
Investment	100,000	100,000	100,000	100,000	100,000	100,000
Return @ 10% (a)	10,000	10,000	10,000	10,000	10,000	10,000
Dividend @ 4% (b)	Nil	4,000	Nil	4,000	Nil	4,000
Capital Appreciation (c)	10,000	6,000	10,000	6,000	10,000	6,000
DDT (d)	Nil	Nil	Nil	1154	Nil	1,154
Tax on LTCG (e)	Nil	Nil	2,369	1,421	2,369	1,421
Post-Tax Return***	10,000	10,000	7,631	7,425	7,631	7,425

* Taxation on STCG in debt funds is assumed @ 35.5350% (highest tax bracket)
** Post-tax returns = (c - e) + (b - d)
*** Post-tax returns = (c - e) + (b - d)
Securities Transaction Tax will be deducted from equity-oriented funds at the time of redemption/switch

Direct Taxes Code

The DTC is an attempt by the Government of India to simplify the direct tax laws in India. DTC will revise, consolidate and simplify the structure of direct tax laws in India into a single legislation. The DTC, when implemented will replace the Income tax Act, 1961 and other direct tax legislations.

The Direct Taxes Code Bill, 2009, was released during August, 2009, inviting opinion from national and international bodies as well as the general public. A Revised Discussion Paper on DTC was subsequently released in June, 2010. The Finance Minister tabled the Direct Taxes Code Bill, 2010 in the Parliament on August 30, 2010. Its implications on mutual funds are outlined below:

The Direct Taxes Code Bill proposes a 5% dividend distribution tax on equity mutual funds and ULIPs. At present, dividends on equity mutual funds are tax-free in your hands. However, the 5% dividend distribution tax would not be a very big blow as you can always opt for growth plans instead of dividend plans of an equity scheme.

DTC has linked the short-term capital gains tax to your annual income (taxed at half the normal slab rates). A short-term capital gains tax of 5% would be applicable if you are in the income group of Rs. 2–5 lakh, 10% in the Rs. 5–10 lakh bracket and 15% for those with income over Rs. 10 lakh.

DTC has maintained the status quo on STT and long-term capital gains tax.

In the case of debt-oriented mutual funds, the dividend received will be added to your income and taxed at normal slab rates as applicable. Currently, dividend from debt mutual funds is taxed at the rate of 25%. As for capital gains tax, the tax rate will be the same for STCG and LTCG. Your gains will be added to your income and taxed according to the tax slab you fall under.

Under the DTC, 80C-type benefits are limited only to term insurance, Provident Fund (PF), Public Provident Fund (PPF) and the New Pension System (NPS). Of these, only the NPS offers some equity exposure – only up to 50% and with a lock-in up to retirement age. ELSS funds are conspicuous by their absence.

In September 2012, after considering the Kelkar Committee's suggestion for a comprehensive review of DTC 2010, DTC 2013 was released. Under the Income tax Act as well as in the DTC Bill, 2010, the dividend distribution tax payable by companies while distributing dividends to shareholders is to be levied at the rate of 15%. This favours high net worth taxpayers who pay only a fraction of their earnings as tax on their investments in the capital market. The draft DTC 2013 proposes to remove this anomaly by levy of

10% additional tax on the resident recipient if the total dividend in his hand exceeds Rs.1 crore. DTC 2013 has retained all other provisions relating to mutual funds in DTC 2010.

The DTC 2013 is presently a draft version which can be implemented only after it is passed by the Indian Parliament. The fate of the DTC 2013 continues to be uncertain.

The tax implications discussed in the book will undergo a change if the DTC Bill comes into effect.

Chapter 21

Systematically Narrow Down Your Choices
Yardsticks to Reach the Final Yard

Having researched for consistent performers with sound credentials, you must have got a long list of such funds. You can quickly whittle down the fund list by using a few criteria such as **costs** (already dealt with in detail in the section on Fund Concepts), **tax implications** (analysed threadbare in the previous chapter), **size, investor concentration and customer service.** We shall focus on the last 3 criteria in this chapter.

Size of the Fund

When it comes to assessing the impact of a scheme's size on its performance, the dynamics vary for debt funds and for equity funds.

Scheme size is an important consideration for income funds (debt funds that invest primarily in corporate debt), but not as much for their 2 cousins, gilt funds and money market funds. Corporates tend to peg the minimum subscription amount in debt at Rs. 5 crore. A portfolio of 10 top-rated holdings is adequately diversified and diversification beyond that does not reduce the risk proportionately. Assuming 10 holdings and a minimum lot of Rs. 5 crore, Rs. 50 crore is the bare minimum you should look for in an income fund. Since there is not an abundance of top-rated paper around, large-sized income funds are compelled to look at paper that does not have the highest rating or Government securities, which offer lower yields compared to corporate paper of identical maturity. Given that just Rs. 300 crore worth of corporate paper is traded in a day, it is easier for a smaller fund than a large-sized fund to meet redemptions. In practice, though, it boils down to how well a fund manager manages its redemptions. An important advantage of a big corpus is that it helps in negotiating better terms in private placement deals. In fact, a performance analysis of income funds shows that schemes with a corpus of over Rs. 500 crore delivered healthy and consistent returns. On the other hand, schemes with a corpus of Rs. 50 crore and below underperformed and failed to deliver consistently. Where debt funds are concerned, size is critical because it has a direct impact on the expense ratio. Larger funds can distribute fixed expenses over a number of investors and bring down the expense ratio. They can also negotiate better rates with issuers of debt paper.

In the context of the present asset sizes of the Indian equity funds, a huge asset size is more of a concern for schemes investing predominantly in small and mid-cap stocks because such stocks happen to be relatively less liquid. Unbridled asset growth of a mid-cap fund should be a warning flag. It can translate into disproportionately high amounts of money being invested into less liquid mid-cap stocks. This could be detrimental to investors' interest if markets experience a sudden decline. A huge size can become a drag on the performance. This is because even a large amount of money invested in a small but promising stock would constitute only a miniscule portion of the fund's portfolio. And should the stock perform very well subsequently, its impact on the fund returns would be minimal. Unlike mid-cap stocks, large cap stocks are much more liquid and have the potential to absorb much higher volumes of transactions without impacting the stock price too much. Smaller funds have the capability of being more agile. This is especially true for small and mid-cap funds. These funds can exit and enter stocks of a smaller market cap without affecting the price of the stock too much. But, if we look at the performance of large mid-cap offerings such as Reliance Growth and Sundaram Select Midcap, this theory is disproved.

In the case of index funds, large size may be an asset. Any inflow can be easily invested without giving rise to significant tracking error. In the case of a small index fund, the same inflow may look substantial and it may not be easy to allocate it without causing a tracking error.

On a closing note, there will be exceptions to all the above observations. Though theoretically there are specific kinds of funds which are better off either as large or small funds, there is no clear-cut trend to prove that a larger fund will perform better than a smaller fund or *vice versa*.

Investor Concentration in the Fund

Most of us assume that each mutual fund is made up of a large number of investors – after all, that is supposed to be the whole logic behind the industry's existence. However, in India, a handful – sometimes just one or two – of investors account for an extraordinarily high proportion of the assets of many funds. In the case of income funds, which constitute 56% of the industry, it is considered to be a norm nowadays that around 59% of the investments come from institutional investors – many of whom tend to make large investments in a few funds. The highest concentration of institutional investors occurs in fixed maturity plans, which are expressly designed for such investments and shorter duration plans. However, all types of funds do have some examples of this kind.

The dominance by a handful of investors indicates the presence of corporate money, which is mostly short-term in nature. Retail investors are vulnerable to the investment decisions of such big investors. If they decide to redeem their holdings at short notice, the scheme might have to resort to panic sales, to the detriment of the remaining small unit-holders. If the single investor exits the scheme, the rest will be left in the lurch. Such schemes should be avoided.

In income funds, the high concentration of institutional investors has little operational impact on the investment management of a fund. In equity funds, this is not the case. A sudden redemption from a large investor can be disastrous, especially if the fund is small and the market is falling. Typically, in such circumstances, trading is thin and the only way a fund manager can generate cash for a sudden redemption is by selling his more liquid stocks, which he may otherwise have wanted to hold on to. The result: the large investor walks away with his cash but the remaining small investors in the portfolio are poorer and the fund manager's track record is affected only because the big guy pulled out.

However, fund managers generally consider large investors to be more stable. They tend to stay in touch directly with large investors to be aware of their redemption plans. Small investors too can just as easily create a run of sorts on a fund at the worst time possible. When the markets move down sharply, small investors can disinvest in a hurry, forcing the fund manager to quickly sell his best stocks. So, if you are planning to invest in a very small equity fund, it may be beneficial to know about the investor concentration it has. But, SEBI guidelines require that funds that do not adhere to the stipulation of a minimum of twenty investors with no single investor accounting for more than 25% of the corpus of a scheme/plan, should be wound up.

Customer Service

Customer service assumes paramount importance in the process of fund selection. Check with friends about easy accessibility, time taken for disbursing payments, regular portfolio updates and investor newsletters. Service standards, speedy solutions to grievances of investors, transparency in actions and the reputation of the fund house are the key factors you should look for.

The long-term characteristics of different mutual funds are given in the following table, which will help you in choosing the right fund(s) suitable for you:

Table 21.1 Picking the Right Fund for You

	Capital Gain Potential	Income Potential	Risk Level	Total Return Potential
Equity Funds				
Aggressive Growth	Very high	Low	Very high	Very high
Growth	High	Low	High	High
Income	Low	High	Medium	Medium
Growth/Income	Medium	Medium	Medium	Medium
Industry Specific	Varies	Varies	Varies	Varies
Precious Metals	High	Low	High	Varies
Global	High	Medium	High	High
International	Very high	Low	High	High
Income Funds				
Government Securities	Low	Medium	Low	Medium
Money Market	Very Low	Low	Very Low	Low

First, ask yourself how much money you want to make and how much risk you can tolerate. When investing in mutual funds, you should pick mutual funds based on your personal objectives and risk tolerance. Before making an investment, make sure that you have done some research and have enough understanding of the fund that you are buying. You can find information about a fund's goals, strategy, performance, management and fee structure in its prospectus. When evaluating a fund, you should compare its relative performance over various periods of time (for example, 1, 3, 5 and 10 years) and in different kinds of economic and stock market environments. A fund manager's experience and record, the fund's level of consistency and its major investment holdings are other important factors to consider. You can also find information and rankings of mutual funds in various publications, the most notable being **'Mutual Fund Insight' of Value Research**.

The following are a few of the websites that have a wealth of information on mutual funds:

www.valueresearchonline.com

www.moneycontrol.com

www.mutualfundsindia.com

www.indiainfoline.com

www.morningstar.com

You researched your resources...systematically scouted for consistent performers with sound credentials...selected the right funds and the best option that would maximise returns. Now that the mirror on the wall has answered your question, you have your wealth-building winners, the final yard we referred to at the outset, ready for action ... actual investment.

SECTION VII
FUND PLANS AND SERVICES

"No life ever grows great until it is focused, dedicated, disciplined."

— Harry Emerson Fosdick

In the same manner, no investment ever grows great until it is focused, dedicated and disciplined. The investment plans, Systematic Investment Plan (SIP), Systematic Withdrawal Plan (SWP) and Systematic Transfer Plan (STP), offered by mutual funds, are focused, dedicated and disciplined approaches to investing, that balance both risk and return and build wealth.

The services offered by mutual funds sans technology and the sea change brought about by technology in the arena of mutual fund investing and the tremendous response by the investing community substantiates the words of Charles Darwin, "It is not the strongest of the species that survives, nor the most intelligent, but the one most responsive to change."

Chapter 22

Mutual Fund Investment Plans
Compounding – the Eighth Wonder of the World

"Our favourite holding period is forever…"

— Warren Buffett

The various investment plans offered by mutual funds are dealt with in brief and elaborated subsequently.

1. **Systematic Investment Plan (SIP):** You are given the option of preparing a predetermined number of post-dated cheques (or a direct debit of the bank account) in favour of the scheme. You are allotted units on a predetermined date specified in the offer document at the applicable NAV.

2. **Systematic Withdrawal Plan (SWP):** It allows you the facility to withdraw predetermined amount/units from your fund at predetermined intervals. Your units will be redeemed at the applicable NAV as on that day.

3. **Systematic Transfer Plan (STP):** It allows you to invest a lump sum amount in one scheme of the fund house and give a standing instruction to transfer sums at monthly intervals (for a minimum period of 6 months) into any other scheme of the fund house. You have the option of specifying a fixed sum to be transferred every month or transferring just the capital appreciation.

4. **Dividend Transfer Plan:** You can choose to transfer your dividend from one scheme to another scheme as and when dividends are paid out (on the ex-dividend date) automatically and units will be allotted accordingly.

5. **Insurance Plan:** Certain schemes offer you insurance cover.

Systematic Investment Plan

The Indian stock market is synonymous with volatility and dynamism. What is the strategy for investors like you to sail smoothly in a storm? Past experience has shown that a disciplined investment plan holds the key to ride the bulls and bears in the market. One of the most disciplined and convenient methods of investing in mutual funds, is the SIP. SIP is a powerful tool, with a strategy of not only preserving capital but also translating into substantial creation of wealth in the long run.

What is a Systematic Investment Plan?

SIP is a method of investing a fixed sum, regularly, in a mutual fund. SIP allows you to buy units on a predetermined date at predetermined intervals at the prevailing NAV on that day. Once you have decided the mutual fund scheme in which you want to invest and on the amount you want to invest and the frequency of investment (monthly or quarterly), you can either give post-dated cheques or auto-debit/ECS (Electronic Clearing System) instruction and the investment will be made regularly. You have to sign up a mandate form based on which the mutual fund will arrange for your account to be debited as per the frequency, amount and date chosen by you. SIPs generally start at minimum amounts of Rs. 500 per month and the upper limit for using an ECS is Rs. 25,000 per instruction. Therefore, if you wish to invest Rs. 1,00,000 per month, you may need to do it on 4 different dates. Every mutual fund specifies the minimum number of payments that should be invested in order to get this facility. It might be 12 cheques of Rs. 500 each or 6 cheques of Rs. 1,000 each. It is mandatory that the cheques should be of the same value. The first cheque can be on any date of the month, but the subsequent cheques should bear any of the dates offered by the mutual fund for SIP.

Let us say that every month you commit to investing, say, Rs. 1,000 in your fund. At the end of a year, you would have invested Rs. 12,000. If the NAV on the day you invest in the first month is Rs. 20, you will get 50 units. The next month, the NAV is Rs. 25. You will get 40 units. The following month, the NAV is Rs. 18. You will get 55.56 units. So, after 3 months, you would have 145.56 units. On an average, you would have paid around Rs. 21 per unit. This is because, when the NAV is high, you get fewer units per Rs. 1,000. When the NAV falls, you get more units per Rs. 1,000. **This is called 'rupee-cost-averaging'.**

Innovative Variations of Systematic Investment Plan

The concept of daily SIP was introduced for the first time in India in September 2008 by Bharti AXA Investment Managers (now BOI AXA Investment Managers). Besides minimising risk and generating greater risk-adjusted returns, it fosters participation of retail investors in small towns and cities. Bharti AXA's daily SIP allows you to invest on a daily basis a minimum amount of Rs. 300 per day. In daily SIP you invest on all days when the stock markets are open, which may vary from 19 to 23 investments per month. It has a lock-in period of one month during which you have to pay the SIP amount without any default. Beyond this period, you can withdraw the amount invested along with the returns at any point of time. If you fail to pay the SIP amount on any particular working day, your investment will not default but your return will be adjusted against the failure of payment for that day. To make the payment hassle-free, auto debit facility has been introduced. The auto debit mode is expensive as opposed to the electronic clearing system. ING Mutual Fund (schemes of ING Mutual Fund form part of Birla Sun Life Mutual Fund w.e.f. October 11, 2014) closely followed Bharti AXA (now BOI AXA) and introduced Zoom Investment Pac (ZIP), a daily SIP in 6 of its schemes, whereby, a predetermined amount, a minimum of Rs. 99, is transferred from ING Liquid Fund (now Birla Sun Life Cash Plus Fund) to such target schemes. The default target scheme is ING Nifty Plus (now Birla Sun Life Top 100 Fund). The exit load/CDSC is applicable as per the existing structure of the respective schemes. Several mutual funds such as IDFC Mutual Fund, Sahara Mutual Fund, Quantum Mutual Fund, HDFC Mutual Fund, L & T Mutual Fund, etc. followed suit. Though the concept looks good, tracking your investment becomes difficult. Your annual statement for the fund would run into several pages. Imagine tracking around 250 transactions a year!

In July 2012, Fundsupermart, the online mutual fund investment portal, launched flexi SIP service, where you can alter the monthly SIP investment within the ECS limit, without any hassle of a fresh ECS bank mandate. In regular SIP you need to cancel your existing SIP, increase or decrease the SIP amount and recreate the SIP. The flexi SIP feature enables you to effortlessly alter your monthly investment to suit your affordability or temporary upheaval in your finances. You only need to choose the funds where you want to make the alterations, the amount you want to invest in those particular funds, date of investment and the maximum ECS limit. You can increase the SIP amount if you want to take advantage of acquiring more units during a market downturn. Likewise, if valuations are stretched, you can make the appropriate changes and channelise your savings into a debt fund till the market cools down. This facility is available for all funds. You can terminate the ECS mandate any time before the agreed tenure. If there are no sufficient funds, the transaction would fail. After 3 consecutive failures of such transactions, the SIP for that fund would be auto-terminated but the bank mandate will still be active allowing you to renew your SIPs without any extra documentation.

Exploding the Myths on SIP

The seemingly simple SIP has been one of the most misunderstood concepts associated with mutual fund investment. Let us now break some myths associated with SIP.

Investment in equity mutual funds should always be done in SIP mode: If you have the maturity to realise that equities are for the long-term and are willing to leave your funds untouched for about 10 years and you have a substantial sum, you can afford to give the SIP route a slip. However, if your horizon is less than 5 years, SIP is the best alternative.

Rupee-cost-averaging in a single equity is a kind of SIP: Rupee-cost-averaging in any single scrip cannot be equated to an SIP. When the market brings down the price of the single scrip, it is giving you information. You need to react to that. Silverline Technologies moved from Rs. 30 to Rs. 1,300 and then to Rs. 7! In this case, if you had started an SIP at a price of Rs. 1,300, today you would be licking your wounds. SIP works in a portfolio (hence a mutual fund) and not in a single scrip.

You cannot invest a lump sum in the same account in which you are doing an SIP: Many people assume that if they are doing an SIP in a particular fund and they have an unexpected surplus, they cannot put that amount in that fund. The fact is, in case you are doing an SIP of

Rs. 10,000 per month in an equity-oriented fund and suddenly you have a surplus of Rs. 1,00,000 and you have a 10-year view on the same, then you can just add it to your SIP account. SIP is just a payment mode, not a scheme!

Fear of prosecution in the event of non-payment of a monthly investment: In an SIP (unlike an EMI), you are buying an investment every month (or quarter). There is no question of prosecuting you for missing one investment. As a matter of discipline, you should not miss any payment.

SIP works for everybody, but does not work for me: A psychological myth. SIP works in a well-diversified equity fund in the long run. When people put forth arguments that it does not work for them, they have either not chosen a good fund or are looking at a 12-month horizon.

Now that the common misconceptions about SIP have been clarified, we shall discuss some unique advantages that elevate this mode of payment to the pedestal that it deserves.

The Proof of the Pudding Lies in the Unique Advantages that SIP Enjoys

No strain on your day-to-day finances: Mutual funds were never meant to be elitist – far from it. The retail investor is as much a part of the mutual fund target audience as the high net worth investor. Investing smaller amounts over a period of time is a lot more convenient, particularly for the salaried class. Given that average per capita income of an Indian is approximately Rs. 95,613 (monthly income of Rs. 7,968) a Rs. 5,000 one-time entry in a mutual fund is still asking for a lot (a little less than the monthly income!). So, if you cannot shell out Rs. 5,000, it is not a huge stumbling block. Take the SIP route and trigger your mutual fund investment with as low as Rs. 500 (in most cases).

Relevance of market timing reduced: Studies have repeatedly highlighted the ability of stocks to outperform other asset classes over the long-term (at least 5 years) as also to effectively counter inflation. So, if equity is such a great investment option, why are so many investors complaining? It is because they either got the stock wrong or the timing wrong. One of the biggest difficulties in equity investing is 'WHEN to invest', apart from the other big question of 'WHERE to invest'. While investing in a good mutual fund solves the issue of 'where' to invest, SIP helps us to overcome the problem of 'when' to invest. Both these problems can be solved through an SIP in a mutual fund with a steady track record.

With an SIP, you are relatively indifferent to the behaviour of the stock markets over a period of time. The truth is none of us can time the market. No one knows when a fund's NAV will rise or fall. When the market is falling, you may feel that it may decline further and that you should wait a while. Often stock markets make a recovery before you notice and the opportunity is lost. When markets are rising, it is scary to invest money. Is it not better that you wait for a correction and then make an investment? But if the correction does not come about, then even this opportunity is missed. And if markets are going nowhere, then what is the point in investing at all? It, thus, makes timing the market totally irrelevant.

Reduces the average cost: In an SIP, you invest a fixed amount regularly. Therefore, you end up buying more number of units when the markets are down and the NAV is low and less number of units when the markets are up and the NAV is high. This is called rupee-cost-averaging. Generally, you would stay away from buying when the markets are down and tend to invest when the markets are rising. SIP works as a good discipline as it forces us to buy even when the markets are low, which actually is the best time to buy.

The magic of compounding unfolds: 'The early bird gets the worm' is not just a part of the jungle folklore. Even the early investor gets a lion's share of the investment booty *vis-à-vis* the investor, who comes in later. The following example illustrates how the power of compounding can do wonders. Imagine A is 20 years old when he starts working. Every month, he saves and invests Rs. 5,000 till he is 25 years old. The total investment made by him over 5 years is Rs. 3 lakh. B also starts working when he is 20 years old. But he does not invest every month. He gets a large bonus of Rs. 3 lakh at 25 and decides to invest the entire amount. Both of them decide not to withdraw these investments till they turn 50. At 50, A's investments have grown to Rs. 46,68,273 whereas B's investments have grown to Rs. 36,17,084. A's small contributions to an SIP and his decision to start investing earlier than B made him wealthier by over Rs. 10 lakh. Benjamin Franklin had rightly said, "Compound interest is the eighth wonder of the world." And no doubt it is. Even if each investment is small, over time, this can add up to a neat kitty.

Helps realise your dreams: Most of you have needs that involve significant amounts of money, such as your child's education, your daughter's marriage, buying a house, or a car. If you are to save for these milestones overnight or even a couple of years in advance, you are unlikely to meet your objective since many of them require a huge one-time investment. As it would not be possible to raise such large amounts at a short notice, you need to build the corpus over a longer period of time, through small but regular investments. This is what SIP is all about. Small investments, over a period of time, result in huge wealth and help fulfil your dreams and aspirations.

An SIP does not assure a profit or protect against a loss but the probability of making a loss through an SIP over a longer period of time is almost negligible. Overall, systematic investment programmes have been recognised historically as an excellent method for developing what could be a substantial investment, i.e. wealth accumulation.

Some Points to Consider Before Deciding On an SIP:

* Ascertain your investment horizon.
* Decide on the periodicity of investment.
* Determine the amount you can comfortably invest in an SIP periodically.
* Pick a scheme according to your risk profile.
* Invest for the long-term.

SIP is an ideal route to embark on your journey in the financial markets. It is the answer to preventing the pitfalls of equity investment while reaping rich rewards. An SIP can be useful for a debt fund as well...to help build a pool of savings. It can be thought of as something similar to a recurring deposit where a part of your savings is automatically deducted from your account.

Think of each SIP payment as laying a brick. One by one, you will see them transform into a building. You will see your investments grow steadily month after month. Being disciplined is, no doubt, the key to successful investing.

Systematic Withdrawal Plan (SWP)

If SIP is for making a disciplined investment in the market, the Systematic Withdrawal Plan (SWP) is a disciplined way of unwinding your investment. If you keep booking profits in predefined successions, you avert the risk of getting stuck should the market fall suddenly. This happens rather frequently in our system where liquidity and, therefore, depth is rather low. The amount of withdrawal can be subject to the minimum limit set by the AMC, your requirements, as well as the corpus invested. You will have to leave instructions with the fund on the periodicity of withdrawal (monthly or quarterly), a date for each withdrawal and the delivery of the money.

Fund houses such as Franklin Templeton Mutual Fund, HDFC Mutual Fund, Birla Sun Life Mutual fund and Kotak Mahindra Mutual Fund offer 2 sub-options within the SWP – Fixed and Appreciation. Under the fixed SWP, you can choose to receive a fixed sum, say, Rs. 1,000 each month, over a specified number of months by way of systematic withdrawals. Under the appreciation option, you can leave instructions with the fund to redeem units only to the extent of the capital appreciation, if any, earned on the units. A few fund houses such as ICICI Prudential Mutual Fund and UTI Mutual Fund offer a trigger facility that is a variant of the Appreciation SWP. The trigger facility saves you the trouble of having to keep track of your investment. You can leave instructions on booking profits on fund holdings when a specified 'trigger', say appreciation, stop loss, etc. is reached.

SWPs are an ideal way to supplement your monthly cash flow, reinvest periodically in other instruments or meet your periodic payment schedules such as your EMIs, insurance premiums, your children's school fees, etc. without leaving your money idle. The SWP could be a good alternative to the dividend option of a mutual fund, because payouts can be timed to your convenience, instead of you having to wait for the fund to declare dividends.

Systematic Transfer Plan (STP)

You have made big money on equity fund investments over a period of time and want to plough the capital gains into safe investment avenues. The **Systematic Transfer Plan (STP) or Drip Investing** could be the answer. STP allows you to make periodic transfers from one fund into another managed by the same fund house. It works out to be a combination of Systematic Withdrawal Plan (SWP) and Systematic Investment Plan (SIP). SWP is an option where the fund house allows you to redeem funds at regular intervals. SIP, on the other hand, allows you to purchase units at regular intervals. The dates as well as the amount to be withdrawn or invested will be predetermined in both the cases. How does the STP work? Let us say, you put a lump sum amount in a debt scheme. You instruct the fund to transfer a specified amount every month to a particular equity fund on a particular date. So, STP is an SWP from a debt fund and a simultaneous SIP into an equity fund. As with an SWP, you have to specify the instalment and the periodicity of the transfer. Fund houses usually offer monthly and quarterly STPs. But a few funds such as ICICI Prudential allow systematic transfers even at weekly intervals. The STP can be a useful facility to rebalance your portfolio or to phase out investments in a fund over a period of time. You can invest a lump sum in a liquid or floating rate or debt fund and leave instructions to transfer a fixed sum every month into an equity fund. While many fund houses permit STPs from debt to equity funds, only a few allow the reverse. Franklin Templeton Mutual Fund, ICICI Prudential Mutual Fund and Birla Sun Life Mutual Fund allow systematic transfers out of their debt schemes into their equity funds, but not the reverse. Kotak Mutual Fund permits two-way STP. STPs too offer a choice between a Fixed and an Appreciation option. **A Fixed option STP** allows you to transfer a fixed sum at periodic intervals into another fund. **The Appreciation STP** is activated only when the capital appreciation on your investment crosses the limit you have set. Since the STP works on the principle of redemption and fresh investment, the tax implication would be the same as capital gains (short-term and long-term) on the redemption of equity or debt funds as the case may be.

How STP Compares with SIP...

Unlike SIP, where you have to cut a number of cheques depending on your investment duration, in STP only a single form has to be filled.

Though there is a link between systematic transfer plan and systematic investment plan, both the options differ from each other by way of the nature of cash flow. STP is as good as SIP and a better option for those of you with large *ad hoc* cash flows to invest. SIP is targeted at those of you with small regular cash flows.

STP – the Star Attraction

STP offers you the security of a liquid fund while trying to enhance returns by investing a part of the funds in equity. STP is basically meant for HNIs, businessmen and corporates. However, any risk-averse individual would do well to invest through STP. This option also helps a fund house build its asset base. The fact that this option gives better returns than a one-time direct investment is also demonstrated by a study by JP Morgan.

STP helps you reach your financial goals by investing a fixed sum in your chosen fund for a predetermined number of instalments. It is an ideal option for those sitting on cash and not wanting to take the risk of lump sum investment in the equity market. This helps mitigate any risk arising from volatility.

Chapter 23

Mutual Fund Investment Services
At Your Service

Interest in and information about investing has increased dramatically. At the outset, it would be appropriate to apprise you of **the eligibility criteria for investment in Indian mutual funds.**

Resident Indian adult individuals, above the age of 18, either singly or jointly (not exceeding 3 names), minors, i.e. persons below the age of 18 (through their parents/lawful guardians), Hindu Undivided Families (HUFs) (the head of the family, called "Karta", invests on behalf of the family), Non-Resident Indians (NRIs)/Persons of Indian Origin (PIO) resident abroad, foreign investors, non-individual investors (the individuals who sign the documents are investing on behalf of organisations/institutions they represent, such as companies/corporate bodies, registered in India, registered societies and co-operative societies, trustees of religious and charitable trusts, trustees of private trusts, partner(s) of partnership firms, association of persons or body of individuals, whether incorporated or not, banks (including co-operative banks and regional rural banks) and financial institutions and investment institutions, other mutual funds registered with SEBI, Foreign Institutional Investors (FIIs) registered with SEBI, international multilateral agencies approved by the Government of India, Army/Navy/Air Force, Para-Military Units and other eligible institutions, Scientific and Industrial Research Organisations, Universities and Educational Institutions) are eligible to invest in mutual funds in India.

The following were not permitted to invest in mutual funds in India until recently:

* An individual who is a foreign national (unless, of course, the person is an NRI or PIO/OCI card holder).

* Any entity that is not an Indian resident, as per FEMA (except when the entity is registered as FII with SEBI, or has a sub-account with a SEBI registered FII).

* Overseas Corporate Bodies (OCBs), i.e. societies/trusts held, directly or indirectly, to the extent of over 60% by NRIs, or trusts where more than 60% of the beneficial interest is held by such OCBs.

SEBI and RBI circulars, dated August 9, 2011, have allowed Qualified Foreign Investors (QFIs), who meet Know Your Client (KYC) requirements to invest in equity and debt schemes of mutual funds either directly (holding mutual fund units in demat account through a SEBI registered DP) or indirectly (holding mutual fund units via Unit Confirmation Receipt (UCR)).

The individual and non-individual investors eligible to invest can invest in any mutual fund scheme, unless the mutual fund comes out with a specific scheme, or a plan within a scheme, that is not intended for any category of investors. **However, for a first-time investor, it is a good practice to check the 'Who can Invest' section of the Offer Document.** Further, in some schemes, only specific classes of non-individual investors are permitted. For instance, some gilt schemes have specific plans, which are open only for Provident Funds, Superannuation and Gratuity Funds, Pension Funds, Religious and Charitable Trusts and Private Trusts. In the case of Exchange Traded Funds, only authorised participants and large investors can invest in the NFO. Subsequently, in the stock exchange, anyone who is eligible to invest can buy units of the ETF.

A vivid description of **the process of investing in a mutual fund** will help you appreciate the services offered by mutual funds.

Launch of NFO

Mutual funds normally come out with an advertisement in newspapers publishing the date of launch of the new schemes. You can also contact the agents and distributors of mutual funds, who are spread across the country, investor service centres of the respective mutual fund, registrar and transfer agent of the fund, or the office of the mutual fund itself for necessary information on NFOs and existing schemes.

Offer Document and KIM

You should read the offer document very carefully. SEBI has prescribed minimum disclosures in the offer document. Due care must be given to portions relating to the main features of the scheme, risk factors, initial issue expenses and recurring expenses to be charged to the scheme, exit loads, sponsor's track record, educational and professional qualifications, work experience of key personnel, including fund managers, performance of other schemes launched by the mutual fund in the past, pending litigations and penalties imposed. An abridged offer document, KIM, which contains very useful information, is required to be given to the prospective investor by the mutual fund along with the application form for subscription to a scheme.

Application Forms

The application form contains a statement to the effect that the investor has read and understood the offer document and he/she abides by the terms and conditions stated in it. It is an important agreement between the investor and the fund and you cannot plead ignorance of the terms and conditions and procedures at a later date. You can download the application form from the respective mutual fund website. Alternatively, you can approach the distributors of mutual funds, investor service centres of the respective mutual fund, registrar and transfer agent of the fund, or the office of the mutual fund itself for the application form.

Registering a Mutual Fund Account and Nomination

You can open the mutual fund account in your name only or the account may be registered jointly. Every investment in a mutual fund can have up to 3 joint holders. When units are held singly, the sole holder is entitled to all the information and notifications as also the dividend payments and the redemption proceeds. In the case of joint ownership, the person first-named in the application form will receive all notices and correspondences with respect to the account. Such person shall hold the voting right, if any, associated with the units. However, all documentation/purchase applications/redemption requests/enrolment forms shall necessarily be signed by all the holders. If the nature of joint holding is 'either or survivor', it is sufficient if one of the holders signs the redemption request.

The AMC is required to provide you an option to nominate a person who will inherit the units held by you in the event of your death. The nomination facility is available only for individuals applying on their own behalf, i.e. singly or jointly.

Filling up the Application Form

While filling up the application form, you must mention your name, address, number of units applied for and such other information as required in the application form. SEBI has made it mandatory for investors in mutual funds to state their bank account numbers in their applications and in redemption requests. You must give your bank account details so as to avoid fraudulent encashment of any cheque/draft issued by the mutual fund at a later date for the purpose of dividend or repurchase/redemption. A cancelled cheque or a photocopy of your cheque leaf is a must if you wish to avail the facility of direct credit/ECS and it is preferable in all cases to ensure that your bank account details and cheque details such as the magnetic ink character reader (MICR) code, Indian Financial System Code (IFSC) are captured accurately. You may refer to an application form to get an idea as to how it is to be filled. Any changes in the address, bank account details, etc. at a later date should be informed to the mutual fund immediately in the transaction form.

If you wish to start an SIP, you need to fill up 2 forms – one to open an account with the mutual fund and the other to specify your SIP details such as frequency, monthly instalment amount and so on.

The application form is to be accompanied by a cheque or demand draft for the amount to be invested. The application should be for at least the minimum amount as mentioned in the KIM attached to the application form.

Payment Mechanism for Purchase of Mutual Fund Units

The mode of payment is prescribed in the scheme information document. Payment should be in the form of a local cheque in the city in which the application form is submitted or by demand draft payable locally. All cheques and drafts should be crossed "A/c. Payee only" and made out in favour of the "mutual fund/scheme" as specified in the instructions accompanying the application form and the PAN number should be written on the reverse. Cash and outstation cheques will not be accepted.

Mutual funds usually do not accept cash. Small investors, who may not be tax payers and may not have PAN/bank accounts, such as farmers, small traders/businessmen/workers are allowed cash transactions for purchase of units in mutual funds to the extent of Rs. 20,000/- per investor, per mutual fund, per financial year. This is subject to compliance with Prevention of Money Laundering Act, 2002 and SEBI Circulars on Anti Money Laundering (AML) and other applicable AML rules, regulations and guidelines. Although investment can be made in cash, repayment in the form of redemptions, dividend payments, etc. can be only through the banking channel. Apart from the above-mentioned exception for small investors, application money needs to come through normal banking channels, as elaborated below.

Application forms for fresh investment/transaction slip for additional purchase is normally accompanied by a **Cheque or Demand Draft (DD)**, drawn in favour of the scheme in which the investment is to be made. Cheques are signed by the account holder, while DDs are signed by the banker. Generally, DDs are accepted only if the investor is from outside the location where the application form/transaction slip is being submitted.

The payment instrument would need to be local, i.e. cheque should be drawn on a local bank account. If it is drawn on an outstation bank account, then the bank should offer the facility of 'at par' payment in the location where the application form and cheque are submitted. If such an 'at par' facility is available, 'payable at par at ... (list of locations/all over India)' would be clearly mentioned in the face or back of the cheque.

Cheques accompanying the investment application are to be signed by the investor. Third-party cheques are not accepted except in special cases such as grandparents/parents making payments not exceeding Rs. 50,000 on behalf of a minor, employer making payments on behalf of employee through payroll deductions and custodian on behalf of FIIs. AMCs are required to put checks and balances in place to verify such transactions. Similarly, DD should clearly mention the place of payment as the location where the application form/transaction slip and payment instrument are being submitted. The payment instrument should not be post-dated (except for future instalments under SIP) and not stale (i.e. cheque date should not be more than 3 months older than the date on which the cheque is to be banked).

NRI/PIO applications need to be accompanied by cheque drawn on an NRO account (for non-repatriable investment) or NRE account (for repatriable investment). If payment from NRI is by DD and investment is on repatriable basis, a banker's certificate will be required to the effect that the DD has come out of money remitted from abroad. When the NRI receives money in his bank account in India, the banker would issue a Foreign Inward Remittance Certificate (FIRC), which is evidence that the money was remitted from abroad.

Remittance can also be made directly to the bank account of the scheme through Real-Time Gross Settlement (RTGS)/ National Electronic Funds Transfer (NEFT) transfers (for transfers within India) or Society for Worldwide Interbank Financial Telecommunication (SWIFT) transfer (for transfers from abroad). While RTGS transfers are instantaneous, NEFT transfers are batched together in the banking system and effected at various times during the day. SWIFT transfers tend to pass through multiple banks in different geographies and multiple levels within the same bank, resulting in delays. Before money is remitted directly to the mutual fund, it is advisable to get the proper bank account details from the AMC/distributor. Further, the application form/transaction slip will need to be accompanied by proof of the remittance.

Electronic Clearing Service (ECS)/Standing Instructions are a convenient form of investment in an SIP. On the specified date, each month, the bank will automatically transfer money from the investor's account to the account of the mutual fund. The bank accepts 'Standing Instructions' (also called 'Direct Debit') if both investor and mutual fund have an account with the same bank. If the 2 accounts are in different banks, then ECS is used.

Application Supported by Blocked Amount (ASBA) is a facility where the investment application is accompanied by an authorisation to the bank to block the amount of the application money in the investor's bank account. The benefit of ASBA is that the money goes out of the investor's bank account only on allotment. Until then, it keeps earning interest for the investor. Further, since the money transferred from the investor's bank account is the exact application money that is due on account of the allotment, the investor does not have to wait for any refund. ASBA, which was originally envisaged for public issues in the capital market, has now been extended to mutual fund NFOs.

M-Banking, i.e. mobile banking is nascent in India. Individual banks may impose per day fund transfer limits. Once people are comfortable with M-banking, this will become a convenient way to invest.

Documentation

Broadly, mutual fund investors need the following documents:

- Attested copy of PAN Card
- KYC Acknowledgement

PAN Card

Your PAN or Permanent Account Number is a 10 digit alpha-numeric number issued by an assessing officer of the Income Tax Department. You will need your PAN for property deals, opening bank accounts, demat accounts, investing in Indian markets, sale of property, claiming refunds on TDS and also to get a telephone connection in India. SEBI order states that investors without a PAN cannot trade through the depository, depository participant, or a broker. So, if you are keen on investing in mutual funds in India, make sure you have your PAN. SEBI has mandated that PAN shall be the sole identification number for all participants in the securities market irrespective of the amount of transaction. The sole exception is Micro SIP of an individual investor if the total amount of all instalments is less than Rs. 50,000 per investor in any rolling 12-month period or in a financial year.

PAN is a proof of your identity. Your PAN card contains a unique 10 digit alpha-numeric number, your name, your photograph, your date of birth, your father's name as well as your signature.

You can apply for your PAN card based on your passport as proof of identity and residence. In case PAN has not been applied for or applied for and not allotted, you should submit a declaration in Form 60/61 prescribed by the IT Department, in duplicate, along with a copy of the proof of address specified in Form 60/61. Today you can get your PAN card with a simple click of your mouse. You can easily download the PAN form from the internet, fill it up, attach the supporting documents and send it to the IT Department. Your PAN card will be delivered to your address within 2 months. If you are an NRI and are in one of the ninety-nine countries for which foreign delivery addresses are accepted then you can apply online and send documents direct to the department. But the printed form and documents must reach them within 15 days of online submission, which may be a challenge!

KYC Acknowledgement

KYC is an acronym for "Know Your Client", a term commonly used for client identification process. KYC policy is an important step developed globally to prevent identity theft, financial fraud, money laundering and terrorist financing. The objective of KYC is to enable financial institutions to know and understand their customers better and help them manage their risks prudently.

SEBI has prescribed certain requirements relating to KYC norms for financial institutions and financial intermediaries, including mutual funds to 'know' their clients. This is in the form of verification of identity and address, providing information of financial status, occupation and such other demographic information and maintaining record of identity and address of investors. An applicant must be KYC compliant while investing with any SEBI registered mutual fund. Previously it was compulsory for all investments of Rs. 50,000 and above to be compliant with the regulatory requirements prescribed under the Prevention of Money Laundering Act, 2002 and SEBI circulars in this regard. The regulations have now been revised. All investors investing in mutual funds are required to be KYC compliant. Investors can execute financial transactions on their folios only if they are KYC compliant.

The AMFI initially facilitated a centralised platform through CDSL Ventures Limited ("CDSL"), a wholly owned subsidiary of Central Depository Services (India) Limited, to carry out the KYC procedure on behalf of all mutual funds.

From January 2012, SEBI has set out revised KYC norms to make the process uniform across the securities market and introduced a common KYC application form for all the SEBI registered intermediaries, viz. mutual funds, portfolio managers, depository participants, stock brokers, etc. Investors who have not completed the mutual fund KYC norms earlier can use the uniform KYC application form to apply for KYC at the time of investment in mutual funds. The intermediary, for example mutual fund, shall perform the initial KYC of its clients and upload the details on the system of the KYC Registration Agencies (KRA). SEBI has instituted a framework of Centralised KRAs for the benefit of investors. Centralised KRAs have made the KYC process simpler for investors. When the client approaches another intermediary, the intermediary can verify and download the client's details from the system of the KRA. As a result, once the client has done KYC with a SEBI registered intermediary, the client need not undergo the same process again with another intermediary.

You can apply for KYC by first downloading the applicable KYC application form from www.camsonline.com or www.camskra.com (separate forms for Individuals and Non-individuals) and filling the KYC form by completing all required details and submitting it along with a self-certified copy of the proof of identity, proof of address (in addition, a document with overseas address proof is required for NRIs), PAN card and photograph for In-Person Verification (IPV) by the AMC, RTA (on behalf of AMCs), or an NISM/AMFI certified and KYD-compliant distributor. The original documents have to be taken along for IPV. The supporting documents will be verified with the original. The original is returned to you, after verification, while the forms and supporting documents are submitted to any SEBI registered intermediary including mutual fund AMCs or to any of the RTA's service centres, who in turn will forward it to any of the centralised KRAs. Once these processes are completed the details are uploaded on the KRAs' servers. The KRA will, in turn, send a letter to you within 10 days confirming the details. Initial KYC is sufficient for you to start investing, while the KRA completes the rest of the process. Intimation about application for/success of Centralised KYC (KYC Acknowledgement) should be carefully preserved and a copy of the same should be attached along with the transaction slip to invest in a mutual fund with which you completed the KYC process. Copies of KYC acknowledgement can be given to other mutual funds, either before or at the time of next investment. First-time investors, who have undergone the common KYC process with another SEBI registered intermediary, shall enclose the KYC acknowledgement along with fresh applications.

Alternatively, visit www.cvlindia.com and click on 'Inquiry on KYC'. A small window will pop up on your screen that will ask for your PAN card number. Fill it up and submit. If your KYC is approved, you will get a notification on the screen saying so. You need to take a printout of it as proof.

You do not need any further KYC for dealing in any part of the securities market (depository, stock exchange transactions, mutual fund transactions, etc.). In the event of change of address or any other information, you need to fill the standard form and follow the prescribed process only once, with any of the intermediaries mentioned above. Based on that, the information will be updated with all the mutual funds and other capital market related parties where you have invested.

In the case of investments by a Power of Attorney (PoA) holder on your behalf, KYC requirements have to be complied with, by both, the PoA holder and you.

If you wish to invest in the name of a minor, you need to fill in a third-party declaration form. Only parents are allowed to invest on behalf of their children. Documents that establish the parent's relationship with the child should be submitted; for example, a passport. If the child has no parents in case of an eventuality, then a court-appointed guardian can invest. If necessary, documentary proof is submitted to establish the relationship between the minor child and the guardian. KYC requirements have to be complied with by the guardian.

SEBI had made it mandatory for all individual investors (existing and new) to provide additional details such as occupation details, gross annual income, net worth and political association, if any, before December 31, 2015. These details were marked in the Scheme Application Form. This was in addition to the standard KYC form. Apart from furnishing these additional details, In-Person Verification had to be completed. If the above details were not provided before December 31, 2015, the KYC status was displayed 'On Hold' and according to the circular of AMFI, the fund house cannot make any transaction in such an account. No new purchase or switch transactions were allowed unless the KYC was updated or a new KYC form was processed.

KYC formalities can now be completed online with direct authorisation of investors, thanks to e-KYC. Currently e-KYC is available only to individual investors with single mode account. The key objective of e-KYC is to reduce turnaround time and paper work. e-KYC formalities can be completed online with hassle-free and paperless procedure. There are no forms to download, no taking print-outs, no signing and no document proofs to be uploaded for all resident individuals. There is not even a need to visit a physical office for verification. Everything can be done in a few simple steps:

1. Enter Basic details

   You have to log into the KRA website and enter basic details such as PAN number, e-mail id, AMC name, bank name, date of birth, mode of holding and tax status. On providing these details, your KYC compliance status will be displayed. If you are not KYC compliant, you are required to add your Aadhaar number and registered mobile number.

2. Aadhaar-based authentication

   After providing the Aadhaar number and registered mobile number, the Aadhaar authentication screen is displayed. An OTP (one-time password) is sent to the registered mobile number. The same needs to be entered on the screen along with pin code. The OTP will be valid for 30 minutes. In the event of non-receipt you need to regenerate OTP to restart the process.

3. Uploading documents

   After Aadhaar authentication, you are required to upload a self-attested copy of e-Aadhaar. Further, you will be required to select consent displayed on the screen for further processing of the request.

4. Verification

   Your Aadhaar and registered mobile number is verified with the Aadhaar database of the UIDAI. Upon successful verification, the screen displays that you are e-KYC verified and can carry out transactions in mutual funds.

You have to log into any one of the KRA website. KRAs are the agencies that offer KYC services to all mutual fund companies. You are required to fulfil KYC requirements with these agencies once and your completed KYC record will be updated into KYC Registration Agency Systems for usage by other intermediaries.

Currently, SEBI permits mutual fund investment of Rs 50,000 each financial year per mutual fund for e-KYC. Once the investment reaches Rs 50,001 in a financial year, you will have to undergo normal in-person KYC verification.

Submitting the Application Form

You can submit completed application forms, along with self-attested copy of the PAN card and copy of the KYC Acknowledgement, at the investor service centres or collection centres of the mutual funds, along with the cheque/DD either directly or through the agents/distributors. The application form, signed by the holders, is tantamount to acceptance of the offer. You cannot claim ignorance of a provision after having signed the application form.

Purchase of Mutual Fund Units

The normal application form, with KIM attached, is designed for fresh purchases, i.e. instances where you do not have an investment account (technically called "folio") with the specific mutual fund. The mutual fund would need the application form with the prescribed documentation and the requisite investment amount, to allot an investment folio in your name. While investing, you need to confirm that the investment is above the minimum investment limit set by the mutual fund for the scheme.

Once you have a folio with a mutual fund, subsequent investments with the same mutual fund do not call for the full application form and documentation. For additional purchases, you need to fill and submit the transaction slip along with the requisite payment. Similarly, you can use the transaction slip in the event of change in any information, e.g. your address. Most mutual funds send a transaction slip (with your folio number pre-printed) along with the Statement of Account. Alternatively, a blank transaction slip (without pre-printed folio number), which is available with the branches of the AMC, distributors and ISCs, or downloadable from the internet, can be used. You need to confirm that the investment is above the minimum investment limit set by the mutual fund for additional purchases in the scheme.

Online transactions facility is given to an existing investor in a mutual fund. You are required to fill the requisite details in an application form.

Based on this, the registrar would allot a user name and password (Personal Identification Number – PIN). You can use this to make additional purchases of units in the mutual fund, or to request redemption of the units held in the mutual fund. Some distributors too, through their websites, facilitate online transactions by investors. For investors directly investing into mutual funds without routing through a distributor, mutual funds/AMCs provide a separate plan called "direct plan". Units under this plan have a lower expense ratio and have a separate NAV.

Demat Account

Dematerialisation is a process whereby your holding of investments in physical form (paper), is converted into a digital record. Your purchase and sale of mutual funds get automatically added or subtracted from the investment demat account, without having to execute cumbersome paperwork. With National Stock Exchange and Bombay Stock Exchange making available screen-based platforms for purchase and sale of mutual fund schemes there has been widespread use of demat facility by mutual fund investors.

The demat facility is typically initiated by the mutual fund, which ties up with a depository (National Securities Depository Ltd. or Central Depository Securities Ltd.). On the basis of this tie-up, you can go to a depository participant (which is generally a bank or a broking house) and demat your investment holding, i.e. convert your physical units into demat units. In order to avail of this facility, the depository participant will insist on your opening a demat account. Usual KYC documentation will be required. However, once the KYC is performed for opening a demat account, no separate KYC is required to be done by the AMC or distributor. If the investor is already KYC compliant, he need not undergo the process again.

On dematerialisation, your holding will be added to your demat account. As and when you sell the units, the relevant number of units will be reduced from your demat account.

Less paperwork in buying or selling the units and correspondingly, accepting or giving delivery of the units, direct credit of bonus and rights units that you are entitled to, into your demat account are some of the benefits that arise from holding a demat account. Change of address or other details need to be given only to the depository participant, instead of separately to every company/mutual fund where you have invested. You also have the option to convert the demat units into physical form. This process is called re-materialisation.

Receipt of Fund Account Statement

After processing of the application form, the registrars will allot an account number or folio number and units and dispatch an account statement to you. Your mutual fund holdings are identified by the account number or folio number. A CAS can also be received by you, if you desire to consolidate your holdings in the mutual fund across schemes.

SEBI has mandated all fund houses to send monthly CAS to their unit-holders with effect from October 2011. Consolidated Account Statement is a single account statement that consolidates financial transactions, holdings at the end of the Statement period, including transaction charges paid to the distributor, in all folios of an investor across all schemes of all mutual funds. A monthly CAS includes only those folios in which financial transactions have taken place during the month, provided the folios have valid PAN numbers available for all the unit-holders, who are also KYC compliant. For example, if an investor has 3 folios and transacts in only 2 folios in a month, the CAS for the month will include only the 2 folios and not the third folio. CAS for folios that do not have a financial transaction in a half-year period ending September or March will be sent in the following month detailing the holding at the end of 6 months. CAS includes all types of financial transactions such as purchase, including NFOs, redemption including maturity and switches, systematic transactions similar to SIP, SWP, STP, etc. dividend payouts or reinvestments, mergers, bonus transactions, etc. Transactions under demat mode are not included and investors should check their demat account statement for the same. CAS will be sent on or before the 10th calendar day of the following month for folios which have been transacted during the previous month. From March 2015, investors can keep track of all their investments in stocks and mutual funds with a single CAS.

In open-end funds, the account statement shows the holdings and the transactions. Mutual funds also provide transaction slips. The account statement is computer generated and has no signature. It is not an instrument that can be traded or transferred. In the case of listed closed-end funds, certificates which are negotiable instruments or depository receipts are received as proof of purchase. Certificates have a folio number and distinctive number and can be held in market lots of fifty units each. It is a very safe way of holding mutual fund units.

Pledging of Mutual Fund Units as Security

Mutual fund units can be offered as security by way of a pledge in favour of Scheduled Banks, NBFCs, or financial institutions. An AMC will note and record such pledged units and you will be required to fill a standard form provided by the AMC for this purpose.

Redemption of Units

You have to make a request to the AMC to redeem any amount or number of units (it can be in parts or in full) according to your desire. The redemption price is the applicable NAV less exit load, if applicable. If you have specified the redemption amount, then that amount divided by the redemption price would be the number of units that will be reduced from your folio. If you have specified the redemption units, then those many units will be reduced from your folio; payment would be made equivalent to the number of units redeemed, multiplied by the redemption price. If, during the process of redemption, the investment holding in the folio goes below the minimum limit set by the mutual fund for the scheme, then all the units may be redeemed and your investment folio will be closed.

The transaction slip or repurchase requisition slip (attached as a tear-off portion of the account statement) can be used for this purpose. You have to send the repurchase requisition slip, duly completed and signed, to the registrar and transfer agents. In the case of closed-end funds you have to send the original certificate, duly discharged by signing on the reverse, to the registrar and transfer agent.

The redemption request has to be submitted at any of the investor service centres as mentioned in the offer document/KIM of the scheme.

Payment Mechanism for Redemption of Units

You have various options for receiving the money, due to you from the scheme on redemption of units. "A/c. payee only" cheques drawn in the name of the sole holder or the first-named holder is a traditional approach, where the receipt of money in your bank account is delayed on account of the processes involved, viz. time taken by the AMC to prepare and send the cheque, time taken by postal authorities/courier to deliver the cheque, time taken by you to deposit the cheque in the bank and time taken by the banking system to transfer the proceeds to your bank account. You can give instructions for the redemption proceeds to be directly transferred to your bank account. Direct credit to your bank account (in case you have an account with the bank in which the AMC has a tie-up) is much faster because the various processes mentioned earlier for payment by cheque, are obviated. It may be noted that for non-resident investors, payment is made by the AMC in rupees. In case the investment has been made on repatriable basis and the investor wishes to transfer the money abroad, the costs associated with converting the rupees into any foreign currency would be to the account of the investor.

Dividends/Redemption/Repurchase Proceeds

A mutual fund is required to dispatch to you the dividend warrants within 30 days of the declaration of the dividend. The redemption or repurchase proceeds are to be dispatched within 10 working days from the date of redemption or repurchase request made by you. In case of failure to dispatch the dividend/redemption/repurchase proceeds within the stipulated time, the AMC is liable to pay interest as specified by SEBI from time to time (15% at present).

Redressal of Complaints

In the offer document of the mutual fund scheme, you would find the name of the contact person, whom you may approach in case of any query, complaint, or grievance. The names of the directors of AMCs and trustees are also given in the offer document. You can also approach SEBI for resolution of complaints. On receipt of complaints, SEBI takes up the matter with the concerned mutual fund and follows up with them till the matter is resolved. Various investor forums also take up the case of individual investors. You can also turn to the judiciary as the last resort.

It would be in your best interest if you take the following precautions while investing in mutual funds:

- Keep a photocopy of the application form;
- Preserve the counterfoil/acknowledgement issued by the collection agency;
- Opt for joint ownership, preferably;
- Clearly state a nominee in the application form;
- Cross your cheques and write your name and application number on the back of the cheque;
- To facilitate consolidation of holdings, you can quote your unique account number; and
- Maintain complete records of your transactions going back many years.

The sundry services offered by mutual funds include phone transactions/information, cheque writing, passbooks, tax information and periodic statements, including statutory information, etc. During the past decade, mutual funds have started offering several value-added services similar to electronic fund transfer facility, investment and repurchase facility through the internet, holding investment in electronic form (demat facility), systematic withdrawal and deposit facility, etc. While all these services have been explained in detail in this chapter, investment through the internet has been dealt with in the next chapter.

NRI Investment in Mutual Funds

Indian citizens, who are working abroad and their family residing abroad, are typical NRIs who invest in India. Some Indians go on to become citizens of foreign countries such as the United States, Canada, Australia, etc. Since India does not permit dual citizenship, they need to give up their Indian citizenship. However, their status as erstwhile Indians, entitles them to invest in mutual fund schemes on full repatriation or non-repatriation basis. As part of the documentation, they will need to provide their PIO (Person of Indian Origin) Card/OCI (Overseas Citizenship of India) Card.

For an NRI to invest in India directly, he needs to show that he is a person of Indian origin. An Indian passport would serve the purpose. Else, he needs to apply for an OCI (Overseas Citizen of India) card, or a PIO

(Person of Indian Origin) card. For this, he needs to show that he was born in India, or any of his previous 2 generations (parents and/or grandparents) were born in India. The process takes anywhere from 3 weeks to 2 months. Simultaneously, the person looking to invest in India needs to apply for a PAN online or otherwise. He will also need to provide documentary evidence of identity proof and address proof, both overseas and in India, so as to comply with KYC norms.

For buying or selling shares, an NRI needs to have a broking or trading account, a demat account and of course, a bank account. Trading or broking account is used to buy or sell shares and mutual funds. Demat account is for holding shares and mutual funds in electronic form. Bank account is held in respect of purchasing shares or mutual funds, to credit dividends and to get the sales and redemption proceeds.

3-in-1 accounts are in vogue allowing him to operate the 3 accounts on a single platform. He can open all 3 accounts with the same bank using a single account opening form and know your client form. Funds can be transferred from the bank account to the trading account while buying securities and to the bank account while selling or redeeming them. It reduces paperwork involving cheques, fund transfers, contract notes, account statements, order placements and branch banking transactions. The bank account is only used for securities transactions to see and block the balance. Net banking is not available with 3-in-1 passwords. The demat account can be debited only for online transactions linked to the trading account and is secured from being debited in favour of any third party. In the case of NRIs, banks allow them to link their NRE/NRO bank accounts, PIS/Non-PIS trading accounts and demat accounts.

Portfolio Investment Scheme (PIS) is a scheme of the RBI under which NRIs can purchase and sell shares and convertible debentures of Indian companies on a recognised stock exchange in India by routing all such purchase/sale transactions through their account held with a designated bank branch. PIS account is applicable only for NRIs and not for resident Indians. It is only for trading in Indian markets and not any other foreign markets. It is applicable only for equity trades and not mutual fund investments. It is a normal savings bank account, which can be opened with any bank in India. Non-PIS is a normal savings bank account for which the transactions are not reported to RBI. This account takes care of selling all those shares, which are not allowed under PIS. Shares acquired under IPO or received as gift or bought as resident Indian can be sold under Non-PIS account. Mutual fund transactions of NRIs are routed through Non-PIS account.

Once the mutual fund investment is made, if it becomes impossible for the NRI to keep track of the money he has invested and react according to the market movements, the NRI can allow his PoA holder to take decisions on his behalf. The PoA holder needs to submit the attested copy of the PoA document (that has the signature of the investor and the PoA holder in it) to the fund house. An NRI can also make an Indian resident as his nominee in the mutual fund scheme and *vice versa*, i.e. an NRI can also be held as the nominee for the investments made by the resident Indian.

For NRIs, the cost of transacting directly in stocks is higher than that for resident Indians. NRIs must use their equity accounts to build a long-term portfolio as active trading turns out to be expensive. Further, restrictions on derivatives also exist. It may be prudent for them to consider mutual funds as a simpler way to start investing in India.

With India being one of the most promising emerging markets, NRIs have a keen interest in being part of the Indian growth story. Here are 7 questions that NRIs tend to grapple with:

Can NRIs Invest in Mutual Funds?

Yes, NRIs can invest in mutual funds in India. But they must do so in Indian currency. The money should be channelised from an account specially designed for NRIs. But all investors, including NRIs, need to have a permanent account number (PAN). NRIs can keep necessary documents, forms and authorisation required to carry out the transactions with their relatives or close friends in India so that the access is swift.

What are the other avenues that NRIs can invest in?

According to RBI rules, NRIs can freely invest on repatriation and non-repatriation basis in Government dated securities/Treasury bills and Non-convertible debentures of a company incorporated in India. The RBI permits NRIs and PIO to buy immovable property in India other than agricultural land/plantation property or a farm house out of repatriable and/or non-repatriable funds. NRIs are not permitted to invest in small savings or PPF.

How Must One Invest so That the Money Can Be Taken Out of the Country?

NRIs/Persons of Indian Origin resident abroad have the facility of investing on repatriable basis, i.e. when they sell the investment, the sale proceeds can be transferred abroad. Payments can be made by inward remittance through funds held in the Non-Resident (External) Rupee Account (NRE) and the Foreign Currency Non-Resident Account (FCNR). Indian rupee drafts or cheques can also be made out from these accounts and submitted along with an account debit certificate from the bank or directly credited to the investor's account. In the case of repatriation, the redemption amount is paid in the local currency, rupee and NRI investors have to bear the currency risk.

NRE accounts must be maintained in Indian rupees but must be opened with funds remitted from abroad. The account can be in the form of a savings or current account or a recurring or fixed deposit. Money can be transferred out of India and interest income is free of income tax. FCNR accounts were opened and maintained in specified foreign currency: Dollars (US, Canadian and Australian), Pound Sterling, Japanese Yen and Euro. According to the Reserve Bank of India, Indians who have non-resident accounts in the country can now hold them in any currency, which is fully convertible. This helps NRIs/Persons of Indian Origin as it gives them more options in the holding of accounts and lessens the risk from fluctuations in major currencies. This account can only be held in the form of a term deposit. Just like the NRE account, the interest income is tax-free.

How Does One Invest on a Non-repatriable Basis?

NRIs can invest on a non-repatriable basis, in which case the proceeds from the sale of those investments cannot be remitted abroad. NRIs wanting to invest on a non-repatriable basis can do so through a Non-Resident Ordinary Rupee Account (NRO). This is a rupee-denominated account and can be in the form of a savings or current account, or a recurring or fixed deposit. This account can be held jointly with an Indian resident. What is interesting about this account is that the interest earned on it is repatriable, net of taxes.

What Is the Tax Impact?

The tax treatment for NRIs is somewhat similar to that for resident Indian citizens. Tax is payable when the units of a fund are sold (capital gain) or dividends are earned. For the financial year 2016–17, in the case of equity funds (those with an equity exposure exceeding 65%), short-term capital gain is taxed at 15% plus surcharge and cess. This is for units of equity funds redeemed within one year of purchase. There is no tax on long-term capital gain. For non-equity funds, the long-term capital gain (for units held for 36 months or more from July 10, 2014) is taxed at 10% without indexation for unlisted units and 20% with indexation for listed units. The short-term capital gain is added to income and taxed at the relevant income tax slab. Dividends are tax-free in the hands of the investor, but a dividend distribution tax is directly levied on a debt fund. The fund will make this payment out of the amount that is set aside for dividends. So, in effect, the investor proportionately receives lesser but tax-free dividend. Equity schemes are exempted from dividend distribution tax. TDS is applicable to NRIs (discussed in detail in Chapter 20).

Does the country of residence have a say on NRI investment in India?

NRI investments need to comply with 2 sets of regulations – India and the country that they are currently resident in. This is important as each country can have a different set of rules. For example, NRIs in the Middle East have no restrictions on where they can invest. On the other hand, USA has severe restrictions on where its residents can invest, even if the residents are not US passport holders.

Can Investments Be Done Online?

Brokers such as ICICI Direct, HDFC Securities, India Infoline, Share Khan, etc. allow NRIs (as well as other investors) to buy stocks and mutual funds online. The flexibility of having an online account is the convenience of monitoring the portfolio and the ease of transactions. NRIs need not fill a form or issue a cheque every time an investment has to be made. They just need to place an order online and the amount gets debited from the linked NRE/NRO account. The account opening and annual charges of online brokers are not very high but are at a premium when compared to the rates offered for domestic investors. Many of the mutual funds' websites also allow online investing (more on this in the next chapter).

Technological advances have ushered in a vast supply of new services that allow you to invest with ease. Mutual fund investors have benefited from these technological advances, as funds have continually offered improved services to meet changing investor needs.

Chapter 24
Advent of Online Investing
Torrential Technological Triumph

Internationally, as well as in India, online investing continues its meteoric rise. Many have debated about the success of e-commerce and its breakthroughs, but it is true that this aspect of technology could and would change the way the financial sector functions. Therefore, mutual funds cannot be left far behind. They have realised the potential of the internet and are equipping themselves to perform better.

With the advent of online trading in mutual funds and the seamless integration of banking, broking and demat accounts, the rigorous formalities connected with application or agreement, point of receipt, the form of payment, continuing payment, physical certificates, registering a mutual fund account and repurchase and redemption options have been either done away with or simplified and taken care of by the online trader. ICICI Direct was the pioneer and a number of online platforms have followed suit. Idbipaisabuilder, Indiainfoline, Myiris, Indiabulls, Sharekhan, Reliancemoney, IL&FSinvestsmart, HDFC bank, NRI InvestIndia, Barjeelgeojit, etc. are online trading platforms for mutual funds that have sprouted in recent years. Online investing is also done through the respective mutual funds' websites.

With increased internet penetration, most financial transactions have gone online. Mutual fund assets traded online is growing rapidly. Such increases in volumes are expected to bring about large changes in the way mutual funds conduct their business. Not only online transactions take less effort, they are also easy to organise. Furthermore, a search for a history of transactions is easily possible. These advantages and much more are available when you buy mutual funds online.

Here are some of the basic changes that have taken place since the advent of online trading:

* **Lower costs:** Mutual funds can bring down their administrative costs to 0.75% if trading is done online. As per SEBI regulations, bond funds can charge a maximum of 2.25% and equity funds can charge 2.5% as recurring expenses. Therefore, if the recurring expenses are low, the benefits are passed on to you. This will enable mutual funds to attract more investors and increase their asset base.

* **Better services and advice:** Mutual funds can provide better advice to you through the internet rather than through the traditional investment routes. Besides, direct dealing with the online trader could help you with your financial planning since you could avail of the resources of the online trader.

* **Easy access:** You enjoy easy access to information about mutual funds. You can transact with funds either directly or through online brokers.

* **Young investors prefer online transactions:** Mutual funds can target investors, who are young and tech-savvy, since servicing them would be easier on the internet.

* **Advertisements over the internet**: There are more sites involved in advertisements for promoting mutual funds. In the USA sites similar to AOL and Morningstar offer detailed research and financial information about the functioning of different funds and their performance statistics and serve as an excellent resource. In India, notable sites include valueresearchonline, ICICIdirect, idbipaisabuilder, indiainfoline, moneycontrol, etc.

* **Research availability:** With several hundred mutual fund schemes on offer, it is tough to decide on which one to buy. Most websites facilitating purchase of mutual funds online offer live research support, which means you can check out the top-performing funds in each category for different time periods. Comparisons can be done right up to the last NAV. In-house research teams also advise you based on your individual investment horizons. This apart, there are ready-made asset allocation models you can use to construct your portfolio based on your age and risk appetite and if you want to keep it simple, you can just mimic these model portfolios. You are also supported with various calculators.

* **Portfolio tracker:** Your entire mutual fund portfolio, be it in equity or debt, is consolidated and can be viewed on a single screen. Your portfolio is updated daily with the latest NAV and you can also see research recommendations against the schemes. This helps you take decisions about your portfolio quickly and with minimum delay.

* **Integrated paperless approach:** In the physical route, you are burdened with paperwork and movement of paper. With online investing, you get the ease of transacting from any corner of the world at any point of time. You can just go online and invest. As internet banking spreads, the integration of your banking account with your mutual fund account also ensures seamless transactions and instant confirmation of transactions. When you transact online, you do not have to wait for paper to know whether your cheque is cleared, or something is missing in your form.

* **Invest in SIP/SWP:** Investing in a systematic investment plan or a systematic withdrawal plan is a pleasure when you do it online. In the case of an emergency, even at the last moment, you can stop a payment. In the physical mode, you would have to fill in forms and send it to the registrar, which would require a minimum of 2 days. An added advantage is automatic reminders that inform you when your SIP gets over.

* **Buy through brokers:** With stock brokers now being allowed to buy and sell mutual fund units through the exchange, you can also buy mutual funds by logging on to your trading account. However, it is yet to catch investors' fancy.

* **Queries:** Some websites give you an opportunity to build communities where you can interact with other investors. The communities provide a platform to clarify doubts on investments in mutual funds, financial planning and such other related areas. For example, you can ask questions on any specific fund and you will be answered by experts either from mutual funds or from the research team of the web site.

These fundamental changes have given rise to a mushroom growth of online investment portals and services. A select few are presented below.

In July 2008, Fidelity Mutual Fund launched an online platform, Funds Network, a technology-powered solution, which provides mutual fund advisers with business tools that support transactional and reporting requirements as well as planning and guidance needs. This platform offers online a range of funds from a number of fund houses. Market development and penetration of mutual funds have been severely limited by the smaller number of agents selling funds especially when compared with the insurance industry's strength in the number of agents. The challenge has been further aggravated by poor acceptance of mutual funds among insurance agents. This facility is aimed to help intermediaries to grow their business by allowing them to focus on customer acquisition, advice and relationship management, without being concerned about back-office and administrative issues. Funds Network is a business partner for mutual fund agents and provides them business coaching to help them grow their business aided by modern management tools. The platform can also be used by you to invest directly or through intermediaries in various mutual fund schemes. Funds Network has a presence in the USA, the UK, Germany and Taiwan.

In April 2009, iFast India launched a financial integrated wealth management platform. This online business-to-business platform offers integrated mutual fund products and services to IFAs. The platform acts as a link and offers a comprehensive platform, including investment management, research, investment training, IT services and back-office functions to the IFAs and financial institutions. The iFAST platform gives IFAs the ability to offer wrap accounts to their clients, where all the unitised investment holdings of a client can be "wrapped" and managed conveniently in one account. iFAST launched Fundsupermart.com, an online platform for mutual fund investment in September 2009. iFAST launched WRAP Product in August 2012 and insurance coverage for iFAST advisers in July 2014.

In June 2009, Birla Sun Life Mutual Fund launched iSIP or internet based SIP that enables you to start your SIP investments online. Being faster, more convenient and providing paperless management of SIPs, iSIP provides many benefits to you. The service is available through Citibank, ING Bank, Axis Bank, etc. You can invest through a current or savings account held with the registered banks. This facility is not available for NRI accounts. The company has leveraged technology platforms through its "Anytime Anywhere" initiative to provide its customers enhanced service experience. It offers you the facility to track your investments through internet based Online Portfolio Management Services, through Interactive Voice Response System on Toll-free numbers and through Mobile Investment Manager. All these services are secure, user-friendly and more importantly available 24x7. The endeavour is to provide you with a full range of convenient service solutions.

In November 2009, SEBI paved the way for funds to be sold on stock exchanges. BSE's platform was christened BSE Star Mutual Fund Platform while NSE's was called the Mutual Fund Service System (MFSS). Asset management companies started selling funds on NSE from November 30, 2009, with UTI being the first to do so. Fidelity, SBI and HDFC fund houses were amongst the first few to start selling funds through BSE, though they also have the same arrangement with NSE and several funds have followed suit. Purchase applications below Rs. one crore are allowed. Both the platforms facilitate purchase and redemption of mutual fund units by investors through NSE or BSE brokers and sub-brokers across its network.

Steps to Purchase Mutual Funds Through Stock Exchanges

Indicated below are steps to purchase mutual funds through stock exchanges.

Step: 1 Getting Started

Open a demat account with a depository participant, who operates as an agent of the two depositories in the country — National Securities Depository (NSDL) and Central Depository Services (CDSL). You would also need to open a trading account with an eligible stock broker (who is registered with the association of mutual funds — AMFI). KYC procedure will be conducted by the depository participant while opening the demat account, if you are not already KYC compliant.

Step: 2 Trading

For buying/redeeming mutual fund units, as in the case of stocks, you will have to send the instruction to your broker, who will, in turn, place the order on the terminal on your behalf, after collecting the money and brokerage from you. During redemption, however, the proceeds are directly credited to your account by the mutual fund.

> **Step: 3 Settlement**
>
> While purchasing units, the transactions are settled on a T+1 basis. Redemptions are done on T+3 for equity mutual funds and T+1 for debt mutual funds. Transactions, however, cannot be initiated after trading hours, as NSE terminals shut at 3 p.m. Under the existing system, you can go to your distributor or the mutual fund after 3 p.m., but it is the next business day's NAV that will be taken into account.
>
> **Step: 4 Keeping Track**
>
> The holding report, which is submitted by the DP (and not the AMC, unlike the existing format) will provide a snapshot of the stocks as well as the mutual fund units that you own, presenting a more holistic picture of your total investments.

This initiative, undertaken by SEBI to provide millions of investors spread across 1,500 towns and cities the ability to transact in mutual funds *via* the 2,00,000 terminals, is a giant step for increasing local participation in India's growing stock markets. Speedy execution and less paperwork are the other advantages. The stock exchange platforms have not taken off in a big way due to the higher costs incurred by investors, the need for opening demat accounts, the short-term viewpoint ingrained in the broker's approach to stock trades, which is diametrically opposite to the long-term view warranted in the case of mutual funds, etc. A cheaper option for new investors is the online portal maintained by mutual funds themselves that do not levy transaction charges. Access to the stock exchange platform was hitherto available to stock brokers only. Mutual fund distributors had to become sub-brokers with a broker in order to transact in mutual funds. Commission was received by the main broker and passed on to the sub-broker. Since 2013, mutual fund distributors have been directly transacting on the stock exchange platform under their own ARNs.

CAMS and KARVY, the two Registrar and Transfer Agents, who between them service 95% of the mutual fund industry, joined hands to launch 'FINNET' in December 2009. Finnet is an "all-in-one engine" product, which facilitates transacting (order placement), execution and customer service on an integrated system.

This software allows IFAs to service their customers by providing enhanced after-sales support. Prior to the launch, Karvy and CAMS had separate software packages to generate online statements and to monitor the asset allocation at the customer or family level. The new system integrates both databases and provides you with a bird's eye view of all your holdings. The lack of regular updates on investments is one problem that many investors face today. The new product offered by these registrars obviates this difficulty. Here is what it offers:

Consolidated account statement: You can request for a single consolidated account statement across your entire holdings in CAMS and Karvy-serviced mutual funds. If you have a registered e-mail address, you can use this service to get an account statement in the PDF format e-mailed to you. In fact, the provider promises the account statement within an hour of request. This statement will divulge the funds held by you, the number of units held, prevailing NAV and the calculated market value.

Consolidated portfolio statement: This statement contains balances by security, cost value, market value, period of holding and return on investment.

Consolidated realised gains statement: This statement will show your investment performance, capital gains and income for the current and previous financial years e-mailed to your registered e-mail address. The best part of all this is that the services come free to you.

For those of you who do not have access to e-mail, turning to independent financial advisers, who have access to the product is a good course. For distributors and independent financial advisers, this product comes at a more affordable cost than the ones being used now. Upgrades are provided automatically.

Here is how Finnet works for a mutual fund agent:

* It makes the job of filling application forms easier and seamless. Once client details are captured through the purchase of one fund product, the details can be used for subsequent transactions by mapping this information into the application forms.

* For instance, if you have invested in a mutual fund scheme and are planning to invest in another, the agent can take a form that has all the basic details filled in to get your signature, along with the cheque.

- A visit to the registrar's office can be done away with. All the distributor needs to do is scan the application form online from his office and send it via Finnet.

- This makes it easier for agents to log in application forms electronically before 3 p.m., the cut-off time for the day's NAV, saving time and transportation costs involved in going to the registrar's office to submit the application form in time for stamping.

- The cheque is to be picked up by a registrar-appointed agency from the distributor's office. The original application forms, however, have to be couriered to the respective registrar within 15 days.

- Your statement of account can be generated the very next day to be forwarded to you. For subsequent transactions such as redemptions, top ups and switch-ins too the distributor can generate the request from this platform.

- If you have multiple accounts within the family and use a common e-mail address in application forms, the product allows generation of a consolidated single statement for the entire family. For investments through systematic investment plan, the platform alerts the distributor when the final instalment is due.

SBI Mutual Fund became the first fund house to introduce a new payment option (for investment) effective March 22, 2010, offering online investment in SBI Mutual Fund schemes through State Bank of India's ATM-cum-Debit Cards. This technically enables all SBI ATM-cum-Debit Card holders to invest in SBI Mutual Fund's schemes even if they do not have SBI Internet banking facility, thereby, adding to a whole new universe of potential investors for SBI Mutual Fund. This facility is available for all SBI Mutual Fund's equity and most of the debt schemes. You can invest amounts, subject to a maximum limit, as periodically decided by SBI. SBI Mutual Fund provides you an online purchase facility, through their website. This mode of payment, besides enhancing reach, brings in customer convenience.

Retail mutual fund investors are experiencing the power of the thumb. Managing mutual funds has become a simpler task with top asset management companies going mobile with their offerings. A host of fund houses have set up 'mobile digital platforms' which allow you to purchase, redeem, or switch your portfolios using a simple Java-enabled cell phone. The setting up of mobile digital platforms is seen as a method to bring you closer to asset management companies by eliminating the extra layer of local distributors and stock brokers (who have now been empowered to buy/sell mutual funds through stock exchanges).

From your perspective, managing mutual fund portfolios using mobile phones is as easy and hassle-free as buying schemes through the internet. Broad requirements for using a 'mobile digital platform' includes a java-enabled mobile phone (priced above Rs. 3,000 in India), an existing folio with the fund house, a net banking option, a fund house-allotted PIN, a link-up with a mobile payment vendor such as Ngpay, Obopay or Meramobi and PAN.

You have to first download the vendor application on your cell phone. The URL for downloading the vendor application is usually sent to your phone (on request) through a text message. Upon downloading the application, the vendor asks you to enter basic identification and bank details. According to IT experts, the data entered is secure as it passes to the vendor's server in a coded capsule format. Once the linkage is set up, buying a mutual fund is as simple as buying a movie ticket using a debit card. On clicking the scheme you want to buy (either on the fund house mobile page or on the vendor page), the vendor routes the request to the net banking site for payment. Once the payment is made, the scheme is added to the existing folio. Both the vendor and fund house mobile page have links to carry out a switch or redemption. All transactions involving money are linked to the net banking facility to standardise the payment mode.

The move to take fund transactions to mobile phones increases the reach of mutual funds to rural areas as well. Mobile phones have a greater penetration in rural India than the internet. There are 924 million mobile users in India with 130 million mobile internet users. However, rapid changes in the industry, say for instance, the entry load ban and fund trading through stock exchanges, have forced some fund houses to defer work on the digital mobile platform.

HDFC Mutual Fund, Birla Sun Life Mutual Fund, Reliance Mutual Fund, L& T Mutual Fund, UTI Mutual Fund, ICICI Prudential Mutual Fund, etc. have launched mobile platforms. The mobile phone platform may sound the death knell to the trend of buying funds through the internet.

In September 2014, CAMS, the leading service solution partner to mutual funds in India, introduced 'Anytime,

Anywhere Mutual Funds,' the next-generation mobility-enabled "on the go" solutions designed to enable mutual fund transaction acceptance and submission from investors' home or office. CAMS launched 4 solutions – CAMS slate, CAMS swift, CAMS scribe and my CAMS.

CAMS slate: This application is used on any tablet/smart phone and acts as an official point of transaction, which is ideal for AMC market representatives, relationship managers and distributors. This app provides customer relationship management (CRM), image capture, KYC completion, additional purchase, redemption and switch, time stamping, etc.

CAMS swift: CAMS swift is a customisable handheld device which is used from anywhere in India where a mobile phone works, in order to accept and submit mutual fund transactions. It is suitable for B-15 penetration where physical official points of transactions are not available. It is a 2G/3G enabled device which has in-built camera, USB Port, printer, SIM and biometric app. It enables KYC and biometric authentication using Aadhar database. It also has a debit card swipe facility which will enable users to accept cash and issue receipts. The device is designed especially for new cadre of distributors who accept small ticket/micro SIPs.

CAMS scribe: It is a digital pen which uses intelligent character recognition (ICR) technology which does away with the process of digitising hand written forms and instructions. It facilitates instant data and image capture and is ideal for AMC sales force and distributors.

My CAMS: This is an app, which runs on Android and iOS devices, which helps in transacting and managing information in a faster, easier and smarter way for mutual fund investors. Through this app you can submit query or register complaint to CAMS customer care centre, order encrypted statements, access account profile, see portfolio details, redeem, invest, switch and do much more.

The introduction of 'Anytime, Anywhere Mutual Funds' using tablets, digital pens, handheld devices and smartphones facilitates mutual fund relationship managers and distributors in reaching out to investors across the country at their doorstep. These devices enable digitisation and near real-time data transfer from virtually any part of the country, assuring you the same day NAV. This, besides being in alignment with market regulator SEBI's vision to encourage retail growth, will foment financial inclusion and help the mutual fund industry grow beyond the urban locations, especially in smaller towns across the country.

The Robo (Adviser) Revolution

If you have watched the famous Hollywood movie 'RoboCop', which features a superhuman law enforcer, then robo-advisers may conjure up images of robots handing out financial advice in synthesised voices. As futuristic as it sounds, that is not the case. Robo-advisory is an automated investment advice platform that provides algorithm-based advice at a very nominal cost, devoid of human intervention. The advice provided through this medium is solely based on client information provided to the system, which leads to the generation of automated portfolio allocation and investment recommendations. The whole premise of this technology is based on the aspect that algorithms can provide sound and logical financial advice at a fraction of a cost of what human advisers charge, without any bias.

How it began...

To start with, robo-advisory made its debut in the US in early 2000. Given the low initial minimum investment, almost negligible management fees and easy access, robo-advisory caught the fancy of many tech-savvy small investors, who otherwise did not have access to established financial advisers. The idea of robo-advisory became a hot cake in the US start-up space because the development of wealth management software was the only big investment required. Very soon, many companies offering proprietary wealth management software cropped up, but very few managed to thrive. Last year alone, venture capitalists collectively poured in $300 million in various companies operating in this space. Betterment, WealthFront, Personal Capital, Future Advisor and SigFig are some of the names which are ruling the roost in the online advisory space, globally. Thanks to their popularity and given the pace at which assets under management ballooned, robo-advisers were soon perceived to give traditional advisers a run for their money. Identifying the vast opportunity, many from corporate America, such as Vanguard and Charles Schwab, too, joined the party. According to global consulting firm A.T. Kearney, robo-advisers are expected to become a $2 trillion industry by 2020, up from around $20 billion till May 2015.

At present, robo-advisory is relatively new in India with FundsIndia, Arthayantra, ScripBox, BigDecisions, MyUniverse from Aditya Birla Money, Tract & Act from ICICI Securities and 5nance from Innovage Fintech, being the only players.

How it differs in India...

There are at least 3 ways in which robo-advisory services, offered in the US and India, differ.

One, the service is typically fully automated in the US. For instance, funds are selected and invested automatically without requiring any effort from the user. The services in India require the user to initiate the transaction and are not on auto-pilot.

Two, investors' money is invested in ETFs in the US, which are passive investments. The robo-advisory services are seen as alternatives to investing in traditional actively managed funds. In India, ETFs are still in early stages and money under robo-advisory is invested in mutual funds which are actively managed.

Three, the fee structure in the US is based on assets under management. For example, Wealthfront charges 0.25% of AUM annually while Betterment charges 0.15 to 0.35% based on the AUM. The fee structure in India is either free or a flat fee that is charged annually plus fixed charges for transactions.

There are other differences as well. Users in the US are used to paying advisory fees, but in India, where advisers could earn commissions, it creates conflict of interest. A shift is needed to get users in India pay for advice or services when a commission-free investment product is enabled online. Also, the advisory service in the US offers a lower cost solution to existing base of investors; in India, robo-advisers hope to increase penetration with affordable advice. Likewise, tax-loss harvesting — selling loss-making investments to offset gains with the aim of reducing tax payments — is an important aspect of robo-advisory services in the US. Tax is not yet a key focus area in India.

Robo-advisory models galore!

Robo-advisory firms in India vary in the way they offer services, but predominantly offer a basket of mutual funds you can invest in. Some operate on an advisory model and charge an advisory fee. You can then invest in mutual funds through the platform for which these platforms also charge convenience fees for facilitating the transaction. The mutual fund investments are in direct plans where the returns are typically higher by up to 1%, somewhat offsetting the additional fees you pay for advisory services. Direct plans save on the commission payable to the distributor.

The second category of firms operates on a distribution model, similar to traditional advisers. They advise on funds and assets to invest in and the transaction is completed through the platform, all for free. The platforms, in turn, earn a commission from the mutual fund house. For instance, FundsIndia. com recommends funds — based on in-house research — to meet your goals. You can use the platform for free, but only to invest in regular plans. If you want to invest in direct plans, you will have to do it independently.

Finally, there are also platforms that have a mixed model. They charge you for the advice in case you opt to transact on your own. Take the case of Arthayantra. It charges an annual fee of Rs.1,000 for financial advice. And you are free to buy the units directly from the fund house. But if you choose to make the investment through its platform, they will waive the service fee and offer you free advice. This is because they facilitate investment in regular option and thereby earn a commission from the fund house.

BigDecisions, on the other hand, (not a robo-advisory in the true sense) only provides guidance through calculators on how much corpus you must build to meet various goals. To invest, it directs you to sites such as FundsIndia. com. Robo-advisers mostly offer a portfolio made up of debt and equity mutual funds. Within this, some firms such as Scripbox only offer a limited set of funds that are pre-selected by their algorithm and in-house experts. Others may provide a wider selection of funds and some also include a wider asset base that includes gold ETFs, bonds and tax saving investments. Some advisers may also provide you advice on keeping your funds in cash based on market condition and a choice of liquid funds. The aim of these platforms, in the near future, is to be a one-stop shop for all financial advice, offering insurance, loan and property and services such as tax filing.

The modus operandi

To get started on a robo-advisory platform, you will have to create an account, add bank details, PAN and KYC details. To make an investment, you need a common account number (CAN) — a single reference for all your mutual fund investments. If you do not have one already, you can get one within 2-4 days, after which you can make purchases on these online platforms.

You have to fill out an online form in the robo-adviser's portal. The questions capture basic information, investment goals and comfort with risk. Online platforms assess your risk profile based on your responses to questions such as how you would react to a market fall. But you are not bound by the recommendations made by the platform. You still have an option to pick a portfolio that is aggressive or passive based on your comfort level. Goals could be broad-based and long term such as retirement and children's education or short-term. Users may be classified into various buckets based on parameters such as age, time horizon, quantum of investment (either lump sum or systematic investment), nature of household (single or dual income, dependants) and risk appetite. The platform's algorithm tells you the amount you must invest and into what categories of funds — diversified equity, gold, or debt. Within these, there may be finer sub-divisions such as blend of large, mid and small cap mutual funds based on your risk profile. While most of the platforms focus primarily on mutual funds, some such as AdviseSure also include property and PPF in their offering.

On an ongoing basis, you can view your portfolio online, get alerts on fund performance, monitor and change your investments. You can also keep a tab on your portfolio's performance. Some services also allow you to meet advisers while others only run online updates. These platforms also review their recommendations periodically. For instance, Scripbox revisits its fund recommendation every year. Bharosa Club evaluates its funds' performance every 6 months.

No free lunch!

For now many of the platforms are free, but this may change in the long term. ArthYanthra, for instance, lets you sign up for free and obtain an assessment of your current financial health. For a more detailed report, you need to pay a fee for personal wealth advisory service, which costs you Rs.360 annually.

Typically, platforms that operate on advisory model charge an annual fee. This covers one-time advice, ongoing portfolio alerts, analysis and enabling transactions. The fee is usually a flat fee but can be a percentage of the assets in some cases. Wixifi offers a single plan where you pay 0.5% of the average daily balance as fee. ORO Wealth, for example, charges a transaction fee of Rs.50 for investments of up to Rs.1 lakh. Thereafter the fee works out to 0.1% of the quantum invested. Bharosa Club, on the other hand, offers 3 different types of plan with fees ranging from Rs.50 per month to Rs.300 per month. Consulting with human advisers, an added feature available with some firms, may be charged additionally. You can also maintain multiple accounts under a single family account. Unovest charges you double the fee for a family account. For Invezta, you only pay an advisory fee if the recommended funds outperform the category average.

The Robo-adviser – dissected

In favour...

Low cost: This is one of the key reasons for the success of robo-advisers overseas and it is likely to do well in India, too. Personal advisers charge a minimum annual fee of Rs. 20,000 or a certain per cent of the assets under management, whichever is higher. For someone whose investible surplus is very low, this fee looks intimidating.

Zero paperwork: You can initiate an investment on the go without getting worried about the paperwork. Before the first transaction is made, the platform will check if you are KYC compliant. In case you do not have a KYC, as is the case with first-time users, the applicant will be asked to fill the application form online, upload scanned copies of supporting documents and get their e-KYC done. Thereafter, with great ease you can swiftly buy or sell any financial product offered on the platform without worrying about recurring paperwork.

Easy interface: Financial planning for most beginners is a worrisome proposition and, as a result, they shy away from investments early on in their earning lives. However, robo-advisory platforms can come to their rescue. Armed with an easy-to-understand interface and sophisticated algorithms, which lay out the path to attain your aspiration, financial planning all of a sudden looks easy and appealing. Given that the investment options are automatically populated based on your risk profile, you can rest assured that no extra in-depth research is required at this stage.

No room for bias: Human beings are bound to be biased. Sometimes, a colleague's bitter experience with, say, stock market investment, can leave you with a bias against equity related instruments. When it comes to robo-advisers, there is no room for emotion-based decisions. The algorithm-based asset allocation plan is purely devised on the basis of the user's goals and the numbers provided to the system. As a result, your portfolio will be free of the in vogue sector fund that makes a splash for a brief period of time.

Money in safe hands: Even though the user has the option of buying multiple financial products from the platform, robo-advisory companies have no access to your funds. When a mutual fund is purchased on any of the platforms, the transaction is between the fund house and your bank account. As a result, even if a company that operates the platform were to face problems, your investments would be in safe hands.

Robo-advisers have the power to address the financial advisory needs of large groups of people similar to the millennial and gen-X investors, currently ignored by traditional systems. Because of their digital nature and low fees, robo-advisers have made advisory services accessible to people with even a few thousands to spare. Use of high technology, speed, simplicity and personalisation make most of the services very appealing to millennials who are digital natives and do not like pouring over finances every day. They can look to make their money start working for them with minimal effort and stress and let the robo-adviser take care of the rest.

...and on the flip side

Limitation in customisation: It is often said that no two individual's financial planning will be similar even if they have similar backgrounds. Nonetheless, in the case of robo-advisory, two different individuals with the same risk profile may end up getting a similar portfolio or asset allocation advice. At this stage, the computer will not take into account the number of dependants on your earnings and other family background, which may impact your savings pattern.

Rigidity in plans: A plan drawn by robo-advisers will not be in a position to address any sudden monetary change in the life of the user. For instance, in case of child birth or job loss, the plan drawn cannot be altered with. However, a financial adviser can make some alterations in line with your requirements without causing much change to your portfolio.

Ultimately, it is portfolio performance that matters. So, the algorithm has to be accurate and better than others in selecting and reviewing recommendations. It is too early to judge or analyse the existing platforms, but as these firms go through more market cycles and recommendations change, the winners will come through.

Is it for you?

If you are a small investor or a beginner, finding a good adviser may be hard. Robo-advisory can help you get started and build a good portfolio. But, if you are a seasoned investor, you may be better off choosing the fund yourself and may want to use the platform to complete the transaction. HNIs investing in mutual funds may find the flat fee structure offered by select platforms attractive. It goes without saying that you have to evaluate the range of asset classes these firms offer, based on your needs. Robo-advisers claim that the fund selection is based on parameters such as performance consistency *vis-à-vis* benchmark, across market cycles, risk-adjusted performance, fund size and fund manager's track record. As in the case of a traditional adviser, be sure you do the necessary due diligence before you sign up for any of these online platforms. Check out the list of services on offer and detailed fee structure. Importantly, look at their disclosures and track record. You also need to understand the limitations of these services. For instance, you may not be able to talk with an adviser when you need to — say, when the market is volatile.

A traditional adviser will always score on personal touch and the face-to-face reassurance he/she can offer in times of need. In addition, the services offer generalised recommendations that apply to the majority. On some of these counts, online platforms may not offer the best value for your need. Even so, given that the trend is fast catching up in India, it is a space that can see a lot of action in the near future. The services may become as ubiquitous as Google maps one day. So, this is just the beginning and the best is yet to come.

Many have a great misconception that investing through online portals similar to Fundsindia, Fundsupermart, etc. offers a host of advantages and is the best and cheapest mode of investment in mutual funds. Of course, they offer you a great convenience of investing online and you can review all investments at one place. Even though these online portals do not charge you anything upfront as cost, they collect the commission from mutual fund companies which will be adjusted to the NAV of the fund.

Stock brokers such as ICICI Direct, HDFC Securities, or Sharekhan offer you investment in mutual funds through online demat accounts. Usually each SIP or investment is charged here directly from your investments. In addition, they receive commission from the respective mutual fund companies. So, this option is costlier than online portals.

The ideal mode of online investing is using the mutual fund company's website. It is a direct method. In the case of new investors in a mutual fund, the first application should be done offline. Once the folio number is generated, a PIN Agreement has to be signed with the mutual fund. Using the Folio Number as the Login id and the PIN as the password, you can start transacting online. Investing through mutual fund websites can be done without any charges. Not only is the distributor bypassed and cost in the form of commissions payable to him is saved, but it is also the most convenient and reliable mode of online investing provided you have the requisite time and knowledge.

SECTION VIII
FUND FAREWELL

"At last, the wheel comes full circle."

— Cassandra Clare

Having been exposed to the different modes of purchasing and redeeming mutual fund units, it is time now to take a look at certain circumstances under which you should redeem or sell mutual fund units. This is as important as purchase since both the actions together complete the money multiplying process of investing in mutual funds.

Chapter 25

Behold, Hold and Fold
Nothing Lasts a Lifetime

You may think that once you invest in a fund, the job of taking care of your investments has been successfully passed on to the fund manager. But this can be a dangerous strategy to adopt. If you think that your work ends when you buy a mutual fund, you are mistaken. You should regularly monitor and review your mutual fund investment. Unlike shares, mutual funds can be reviewed once a quarter.

How Do You Keep Track of Your Fund's Performance?

All AMCs provide you with their annual report, half-yearly report (unaudited results) and monthly fact sheet/newsletter. Over and above these, there is public disclosure of the NAVs of a scheme on the AMFI website and the AMC's own website, as well as in the financial dailies. While NAV tells you very little other than how well your investments are doing, it is basically the portfolio disclosure made through the fact sheets/newsletters and AMC reports that you should be interested in. You can actively monitor your mutual funds to ensure that you keep as much of your profit as possible. Your portfolio pulls together all the information you will need to stay on top of your funds and avoid being caught off guard by negative price movements. In addition, try to gauge the fund's performance *vis-à-vis* its benchmark and its peers (at least to the extent possible). The fund manager will not tell you when to exit the fund. This is something you will have to decide yourself based on the information available. So, keep track of the fund's performance. After all, it is your money and you should know what the fund is doing with it.

An important point you need to understand is that mutual funds are not synonymous with stocks. So, **a decline in the stock market does**

not necessarily mean that it is time to sell the fund. Stocks are single entities with rates of return associated with what the market will bear. Mutual funds are not singular entities. They are portfolios of financial instruments, such as stocks and bonds, chosen by a fund manager in accordance with the fund's strategy. Relying only on market timing to sell your fund may be a useless strategy since a fund's portfolio may represent different kinds of markets. Besides, mutual funds are geared towards long-term returns. A rate of return that is lower than anticipated during the first year is not necessarily a sign to sell.

But **holding on to a persistently losing fund is the most crucial mistake you might make**. Sometimes you become emotionally attached to the fund and tell yourself that the fund is bound to turn around or that you are a long-term investor and just need to stick it out and you sit back and watch these losing funds drain money out of your portfolio. But you do not have to suffer the same fate as that of the fund. For most investors, especially those with equity exposure and long-term perspectives, 'buy and hold' is the easiest strategy and one that has proven effective on a historical basis. **What 'buy and hold' really means is staying the course through short-term market dips.** However, there is a time when selling a fund is not so bad an idea. Remember mutual funds are bought to be held for a lifetime, if possible. But you obviously do not want to marry your mutual fund as things may change even if you are a long-term investor. There are times to admit an error.

Do keep in mind that even if your fund is geared to yielding long-term rates of returns, that does not mean that you have to hold onto the fund through thick and thin. The purpose of a mutual fund investment is to increase your wealth over time and not to demonstrate your loyalty to a particular sector or group of assets or a specific fund manager. **The key to successful mutual fund investing is the knowledge as to when to hold them and when to fold them.**

We shall discuss some situations that are not necessarily indications that you should fold, but situations that should raise a red flag.

A fund once bought cannot be held for eternity. There are certain circumstances that wave a red flag signalling the need to part with your prized possession. They can be those related to you as a person, who has a definite investment objective in mind as well as a certain risk tolerance and of course, reasons related to the fund's management and performance. We shall take up the **'You' related factors** in the first place.

Why did you buy the fund in the first place? What is the time horizon for which it was bought?

If the fund is not fulfilling its purpose or in case it has already fulfilled its purpose, it may be time to sell. In case the appreciation you had expected has been achieved in a shorter time than expected, then go ahead and sell. In case you had bought for the long-term so as to cream capital appreciation or for its past dividend record and it has slipped up, then there is no reason for you to continue to hold the same.

Financing a Need

We all invest money with a view to financing some need or a desire in the future. Say, you plan to buy a car or a house; or need to pay your child's fees; or maybe you want to take a vacation abroad. All this would require you to liquidate some of your investments. However, a proper choice is essential in deciding as to which fund(s) is (are) to be sold. You can sell the funds, whose performance has not been encouraging or whose tax impact is significant or where the amounts are not very large, etc. Or, sometimes possibly it may be better to borrow rather than to sell a good investment.

Rebalancing the Portfolio

We all have a certain asset allocation across various investment options such as debt, equity, real estate, gold, etc. A change in your financial position may require you to rebalance your portfolio. Suppose you presently have a well-paid job and are unmarried with no liabilities, you can take a much higher exposure in equity funds. But, with marriage and kids, your responsibilities may increase and this would require you to reduce your equity risk to more manageable levels. The portfolio balance changes with time, due to different assets growing at different rates. Your equity portion may have appreciated much faster than your debt, distorting the original balance. In such circumstances, you would need to sell equity and reinvest in debt to restore the original balance.

Adding a New Asset Class to your Portfolio

A new asset class has been introduced in the market – a capital protection fund or a gold fund – and you want to take advantage of it. You may have to sell a part of your existing investment and invest the proceeds in this new asset class.

A Change in your Personal Circumstances or Investment Objective

Depending on your investment life cycle stage, in case your long-term goals have now become short-term, shifting assets to more conservative investments may be required. So, there is no harm in shifting from equity funds to debt funds. If you are now in a different stage in your life, where you are getting closer to retirement, you might want to sell or switch aggressive growth funds for more sedate growth and income funds.

If There Are Changes in Your Risk Tolerance

There is a mismatch between your risk profile and that of the fund. The change in the risk profile could have happened due to change in personal circumstances/fortunes, or due to age, change of job, etc. You might want to sell or switch aggressive growth funds for more sedate growth and income funds.

There could, of course, be other reasons to sell, more specific to your circumstances. **The basic idea is to define beforehand certain rules for yourself for selling your investments.** This would reduce the day-to-day dilemma and *ad hoc* decision-making, thereby making investing more scientific and unemotional.

Evaluating your funds' performance in conjunction with your financial situation every quarter is the basic prerequisite while reviewing your mutual fund portfolio. Having elaborated the 'You' related factors, we now move over to the **'Fund' related factors** as to why you would want to sell your mutual fund.

Poor Performance

In the first place, compare the fund *vis-à-vis* itself at varying time periods. Obviously, a fund should be sold due to poor performance. Be careful not to sell a fund because of poor short-term performance. One bad quarter or even a sub-par year is not sufficient justification to ditch a fund, especially if it has a good long-term performance record. Usually **2 to 3 years of unexplained or dramatic underperformance** are appropriate indicators.

Change in Style or Objective of the Fund

If you researched your fund before investing in it, it is most likely you invested in a fund that accurately reflects your financial goals. If your fund manager suddenly starts investing in financial instruments that do not reflect the mutual fund's original goals, you may want to re-evaluate the fund you are holding. In case there has been a change in the fund's investment objective or strategy, you are justified in selling it. If you bought a fund for exposure to large blue-chip companies and all of a sudden it starts buying small start-ups, that is a definite red flag! Or, if you bought a fund that buys undervalued companies and it starts buying companies at any price, whose earnings are growing rapidly...another red flag. Note that funds are typically required to notify unit-holders of any changes to the original prospectus. Some funds may change their names to attract more customers. When a mutual fund changes its name, sometimes its strategies also change. **If you are not comfortable with the change in the direction of the fund, sell it.**

Change in the Fund Manager

While investing, one of the criteria is to evaluate the expertise, knowledge, experience and past performance of the fund manager. However, while the fund manager is a key player in managing your money, you should not forget the contribution of the research team, the investment committee, the top management and AMC's investment philosophy. Therefore, a change in the fund manager need not necessarily mean that you should exit the fund. But it may be worthwhile keeping the fund under a close watch. If the fund mimics a certain index or benchmark, it may be less of a worry as these funds tend to be less actively managed. For other funds, the prospectus should indicate the reason for the change in the manager. If the prospectus states that the fund's goal will remain the same, it may be a good idea to watch the fund's returns over the next year. You could also research the new manager's previous experience and performance. Give the new fund manager time, particularly if he has an investment philosophy similar to that of the previous manager. If there is **a perceptible decline in the performance** or if the **new fund manager has a different investment strategy**, you may consider selling.

Change in the Fund's Size

Sometimes the size of the fund starts affecting the returns. **The bigger the fund, the harder it is for a portfolio to move assets effectively.** Note that usually the fund size becomes more of an issue for focused funds or small cap funds, which either deal with a smaller number of shares or invest in stocks, which have low volume and liquidity. Certain mid-cap funds take a voluntary step to stop accepting fresh money into the fund, when the size becomes too large to manage. This is because (i) the mid-cap space is limited, (ii) even small purchases of such stocks send their prices soaring and (iii) too large a holding in such stocks will be difficult to offload when required. Here, of course, the funds may take a proactive step to protect the returns of the existing investors. But, if the funds themselves do not take such a step, you should take appropriate steps at the right time.

Comparative evaluation of the fund in question is the final trigger that goads you to say good bye to your fund.

Consistent Underperformance

It is important to base your decision on relative performance. You should compare the fund's performance against the most appropriate peer group – other funds having similar investment objectives or strategies. Comparing "apples to apples" is the only fair way to see if a fund is doing well or underperforming. Moreover, if your growth fund lost money in any year, it may not be such a bad thing if the index lost more than that. But the key is to look at long-term returns. In the short-term, there could be a genuine reason for underperformance – some of the investments may be from a long-term perspective, certain sectors may have been under-performers, contrarian investments take time to catch market fancy, etc. But if the performance of the fund continues to be consistently below par over long periods of time, then it may be worthwhile considering switching over to a better performing fund. When evaluating performance, be sure to measure returns against a fund's benchmark. If a fund fails to match its benchmark for 2 years in a row, that is a good enough reason to reconsider owning it. Similarly, if your fund has lagged across a market cycle (falling more than the indices in 2008 and rising much less in 2009, for instance), that too is a good reason to sell. If possible, you should also try and assess the reasons for poor performance. Exceptionally poor comparative performance should be a signal to sell the fund.

Increase in Fund Expenses

Increase in fees to the manager represents a reduction of income to you and is unlikely to be offset by higher returns. When a fund's expense ratio rises significantly, particularly in bond and money market funds, look at moving to a lower cost alternative where expenses will not be a principal factor in the fund's performance. For many funds, back end loads tend to be higher when you liquidate your units earlier rather than later. So, you need to determine if liquidating your units now is optimal.

Change in Taxation Policy

A change in the tax policy could become a reason to sell and reinvest somewhere else.

You invested in balanced funds since your risk profile is such that you can take around 50:50 equity to debt exposure. But when the **tax laws changed** wherein a fund would be classified as an equity-oriented fund only if the equity component is more than 65%, the balanced funds would have to increase the equity component to 65% so that they continue to enjoy the lower tax applicable to equity funds. But with 65% equity, it becomes riskier. Hence, it could be time to exit.

If your fund has suffered significant capital losses and you **need a tax break** to offset realised capital gains of your other investments, you may want to redeem your mutual fund units in order to apply the capital loss to your capital gains.

Selling a mutual fund is not something you do impulsively without a great deal of thought and consideration. Remember that you originally invested in your mutual fund because you were confident in it. So, make sure you are clear about your reasons for letting it go. However, if you have carefully considered all the pros and cons of your fund's performance and you still think you should sell it, do it and do not look back.

SECTION IX
FUND ADVICE

"Don't follow any advice, no matter how good, until you feel as deeply in your spirit as you think in your mind that the counsel is wise."

— Joan River

This caveat assumes paramount importance in view of the fact that there is a mushroom growth of financial advisers and some of them have the dubious distinction of operating out of vested interests.

Barring those investors who can fend for themselves, the others can place their trust on financial advisers who conform to high standards that we will discuss in the concluding chapter.

Financial advisers are in a position of power. They could be agents of change in our society. They could be nice little gardeners who take care of the garden and investors can be the flourishing plants that adorn it.

Chapter 26

Do You Need a Financial Adviser?
A Caring Gardener...

When it comes to mutual fund investments, do you feel like a rudderless ship without a plan or a map? Or, do you feel that you have a pretty good sense of where you are going? Maybe, you are somewhere in between. How do you know whether you should hire an expert or do it yourself? You may be capable of doing the job yourself if you are willing to do some homework. But **unless you have the time, ability, discipline and desire to manage your portfolio, a good financial adviser can be a tremendous asset – if not a necessity.** He can help you know where you are going so that you can end up where you need to be. Most of you would not think twice about hiring an attorney or finding a good medical doctor. A good financial adviser should fit into the same category.

The necessity for a financial adviser stems from the following factors:

Accords Top Priority to Understanding You and Your Goals

Financial advisers make it their business to learn who you are, where you are with your fund investment programme and where you want to go. From this getting-to-know-you process, your adviser can offer customised investment strategies for:

- enhancing your after-tax return opportunities,
- funding your children's education,
- funding your daughter's marriage,
- planning for your parents' financial needs in later years and
- planning for retirement.

Your financial adviser can help you create a long-term investment plan that fits both your objectives and your budget requirements... right down to how much you need to invest per month to attain your goal.

Recommends Funds Tailored to Your Individual Needs

Mutual funds offer professional management, diversification and liquidity. But how do you choose among the hundreds of funds out there? Your financial adviser can help you see how well a fund's objectives, track record and management style match your specific needs and goals by keeping you informed about -

* how much aggressiveness the fund's managers will assume to achieve their objectives,
* the fund's performance compared to other funds with similar objectives,
* how the fund has done in bullish as well as in bearish markets,
* the fund's performance against its benchmark investment indices over different time periods and
* the types of securities the fund invests in and how those securities can affect its performance.

Aids You in the Allocation of Your Assets

Against the backdrop of your objectives, time horizon and risk tolerance, your financial adviser assists you in allocating your money to the different funds so as to enable you to savour the different fund flavours and achieve the desired diversification.

Reviews and Rebalances Portfolio Regularly

Just as you do a periodical health check-up according to changing lifestyle and age, it is prudent to meet with your financial adviser regularly. Plan a comprehensive appraisal of your mutual fund investments with your financial adviser at least once in 3 months. Armed with a thorough understanding of your financial goals and objectives, coupled with his understanding of financial products and markets, your adviser would be well-positioned to bring suitable new investment opportunities to your attention. He can keep you abreast of changes to the investment and tax environment that may affect your plans and recommend any necessary adjustments. So, when you do make a change in your investment portfolio, there is a logical reason behind it. That way you will be sure that your money is invested wisely every step of the way.

Offers Customisation With Convenience

What does it take to develop a personalised investment programme, monitor your investments and keep track of all the paperwork too? More time than your busy schedule may allow. Your financial adviser offers a professional approach to your customised investment programme that may not demand a lot of work or time on your part and a level of knowledge and expertise that may be difficult for you to achieve on your own.

Waning Want for Financial Advisers

The IFA survey conducted by IIMS Dataworks on mutual fund retail sales and distribution practices shows that extensive brand and product advertising by companies is having some impact, but not to the extent of growing mutual fund customer base to mass market size. The asset management firms need to come together to devise strategies to educate both existing and potential investors. IFAs, in the survey, report that most of their new customers are referred by their existing mutual fund investors. In other words, most new customers are acquired by existing customers 'talking up' the market. Rough weather in markets and high inflation resulted in a slowdown of business for many IFAs. Consequently, the IFA community is under some stress and is willing to consider adjusting traditional business practices. An indicator of this is that many financial advisers are now willing to consider reduced financial incentives.

The status of the business of the IFAs in the aftermath of SEBI's much-hyped entry load abolition on direct investments during January 2008 resulted in a severe dent. 33% of the IFAs admitted to a significant impact of the zero entry load on their business volumes. The abolition of entry loads for all mutual fund schemes with effect from August 1, 2009 by SEBI was another severe blow.

The advent of online investing offered an opportunity to mutual funds to deal directly with investors. Direct transactions curtailed the commission costs involved in distribution. Intelligent investors have severed their dependence on IFAs and have discovered speed, flexibility and convenience in entering into transactions instantaneously through the internet. This has questioned the very survival of IFAs, who focus on selling financial products, but add no other value to investors. Professional IFAs, who have befittingly taken the path of value-added advice and excellent service level to retain their customer base and develop new customer relationships, are few and far between. Many of them offer transaction support through their own websites. A majority of investors in the market need genuine advice. The future of IFAs lies in catering to the needs of such investors, either personally or through a dedicated team with the support of technology.

The financial crisis, coupled with SEBI regulations and the advent of online investing has shadowed the sheen from the profession of financial advisers. Nevertheless, it is up to you to repose confidence in them and avail of their services. The role of a genuine and efficient financial adviser can never be undermined.

A note of caution before you proceed. There are advisers misguiding the naive and easily susceptible clients and pushing them to unsuitable and high commission investments, say insisting on investment in high commission paying, not so liquid capital protection-oriented funds as opposed to low commission paying open-end monthly income plans. You should be aware of the marketing gimmicks adopted by certain advisers, whose primary aim is marketing the funds as mere products earning substantial profits for them rather than matching your profile and requirement to the objectives of the fund. In the words of Bogle, "as long as there are believers in witchcraft, the purveyors of witches' brew will create and peddle elixirs and panaceas, engendering costly and counterproductive investment choices that inevitably come to grips with yesterday's realities, not tomorrow's."

Your portfolio is more than just a list of mutual funds. It is your financial future. If you do not have the time or inclination to closely manage it, a well-chosen adviser can be a reliable ally in achieving long-term financial freedom.

Chapter 27

How to Choose Your Financial Adviser
...Who Nurtures Plants That Bear Fine Fruits

At the outset, answer this question: "Am I comfortable with brand names or independents?" When you start scouting for a financial adviser, there will be big names that may crop up. They can be impersonal and corporate mandates can drive sales of proprietary products. Conversely, independent financial advisers, who are self-employed and unaffiliated with major companies, are unencumbered by corporate policies and may have more flexibility in terms of their product offerings. **You want to be sure that you are going to get someone, who works with you, listens to your needs and concerns, will be honest and will look out for your best interests. Get names from people you trust.** Ask people whose judgement you respect (friends, neighbours, family, or colleagues) for the name of their financial adviser. If the endorsement is enthusiastic, then one may be enough. If not, get 3 names and begin the selection process by phone. First impressions count. If your first impression is positive, arrange for a meeting with the adviser.

A few vital concerns that you must consider while choosing a financial adviser are:

Background and Experience

Try to learn as much as possible about the adviser's background and experience. What is his educational background? Does he have qualifications in specific areas of study and professional licences to provide services? How long has he been doing this? There is something about the passage of time that tends to shake out the incompetents. As the industry undergoes its normal ebbs and flows, those participants who cannot perform are weeded out, either voluntarily or otherwise. And those are exactly the persons you do not want advising you.

The Adviser's Practice

Find out about the adviser's practice. Has the adviser worked with clients whose situation is similar to yours? How many clients does the adviser currently have? What is the product basket offered? Does he have resources in terms of research and support? Does the adviser have minimum limits for investment assets, net worth, or income? Does he maintain client confidentiality?

Investment Pattern Compatible with Yours

As an ideal investment goal, let your adviser's personal portfolio of investments reflect your own. The adviser should work with you to set target rates of return, focus on risk in selecting your portfolio and rebalance it periodically. Keep abreast of your adviser's financial activities regularly.

A Mode of Payment that Avoids Conflict of Interest

The issue of adviser compensation should be explored and fully understood. How is he compensated (hourly, retainer, percentage of assets, or commissions)? Are there financial incentives for the adviser to recommend certain financial products? The adviser should be compensated on a fee-only basis rather than by brokerage commissions. Advisers, who work on commissions, are more likely to recommend frequent transactions in your portfolio. A fee-only adviser has fewer conflicts of interest and is, therefore, more likely to have your best interests in mind.

A Feel for Working With the Adviser

You should try to get a feel for what it would be like to work with your adviser. You should decide about the process and frequency of consultations once you hire the adviser.

Verification of the Basis for Confidence

Often misplaced confidence is the primary cause of financial disaster for many of you. Of course, it is mostly preventable. Just as a leopard does not change its spots, persons with unsavoury backgrounds tend to repeat their underhand actions. So, how does this translate? Consider no adviser on whom you have not obtained (a) an exemplary personal credit report, (b) a clean record for disciplinary actions and lawsuits and (c) personal recommendations from at least 3 current clients of adequate duration.

Have you ever made a decision based on a "gut" feeling or instinct? While all the items listed above are of supreme importance in finding the best financial adviser for you, the value of **the gut test** should not be overlooked. Does the adviser seem to be client-centred? Does he appear interested and whether he can serve you efficiently and effectively given his experience and expertise? Does the adviser seem to be overly anxious to have you as a client or does he express a desire to determine if the two of you will be a good "fit?" Does the person seem to have time for you regardless of how much money you have to invest? Does he or she really listen to you and seem to respect your opinions? Does the person use financial jargon or explain investments to you in clear terms? While harder to measure and define, these intangibles are important in the selection of a financial adviser, who is right for you.

The foregoing, though admittedly a skeletal view of the financial adviser selection process, provides the crucial ingredients. **Gauge your level of comfort with the adviser as you are looking for a long-term relationship.** Never hesitate to ask whatever is on your mind however foolish the questions may sound. Always remember that it is your money and your future.

Epilogue

"Every moment was a precious thing, having in it the essence of finality."

— Daphne du Maurier

When I started writing this book, it was my endeavour to demystify the concept of mutual funds so that even a layman can reap the benefits it offers and build his wealth. Now, when the time has come to draw down the curtains, I sincerely believe that I have succeeded in my task. The mysterious monster of mutual fund has been reduced to mundane existence with the mantra for mutual fund investing having been passed on to the world at large.

We undertook a long but pleasant journey – initiation of the idea of mutual funds, constituents and structure, clarification of the concepts associated with it, savouring of the fund flavours, the *raison d'etre* for traversing the mutual fund route, working our way up with our wealth-building winners, purchase, redemption, SIP and finally the factors that should figure in the choice of the right financial adviser. This culminates in the successful completion of the mutual fund investment journey. Now that we have completed a full circle, it is time to bid adieu.

Armed with this treasure trove of knowledge about mutual funds, you can now embark on a safe and profitable journey into the world of mutual funds. Happy investing!

www.ingramcontent.com/pod-product-compliance
Lightning Source LLC
Chambersburg PA
CBHW020627220526
45464CB00001B/47